Virginia
with Washington, DC
Atlas & Gazetteer™

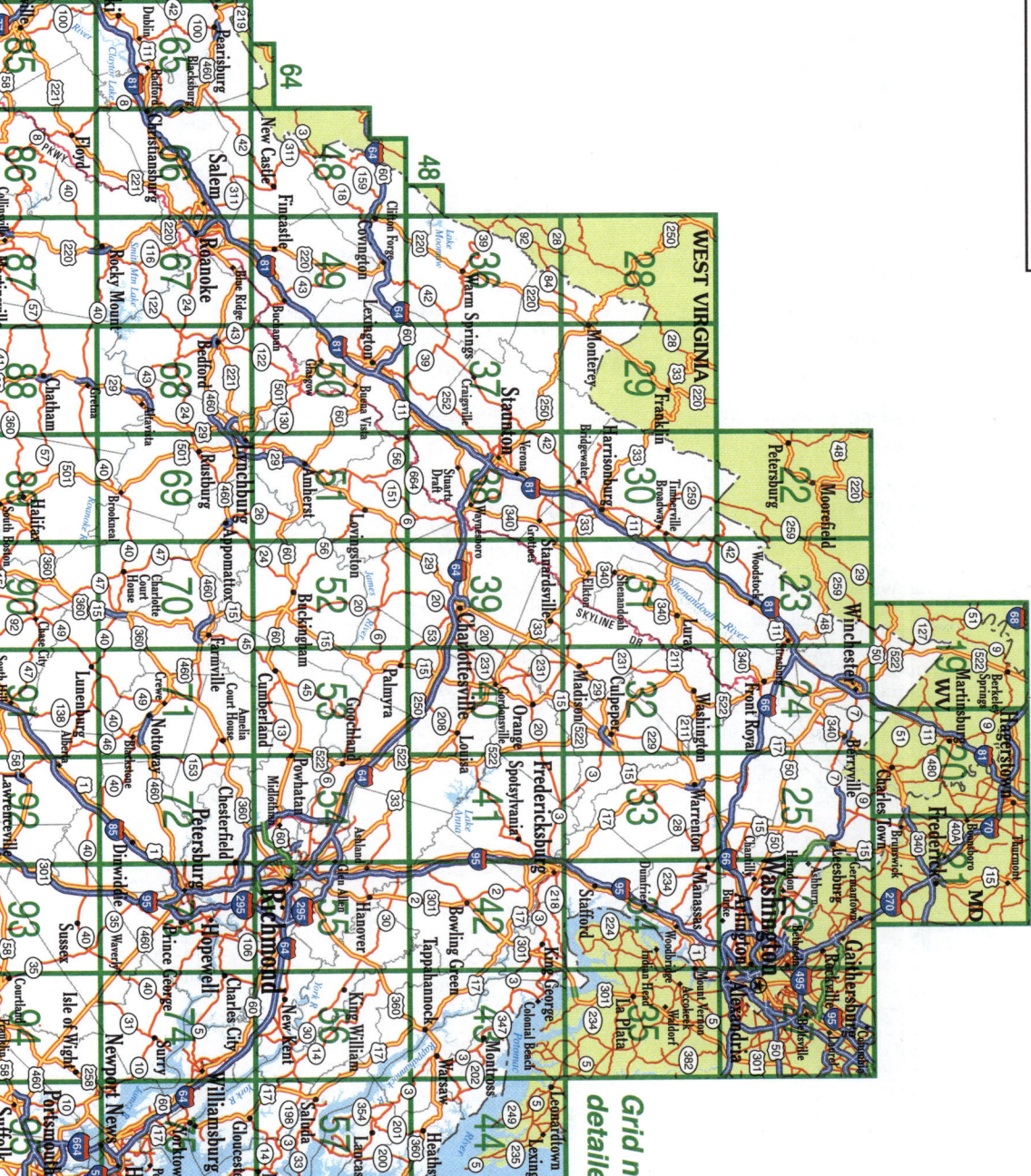

1 inch equals 3.5 miles

Table of Contents

THE ATLAS
- Detailed Topo Maps 19–96
- Washington, DC Metropolitan Area Map 16–18
- Index of Placenames 2–3
- Index of Selected Geographic Features 4–5
- Legend .... Inside Front Cover

THE GAZETTEER
- Introduction 6
- Campgrounds 11
- Family Outings 8–9
- Freshwater Fishing 12–13
- Saltwater Fishing 13
- Hunting 7
- Outdoor Adventures 14–15
- Recreation Areas 10–11
- Unique Natural Features 15

Grid numbers refer to detailed map pages

No portion of this atlas may be photocopied, electronically stored or reproduced in any manner without written permission from the publisher.

Important Notices
Garmin has made reasonable efforts to provide you with accurate maps and related information, but we cannot exclude the possibility of errors or omissions in sources or of changes in actual conditions. GARMIN MAKES NO WARRANTIES OF ANY KIND, EITHER EXPRESS OR IMPLIED, INCLUDING THE WARRANTIES OF MERCHANTABILITY AND FITNESS FOR A PARTICULAR PURPOSE. GARMIN SHALL NOT BE LIABLE TO ANY PERSON UNDER ANY LEGAL OR EQUITABLE THEORY FOR DAMAGES ARISING OUT OF THE USE OF THIS PUBLICATION, INCLUDING, WITHOUT LIMITATION, FOR DIRECT, CONSEQUENTIAL OR INCIDENTAL DAMAGES.

Nothing in this publication implies the right to use private property. There may be private inholdings within the boundaries of public reservations. You should respect all landowner restrictions.

Some listings may be seasonal or may have admission fees. Please be sure to confirm this information when making plans.

Safety Information
To avoid accidents, always pay attention to actual road, traffic and weather conditions and do not attempt to read these maps while you are operating a vehicle. Please consult local authorities for the most current information on road and other travel-related conditions.

Do not use this publication for marine or aeronautical navigation, as it does not depict navigation aids, depths, obstacles, landing approaches and other information necessary to performing these functions safely.

California Prop 65 Warning
⚠ WARNING: Cancer and Reproductive Harm - www.p65warnings.ca.gov

NINTH EDITION
Copyright © 2021 Garmin Ltd. or its Affiliates. All rights reserved.
2 DeLorme Dr. Suite 200, Yarmouth, Maine 04096
www.garmin.com/DeLormeAtlas
Printed in Canada.

Index of Placenames

A

Abbott 66 A4
Abingdon 82 D2
Accomac 59 C8
Accotink 34 B5
Achilles 75 C8
Afton 38 E4
Airlie 33 A7
Alberene 39 F7
Alberta 92 B1
Aldie 25 D9
Alexandria 27 F6
Alfonso 57 A7
Alleghany 48 B3
Allison Gap 82 B4
Altavista 68 E4
Alton 89 F7
Amelia Court House 71 B10
Amherst 51 D7
Amissville 32 B5
Ammon 72 C2
Amonate 63 D6
Andersonville 52 F2
Andover 80 A2
Annandale 26 F4
Appalachia 80 B2
Apple Grove 41 F6
Appomattox 69 B9
Aquia Harbour 34 E2
Ararat 85 F9
Arcola 25 D10
Ark 57 F7
Arlington 26 E5
Aroda 40 A2
Arrington 51 C8
Arvonia 52 C5
Ashburn 26 C1
Ashland 55 B6
Assawoman 59 A9
Atkins 83 B8
Atlantic 46 F4
Augusta Springs 37 D9
Austinville 84 B5
Axton 87 E9
Aylett 55 B10

B

Bacova 36 D2
Baileys Crossroads 26 F5
Banco 32 E1
Bandy 62 D5
Barboursville 40 C1
Barhamsville 56 F3
Barren Springs 85 B6
Baskerville 91 D6
Bassett 87 C6
Bastian 64 D2
Basye 22 F5
Batesville 39 E6
Battery Park 75 F6
Bealeton 33 C7
Beaumont 54 C1
Beaverdam 41 F8
Beaverlett 75 A10
Bedford 68 B1
Bee 61 E9
Bellamy 80 E3
Belle Haven 59 E6
Belspring 65 D8
Ben Hur 79 D8
Bena 75 C8
Bent Mountain 66 D4
Bentonville 24 F1
Bergton 30 A3
Berryville 24 B5
Beulahville 55 A9
Big Island 50 E3
Big Rock 61 A9
Big Stone Gap 80 B2
Birchleaf 61 D8
Birdsnest 58 F5
Bishop 63 C7
Blacksburg 66 C1
Blackstone 71 E10
Blackwater 79 E9
Blackwater 96 F2
Blairs 88 E3
Bland 64 E2
Bloxom 59 A8
Blue Grass 29 D6
Blue Ridge 67 A8
Bluefield 63 C10
Bluemont 25 B7
Bohannon 75 A9
Boissevain 63 C9
Bon Air 54 E5
Boones Mill 67 E6
Boston 32 D3
Boston 58 D5
Bowling Green 42 D2
Boyce 24 B4
Boydton 90 E5
Boykins 93 F9
Bracey 91 F8
Branchville 93 F8
Brandy Station 33 D6
Breaks 61 B8
Bremo Bluff 53 C6
Brentsville 34 B1
Bridgewater 30 F2
Brightwood 32 E2
Bristol 81 F9
Bristow 33 A10
Broad Run 25 F8
Broadford 82 A5
Broadway 30 C5
Brodnax 91 D9
Brokenburg 41 C8
Brooke 34 F2
Brookneal 69 F8
Brosville 87 E10
Brownsburg 37 F9
Brucetown 20 F1
Bruington 56 B2
Brumley Gap 82 C1
Brunswick 92 E1
Buchanan 49 E9
Buckingham 26 E5
Buckingham 52 E3
Buckner 41 E7
Buena Vista 50 C3
Buffalo Junction 90 F2
Bull Run 25 F10
Bumpass 41 E8
Burgess 44 F4
Burgess 57 A9
Burke 26 F3
Burkes Garden 63 E9
Burkeville 71 D7
Burr Hill 33 F6

C

Callaghan 48 A4
Callands 87 C10
Callao 44 E2
Callaway 66 F5
Calverton 33 C8
Cana 85 E7
Cape Charles City 76 C3
Capeville 76 D4
Capron 93 D9
Cardinal 75 A9
Caret 43 E7
Carrollton 95 A7
Carrsville 94 D4
Carson 73 F7
Cartersville 53 C8
Casanova 33 B8
Cascade 87 F9
Castleton 32 C3
Castlewood 81 B8
Catawba 66 A4
Catawba 89 A8
Catharpin 25 F9
Catlett 33 B9
Cauthornville 56 A1
Cave Spring 66 C5
Caylor 78 E4
Cedar Bluff 62 E4
Centenary 52 C3
Center Cross 56 B4
Central Point 42 E5
Centreville 26 F1
Ceres 63 F9
Chamberlayne Heights 55 D6
Chamberlayne 55 D6
Champlain 43 E6
Chance 43 D6
Chantilly 26 E1
Charles City 74 B1
Charlotte Court House 70 E1
Charlottesville 39 D9
Chase City 90 C4
Chatham 88 C3
Check 66 F4
Cheriton 76 B4
Chesapeake 95 C10
Chester Gap 24 F3
Chester 73 B6
Chesterfield 72 A5
Chesterfield 95 B10
Chilhowie 82 C5
Chincoteague 47 F6
Christchurch 57 D7
Christiansburg 66 D1
Christiansburg 65 D10
Chula 72 A1
Church Road 72 D4
Church View 56 C5
Churchville 38 B1
Claremont 26 F5
Claremont 74 C2
Clarks Gap 25 B9
Clarksville 82 C4
Clarksville 90 E2
Claudville 85 F10
Claypool Hill 62 E4
Clear Brook 19 F10
Cleveland 81 A10
Clifford 51 D7
Clifton Forge 49 A8
Clifton 34 A2
Clinchco 61 D7
Clinchport 80 E2
Clintwood 61 D5
Clover 27 F6
Clover 90 B1
Cloverdale 67 A7
Cloverdale 95 C10
Cluster Springs 89 E8
Cobbs Creek 57 F9
Cobham 40 D1
Coeburn 81 A6
Coleman Falls 50 F4
Coles Point 44 C1
Collinsville 87 D7
Cologne 56 E5
Colonial Beach 43 B7
Colonial Heights 73 C6
Columbia 53 B8
Concord 69 B8
Copper Hill 66 E4
Corbin 42 B2
Courtland 94 D1
Covesville 39 F6
Covington 49 B6
Craddockville 58 E5
Craigsville 37 D8
Crewe 71 D8
Criders 30 A2
Crimora 38 C4
Cripple Creek 84 C2
Critz 86 E4
Crockett 84 B1
Cross Junction 19 E8
Crozet 39 D6
Crozier 54 D2
Crystal Hill 89 B9
Cullen 70 E2
Culpeper 32 D5
Cumberland 53 F6

D

Dahlgren 43 A6
Dale City 34 B3
Daleville 67 A7
Damascus 82 E4
Dante 81 A8
Danville 88 F3
Darlington Heights 70 D2
Davenport 61 E10
Davis Wharf 58 E5
Dayton 30 E3
Deerfield 37 B7
Delaplane 24 E5
Deltaville 57 E7
Dendron 74 F2
DeWitt 72 F4
Diggs 57 F10
Dillwyn 52 E4
Dinwiddie 72 E4
Disputanta 73 E9
Doe Hill 29 E7
Dogue 42 B4
Dolphin 92 C2
Donovans Corner 34 A3
Doran 62 E3
Doswell 55 A6
Drakes Branch 70 F2
Draper 65 F6
Drewryville 93 D8
Dry Fork 81 A7
Dry Fork 88 D3
Dryden 79 C10
Dublin 65 E7
Duffield 80 D2
Dugspur 85 C8
Dumfries 34 C3
Dundas 91 A9
Dungannon 81 C6
Dunn Loring 26 E4
Dunnsville 56 A4
Dutton 57 F8
Dyke 39 B8

E

Eagle Rock 49 D8
Earlysville 39 C9
East Stone Gap 80 B3
Eastville 76 B4
Ebony 91 F10
Edgerton 92 C2
Edinburg 23 F8
Edwardsville 44 F4
Eggleston 65 B8
Elberon 74 E3
Elk Creek 84 D1
Elk Hill 53 C8
Elkton 31 E7
Elkwood 33 D6
Elliston 66 C3
Elmo 89 E6
Emory 82 C3
Emporia 92 E5
Esmont 52 A2
Etlan 32 D1
Evergreen 69 B10
Evington 68 C4
Ewing 78 E4
Exmore 59 E6

F

Faber 52 A1
Fairfax Station 26 F3
Fairfax 26 F3
Fairfield 50 A4
Fairlawn 65 D9
Falling Spring 36 F1
Falls Church 26 E4
Falls Mills 63 C10
Falmouth 42 A1
Fancy Gap 85 E7
Farmville 70 B4
Farnham 44 F1
Ferrum 86 A5
Fieldale 87 D6
Fife 53 B9
Fincastle 49 F7
Fishers Hill 23 D10
Fishersville 38 D3
Five Mile Fork 41 A10
Flint Hill 32 A3
Floyd 86 B1
Foneswood 43 D8
Ford 72 D3
Forest 68 A4
Fork Union 53 B6
Fort Belvoir 34 A5
Fort Blackmore 80 C4
Fort Defiance 38 B3
Fort Lee 73 C7
Fort Mitchell 90 A4
Foster 57 F9
Franconia 34 A4
Franklin 94 E2
Franktown 58 F5
Fredericksburg 42 A1
Free Union 39 C8
Freeman 92 D3
Fries 84 D4
Front Royal 24 E2
Fulks Run 30 B4

G

Gainesville 25 F9
Galax 84 E4
Garrisonville 34 E1
Gasburg 92 F1
Gate City 80 E4
Glade Spring 82 C4
Gladehill 67 F8
Gladstone 51 E9
Gladys 69 D6
Glasgow 50 D2
Glen Allen 54 C5
Glen Lyn 64 A5
Glen Wilton 49 B7
Gloucester Point 75 C8
Gloucester 75 A7
Goldbond 65 A8
Goldvein 33 E9
Goochland 54 C1
Goode 68 A3
Goodview 67 C9
Gordonsville 40 C2
Gore 19 F7
Goshen 37 E6
Grafton 57 E8
Graves Mill 31 E10
Grayson 82 F5
Great Falls 26 D3
Green Bay 41 E8
Green Bay 71 D6
Greenbackville 47 E6
Greenbush 59 B7
Greenville 38 E1
Greenway 26 D4
Greenwood 38 D5
Greenwood 55 C6
Greenwood 96 B1
Gretna 88 A3
Grimstead 57 F10
Grottoes 38 A5
Grundy 61 C10
Guinea 42 C1
Gum Spring 54 B1
Gwynn 57 F10

H

Hacksneck 58 D5
Hadensville 53 A10
Hague 44 D1
Halifax 89 C8
Hallieford 57 F9
Hallwood 59 A8
Hallwood 75 E10
Hamilton 25 B8
Hampton 75 F9
Handsom 94 E1
Hanover 55 B7
Harborton 59 D6
Hardy 67 C8
Hardyville 57 E9
Harman 61 B9
Harrisonburg 30 E4
Hartfield 57 E8
Hartwood 33 F10
Hayes 75 C7
Haymarket 25 F9
Haynesville 43 F10
Haynesville 44 F1
Haysi 61 D8
Haywood 32 E2
Head Waters 37 A8
Healing Springs 36 E2
Heathsville 44 F3
Henry 87 C6
Herndon 26 D2
Hewlett 41 F10
Highland Springs 55 E8
Hightown 28 E5
Hillsville 85 C7
Hiltons 81 E6
Hinton 30 E3
Hiwassee 85 A7
Hoadly 34 B2
Hollins 67 B6
Honaker 62 F2
Hood 31 F10
Hopewell 73 B8
Horntown 46 E5
Horsepen 63 C7
Hot Springs 36 E2
Howardsville 52 B1
Huddleston 68 D2
Hudgins 57 F9
Hume 24 F4
Huntly 24 F3
Hurley 62 A1
Hurt 68 E4
Hustle 43 D6

I

Independence 84 E1
Index 43 B6
Indian Valley 85 B9
Ingram 89 D6
Iron Gate 49 B8
Ironsides 34 D5
Irvington 57 C9
Isle of Wight 94 B5
Ivanhoe 84 B4
Ivor 94 B3
Ivy 39 D7

J

Jamaica 56 C5
James Store 57 F8
Jamestown 74 D4
Jamesville 58 E4
Jarratt 93 C6
Java 88 B5
Jeffersonton 33 B6
Jenkins Bridge 46 F3
Jersey 42 B5
Jetersville 71 B8
Jewell Ridge 62 D4
Jewell Valley 62 C4
Jonesville 79 E8
Jordan Mines 48 C4

K

Keeling 88 D4
Keen Mountain 62 D2
Keene 52 A3
Keezletown 30 E5
Keller 59 D6
Kenbridge 91 A8
Kent 84 A3
Kents Store 53 A8
Keokee 80 B1
Keswick 39 E10
Keysville 70 F3
Kilmarnock 57 C9
King and Queen Court House 56 C3
King George 42 A4
King William 56 C1
Kinsale 44 E1
Kire 64 A2
Konnarock 83 E6

L

La Crosse 91 D8
Lacey Spring 30 D5
Lackey 75 C7
Ladysmith 41 E10
Lahore 40 B5
Lake Monticello 39 F10
Lake Monticello 40 F1
Lake Ridge 34 B3

Lakeside 55 D6
Lambsburg 85 F6
Lancaster 57 B8
Laneview 56 B5
Laurel Fork 85 D9
Laurel Park 87 D8
Laurel 54 D5
Lawrenceville 92 D1
Laymantown 67 A7
Lebanon Church 23 C10
Lebanon 82 B1
Lee Mont 59 B7
Leesburg 25 B10
Leon 32 E3
Lewisetta 44 E3
Lexington 50 B2
Lightfoot 74 B4
Lignum 33 E7
Lincoln 25 B8
Linden 24 E4
Linton Hall 33 A9
Linville 30 D4
Little Plymouth 56 D4
Lively 57 B7
Loch Lomond 34 A1
Locust Dale 32 F3
Locust Grove 41 A6
Locust Hill 57 D7
Locust Hill 84 A4
Locustville 59 D7
Long Island 69 E6
Loretto 43 D6
Lorton 34 B4
Lottsburg 44 E2
Louisa 40 E4
Lovettsville 21 F6
Lovingston 51 B9
Lowesville 51 C6
Lowmoor 49 B7
Lowry 68 B2
Lunenburg 91 A6
Luray 31 B9
Lynch Station 68 D4
Lynchburg 69 A6
Lyndhurst 38 E3

M

Machipongo 76 A4
Macon 53 E10
Madison Heights 69 A6
Madison Mills 40 A3
Madison 32 F1
Madisonville 70 D1
Maidens 54 C1
Manakin 54 D3
Manassas Park 26 F1
Manassas 34 A1
Mangohick 55 A8
Mannboro 72 C2
Manquin 55 C9
Mappsville 59 A9
Marion 83 B7
Marionville 58 F5
Markham 24 E5
Markham 88 B5
Marshall 25 E6
Martinsville 87 D7
Maryton 42 B2
Maryus 75 C9
Mascot 56 D5
Massanutten 31 F6
Massies Mill 51 B8
Mathews 57 F10
Mattaponi 56 E4
Maurertown 23 E9
Mavisdale 62 D1
Max Meadows 84 A4
Maxie 61 B9
McClure 61 E7
McCoy 65 C8
McDowell 29 F7
McGaheysville 31 F6
McKenney 72 F3
McLean 26 D4
Meadows of Dan 86 D1
Meadowview 82 C3
Mearsville 59 A8
Mechanicsburg 64 D4
Mechanicsville 30 B5
Mechanicsville 55 D7
Meherrin 70 E5
Melfa 59 D7
Mendota 81 D8
Meredithville 91 C10
Merrifield 26 E3
Merrimac 65 D10
Merry Point 57 C8
Middlebrook 37 D10
Middleburg 25 D7
Middletown 24 C1
Middletown 58 F5
Midland 33 C8
Midlothian 54 F4
Milford 42 E2
Millboro 36 E5
Millers Tavern 56 A2
Millwood 24 C4
Mine Run 41 A6
Mineral 41 E6
Mint Spring 38 D1
Mitchells 32 F4
Mitcheltown 36 E3
Mobjack 75 A9
Moccasin Gap 80 E5
Modest Town 59 A9
Mollusk 57 C7

Moneta 67 D10
Montclair 34 C2
Montebello 51 A6
Monterey 29 F6
Montpelier Station 40 B2
Montpelier 54 A3
Montrose 55 E7
Montross 43 D9
Montvale 67 A9
Moon 57 F10
Morattico 57 B6
Morrisville 33 D8
Moseley 54 F2
Mount Airy 88 A5
Mount Crawford 30 F3
Mount Holly 43 D10
Mount Jackson 31 A7
Mount Solon 30 F1
Mount. Sidney 38 A3
Mouth of Wilson 83 F9
Mustoe 36 A5

N

Narrows 65 B6
Naruna 69 E7
Nassawadox 58 F5
Nathalie 89 A8
Natural Bridge Station 50 D1
Naxera 75 B8
Nellysford 38 F4
Nelson 90 F1
Nelsonia 59 A8
Nethers 32 C1
New Canton 53 C6
New Castle 48 F4
New Church 46 E4
New Hope 26 F4
New Kent 56 E2
New Market 31 B6
New Point 75 B10
New River 65 D8
Newbern 65 E7
Newington 34 A4
Newport News 95 A8
Newport 37 E9
Newport 65 B10
Newsoms 93 E10
Newtown 31 E7
Newtown 42 F5
Newtown 50 B2
Newtown 57 B8
Newtown 95 C10
Nickelsville 81 D7
Ninde 43 A6
Nokesville 33 B10
Nora 61 E7
Norfolk 95 B10
Norge 74 A4
North Chesterfield 54 F5
North Garden 39 F7
North Shore 67 E10
North Springfield 26 F4
North Tazewell 63 E7
North 57 F9
Norton 80 A4
Norwood 68 A3
Nottoway 71 E8
Nuttsville 57 B7

O

Oak Hall 46 F4
Oakpark 32 F3
Oakton 26 E3
Oakwood 26 E5
Oakwood 62 C1
Oakwood 96 A1
Occoquan 34 B3
Oilville 54 C2
Oldhams 43 E10
Onancock 59 C7
Onemo 75 A10
Onley 59 C7
Ophelia 44 F5
Orange 40 B3
Ordinary 75 B7
Oriskany 49 D6
Orkney Springs 22 F5
Orlean 32 A5
Oyster 76 B4

P

Paeonian Springs 25 B9
Paint Bank 48 E2
Painter 59 D6
Palmyra 33 A6
Palmyra 95 D6
Pamplin City 70 C1
Pardee 60 F3
Paris 24 D5
Parksley 59 B8
Parrott 65 D8
Partlow 41 D9
Patrick Springs 86 E3
Paynesville 62 B3
Paytes 41 B7
Pearisburg 65 B6
Pembroke 65 B8
Pender 26 E2

Penhook 87 A10
Penn Laird 30 F5
Pennington Gap 79 C9
Petersburg 73 C7
Phenix 70 E1
Philomont 25 C8
Pilgrims Knob 62 C2
Pilot 66 F1
Pimmit Hills 26 E4
Piney River 51 C7
Pittsville 88 A2
Pleasant Valley 26 E1
Pleasant Valley 30 F4
Pocahontas 63 B9
Pohick 34 A4
Poquoson 75 E9
Port Haywood 75 A10
Port Republic 38 A5
Port Royal 42 C4
Portsmouth 95 C10
Pound 60 E4
Pounding Mill 62 E5
Powhatan 53 E10
Pratts 32 F1
Prince George 73 C8
Prospect 70 B3
Providence Forge 56 F1
Pulaski 65 F6
Pungoteague 59 D6
Purcellville 25 B8
Purdy 92 C4

Q

Quantico 34 D3
Quicksburg 31 B6
Quinby 59 E7
Quinque 39 B10
Quinton 55 E10

R

Radford 67 D10
Radford 65 E9
Radiant 40 A2
Randolph 90 B1
Raphine 37 F10
Rapidan 40 A4
Raven 62 E3
Rawlings 92 A2
Rectortown 25 E6
Red Ash 62 E3
Red House 69 D10
Red Oak 90 C2
Redwood 67 F8
Reedville 57 A10
Regina 57 B9
Remington 33 D7
Republican Grove 89 A7
Rescue 75 F7
Reston 26 D2
Reva 32 D3
Rhoadesville 40 A5
Rice 71 C6
Rich Creek 65 A6
Richardsville 33 F8
Richlands 62 E4
Richmond 55 E6
Ridgeway 87 F7
Ridgeway 89 C6
Rileyville 31 A10
Riner 65 E10
Ringgold 88 F4
Ripplemead 65 B7
Riverton 24 D2
Rixeyville 32 C5
Roanoke 67 C6
Rochelle 40 A1
Rockbridge Baths 37 F8
Rockdell 82 B2
Rockville 54 C3
Rocky Gap 64 C2
Rocky Mount 67 F6
Rollins Fork 42 C4
Rose Hill Farms 34 A5
Rose Hill 26 F5
Rose Hill 78 E5
Rosedale 82 A2
Roseland 51 B8
Round Hill 25 B7
Rowe 62 D1
Ruby 33 D10
Ruckersville 39 B10
Rural Retreat 83 B10
Rustburg 69 C6
Ruther Glen 42 F1
Ruthville 74 A1

S

Saint Charles 79 C9
Saint Paul 81 B8
Saint Stephens Church 56 B1
Salem 66 C5
Saltville 82 B4
Saluda 57 D6
Sandston 55 E8
Sandy Hook 54 B1
Sandy Level 87 F9
Sanford 46 F3
Saxe 90 A2
Saxis 46 F2

Schley 75 A8
Schuyler 52 B1
Scottsburg 89 C10
Scottsville 52 B3
Seaford 75 D8
Sealston 42 A3
Seaview 76 C4
Sebrell 93 C10
Sedley 94 C2
Selma 49 B7
Seven Corners 26 E5
Seven Mile Ford 83 C6
Severn 75 B9
Shackleford 56 E4
Shadwell 39 E10
Sharps 56 A5
Shawsville 66 D2
Shenandoah 31 E7
Sherando 38 E3
Shipman 51 C9
Shortt Gap 62 D3
Simpsons 66 F3
Singers Glen 30 C4
Skippers 92 F5
Skipwith 90 D4
Smithfield 95 A6
Somerset 40 B2
Somerville 33 D9
South Boston 89 D8
South Hill 91 D8
South Hill 95 C10
Sparta 42 E4
Speedwell 84 C1
Spencer 86 E5
Sperryville 32 B2
Spotswood 37 F10
Spotsylvania 41 B9
Spout Spring 69 B9
Spring Creek 30 F2
Spring Garden 88 C4
Spring Grove 74 D2
Springfield 26 F4
Stafford 34 E2
Staffordsville 65 C7
Stanardsville 39 A9
Stanley 31 C8
Stanleytown 80 C3
Stanleytown 87 D6
Star Tannery 23 C9
State Farm 54 D2
Staunton 38 C2
Steeles Tavern 37 F10
Stephens City 24 B1
Stephenson 19 F10
Sterling 26 D1
Stevensburg 33 E6
Stevensville 56 C2
Stonega 80 A2
Stony Creek 93 A6
Strasburg 23 D10
Stuart 86 E2
Stuarts Draft 38 E2
Studley 55 C8
Sudley 26 F1
Suffolk 95 D7
Sugar Grove 83 C9
Sumerduck 33 E8
Supply 42 D5
Surry 74 D3
Susan 75 A10
Sussex 93 A8
Sutherland 72 D5
Sutherland 80 A4
Sutherlin 88 E5
Sweet Briar 51 E7
Swoope 37 C10
Swords Creek 62 F3
Syria 32 D1

T

Tangier 58 A3
Tannersville 83 A6
Tappahannock 43 F8
Tasley 59 C7
Tazewell 63 E7
Temperanceville 46 F4
Thaxton 67 B10
The Plains 25 E7
Thornburg 41 C10
Timberville 30 B5
Tiptop 63 D8
Toano 74 A4
Toga 52 F2
Toms Brook 23 D9
Topping 57 D8
Townsend 76 D4
Trammel 61 F8
Trevilians 40 D4
Triangle 34 D3
Triplet 92 E2
Trout Dale 83 D8
Troutville 67 A7
Troy 40 F2
Turbeville 89 E7
Tyro 51 A7
Tysons Corner 26 E4

U

Union Hall 67 F9
Union Level 91 D7
Unionville 40 B5
Upperville 25 D6
Urbanna 57 D6

V

Valentines 92 F2
Vansant 61 C10
Vernon Hill 89 D6
Verona 38 B2
Vesta 86 D1
Vesuvius 37 F10
Victoria 71 F7
Vienna 26 E3
Viewtown 32 B4
Villa Heights 87 D6
Village 44 F1
Villamont 67 A8
Vinton 67 C7
Virgilina 89 F10
Virginia Beach 96 B4
Volens 89 A7
Volney 83 E9

W

Wachapreague 59 D7
Waiteville 64 A3
Wake 57 E8
Wakefield 94 A2
Walkerton 56 C1
Wallace 81 E10
Wallops Island 59 A10
Wardtown 58 E5
Ware Neck 75 A8
Warfield 92 B1
Warm Springs 36 D3
Warner 57 D6
Warrenton 33 A7
Warsaw 43 E9
Washington 32 A2
Water View 57 C6
Waterford 25 A9
Wattsville 46 F4
Waverly 73 F10
Waynesboro 38 D4
Weber City 53 B6
Weber City 80 E5
Weedonville 42 A4
Weems 57 D8
Weirwood 58 F5
West Augusta 37 A9
West Point 56 E4
West Springfield 34 A4
Westlake Corner 67 D9
Westmoreland 39 D9
Weyers Cave 38 A3
White Hall 39 C7
White Marsh 75 B7
White Plains 91 E10
White Post 24 C3
White Stone 57 D9
Whitetop 83 F6
Whitewood 62 C3
Wicomico Church 57 A9
Wicomico 75 B7
Wilderness 41 A8
Williamsburg 74 C5
Williamsville 37 B6
Willis Wharf 59 E6
Willis 81 B10
Willis 85 B10
Wilsons 72 D1
Winchester 24 A3
Windsor 94 C5
Wingina 52 D1
Winterpock 72 B3
Wirtz 67 E7
Wise 80 A5
Withams 46 F3
Wolford 62 A2
Wolftown 31 F10
Woodbridge 34 B4
Woodford 42 C1
Woodlawn 73 C6
Woodlawn 85 D6
Woodstock 23 E8
Woodville 32 C2
Woolwine 86 C2
Wylliesburg 90 B2
Wyndham 54 C4
Wytheville 84 A3

XYZ

Yale 93 B8
Yorktown 75 C7
Zacata 43 C9
Zanoni 75 A8
Zuni 94 B4

Index of Selected Geographic Features

A

Abbs Valley 63 C9
Abbs Valley Ridge 63 C8
Abrams Mountain 2,051 ft 31 E8
Acre of Rocks 2,277 ft 66 C2
Ad Cox Knob 3,448 ft 49 B9
Adams Peak 2,976 ft 50 A5
Aggies Mountain 3,360 ft 50 A5
Allegheny Mountain 48 A3; B1
Angels Rest 3,633 ft 65 B6
Anthony Knobs 2,398 ft 49 B9
Aps Knob 2,895 ft 48 F4
Archer Knob 3,409 ft 37 C8
Arkansas Hill 2,651 ft 62 F4
Austin Mountain 2,658 ft 38 A5

B

Back Creek Mountain 3,835 ft 36 C3
Back Creek Mountain 2,804 ft 49 D9
Bald Hill 2,840 ft 63 E8
Bald Knob 3,688 ft 30 C2
Bald Knob 4,240 ft 36 F2
Bald Knob 3,894 ft 49 A7
Bald Knob 3,283 ft 49 C6
Bald Knob 4,040 ft 50 B5
Bald Knob 4,361 ft 65 B9
Bald Knob 2,580 ft 82 C4
Bald Knob 3,255 ft 83 D7
Bald Mountain 48 E5
Bald Rock 3,606 ft 62 F5
Bald Rock 2,149 ft 81 B7
Bald Rock 2,460 ft 84 D4
Bald Rock 3,865 ft 82 A4
Bald Rock 3,920 ft 83 D10
Baldwin Mountain 2,440 ft 62 D1
Banks Mountain 2,160 ft 50 C5
Barren Rock 4,380 ft 29 E6
Barringer Mountain 2,342 ft 65 D10
Barton Mountain 3,280 ft 83 D7
Batick Mountain 3,050 ft 48 B3
Battle Knob 3,296 ft 63 E7
Beamer Knob 3,386 ft 85 E6
Bear Church Rock 3,035 ft 31 E10
Bear Knob 2,220 ft 66 B3
Bear Knob 2,400 ft 82 D5
Bear Knob 3,386 ft 85 A8
Bear Mountain 4,470 ft 28 E4
Bear Mountain 3,530 ft 29 F6
Bear Wallow 3,240 ft 48 C4
Bearcamp Knob 4,170 ft 28 D5
Beards Mountain 36 F3
Bearfence Mountain 3,606 ft 31 E9
Beartown Mountain 4,689 ft 82 A3
Bearwallow Mountain 2,937 ft 49 B7
Bearwallow 2,400 ft 49 C9
Bee Mountain 3,034 ft 51 A7
Beech Lick Knob 3,280 ft 30 A2
Beech Mountain 4,966 ft 83 E6
Bell Hill 3,054 ft 63 C9
Bench Mountain 2,930 ft 85 A8
Bettys Knob 2,713 ft 82 B5
Big A Mountain 3,706 ft 62 F1
Big Bald Knob 4,120 ft 29 F9
Big Butt 3,455 ft 37 F7
Big Doubles 3,488 ft 63 F7
Big Flat Mountain 3,389 ft 39 B6
Big Flat Top 3,060 ft 80 B5
Big Hill 2,730 ft 37 A7
Big Knob 2,894 ft 37 E8
Big Knob 4,072 ft 49 A6
Big Knob 3,148 ft 80 E5
Big Mountain 3,697 ft 65 A8
Big Piney Mountain 2,945 ft 36 D4
Big Piney Mountain 2,145 ft 50 D4
Big Ridge 80 E1
Big Rocky Row 2,992 ft 50 D3
Big Schloss 2,964 ft 23 D7
Big Spy Mountain 3,160 ft 38 F1
Big Tom 2,358 ft 31 D10
Big Turkey Knob 3,320 ft 83 A10
Biggs Mountain 2,860 ft 49 C9
Black Hill 2,529 ft 83 A7
Black Lick Mountain 3,412 ft 30 B2
Black Mountain 3,560 ft 60 F1
Black Mountain 4,145 ft 80 A1
Black Rock Mountain 3,446 ft 38 F3
Black Rock 2,894 ft 36 D4
Blackburn Knob 3,606 ft 83 F8
Blue Knob 2,680 ft 67 A8
Blue Ridge 24 F3; 25 C6; 31 D10;F8; 32 B1; 38 F3; 39 B6; 49 F8; 50 D3; 66 F4; 67 B8;D6; 85 F6;F10; 86 B3
Bluff Mountain 3,520 ft 31 E10
Bluff Mountain 4,859 ft 83 E7
Bobbitt Knob 3,008 ft 85 D7
Bolar Mountain 2,725 ft 36 E1
Bold Camp Mountain 2,789 ft 60 E5
Bolton Mountain 2,135 ft 51 A8
Bonner Mountain 3,690 ft 36 D4
Boston Knob 2,560 ft 50 A5
Bother Knob 4,344 ft 29 D10
Bowling Green Mountain 2,800 ft 84 C1
Bradshaw Mountain 2,400 ft 62 B3
Brannom Knob 3,260 ft 85 A7
Branscomb Hill 2,700 ft 85 D9
Bratton Mountain 2,283 ft 37 F6
Breedlove Knob 2,160 ft 31 C10
Brierpatch Mountain 3,634 ft 84 D2
Broad Run Mountain 2,964 ft 48 F5
Broad Top 2,735 ft 30 B3
Browder Mountain 2,040 ft 81 F7
Brown Mountain 2,569 ft 39 A6
Brown Mountain 2,487 ft 50 C4
Browns Peak 3,405 ft 64 F1
Bruisers Knob 3,448 ft 66 B1
Brumley Mountain 4,220 ft 82 B1
Brush Mountain 3,104 ft 66 B1
Brushy Butt 3,560 ft 83 D9
Brushy Knob 2,210 ft 49 A8
Brushy Mountain 3,553 ft 30 C2
Brushy Mountain 3,846 ft 36 E
Brushy Mountain 3,160 ft 48 A3
Brushy Mountain 3,570 ft 49 A10
Brushy Mountain 2,711 ft 49 C10
Brushy Mountain 2,933 ft 63 F9
Brushy Mountain 2,428 ft 67 A6
Brushy Mountain 2,870 ft 65 A10
Brushy Mountain 83 A6
Brushy Ridge 3,895 ft 37 A7
Brushy Top 4,072 ft 65 A8
Bryant Mountain 2,562 ft 38 F3
Bryants Knob 3,205 ft 83 A8
Buchanan Mountain 3,400 ft 83 C9
Buck Hill 2,130 ft 38 A1
Buck Hill 3,305 ft 37 A6
Buck Knob 3,174 ft 60 E4
Buck Knob 4,000 ft 28 C5
Buck Mountain 3,665 ft 29 E10
Buck Mountain 3,087 ft 29 F7
Buck Mountain 3,360 ft 50 B5
Buck Mountain 3,680 ft 83 E10
Buck Mountain 4,670 ft 83 E10
Buck Mountain 4,670 ft 84 E1
Buckeye Mountain 2,884 ft 65 C8
Buckhorn Knob 2,200 ft 49 A8
Buckhorn Mountain 63 D8,10; 64 C1
Bucks Elbow Mountain 3,163 ft 39 D6
Buffalo Clover Knob 3,008 ft 30 A2
Buffalo Mountain 3,971 ft 85 C10
Buffalo Ridge 51 E8
Bull Hill 2,120 ft 81 A7
Bull Mountain 86 D3
Bull Run Mountains 25 E8
Bullpasture Mountain 3,320 ft 29 F7; 37 A6
Burkes Garden 63 E9
Burns Knob 2,339 ft 30 A2
Burnt Hill 2,126 ft 37 E10
Bush Mountain 3,527 ft 31 E9
Bush Mountain 2,688 ft 31 F7
Bushy Mountain 64 E3
Butt Mountain 65 A8
Butt Of Powell Mountain 2,859 ft 80 D1
Buzzard Hill 2,883 ft 84 F1
Buzzard Rock 5,095 ft 83 E6
Buzzard Rocks 2,374 ft 31 E9
Buzzards Roost 3,524 ft 67 A10
Byrd Knob 2,760 ft 37 E8

C

Cabes Hill 2,047 ft 66 E2
Cahas Mountain 3,571 ft 66 E5
Caldwell Mountain 2,830 ft 49 E6
Calf Mountain 2,979 ft 38 D5
Calfee Knob 2,813 ft 65 F10
Camp Mountain 3,294 ft 49 C10
Campbells Mountain 2,414 ft 67 A9
Capola Mountain 1,800 ft 23 D8
Carpenter Mountain 2,690 ft 49 C6
Carr Mountain 3,109 ft 30 B2
Carter Mountain 3,040 ft 63 F8
Carter Mountain 3,040 ft 83 A8
Carter Mountain 2,344 ft 86 E2
Carters Mountain 1,580 ft 39 F8
Castle Rock 2,374 ft 39 F6
Cat Knob 3,701 ft 31 E9
Catawba Mountain 2,360 ft 66 B3
Catback Mountain 2,612 ft 31 A8
Catlett Mountain 3,160 ft 32 C1
Catoctin Mountain 25 A10
Cave Hill 2,772 ft 84 C1
Cedar Bluff 2,762 ft 85 E10
Cedar Knob 2,487 ft 29 F7
Cedar Knob 2,487 ft 37 A7
Cedar Mountain 3,333 ft 39 B6
Cellar Mountain 3,640 ft 38 F1
Chapman Mountain 2,871 ft 31 D9;E10
Charlie Taylor Mountain 2,147 ft 50 B4
Chesnut Mountain 3,107 ft 49 F10
Chestnut Knob 3,205 ft 48 A2
Chestnut Knob 3,374 ft 84 C3
Chestnut Knob 2,932 ft 85 B7
Chestnut Mountain 2,663 ft 50 F1
Chestnut Mountain 2,795 ft 64 F5
Chestnut Mountain 4,040 ft 82 E5
Chestnut Mountain 3,540 ft 83 C8
Chestnut Oak Knob 2,798 ft 37 A9
Chestnut Ridge 3,280 ft 37 D6
Chimney Mountain 2,713 ft 65 F8
Chimney Mountain 2,713 ft 85 A8
Chimney Rock Mountain 2,440 ft 50 B3
Chimney Rock 2,651 ft 38 B5
Chimney Rock 3,638 ft 48 F3
Chimney Rock 3,204 ft 51 A7
Chimney Rock 3,638 ft 66 A3
Chimney Rock 4,080 ft 63 E6
Chimney Rock 4,280 ft 63 D8
Chimney Rock 2,600 ft 80 B4
Chimney Rock 2,800 ft 85 A8
Chimney Rocks 3,330 ft 84 A3
Chisel Knob 3,040 ft 85 E6
Church Mountain 2,890 ft 30 A4
Clark Mountain 3,040 ft 82 E5
Claypool Hill 2,451 ft 62 E4
Clinch Mountain Spur 82 A3
Clinch Mountain 63 F7; 80 E5;F1; 81 D8
Clover Hollow Mountain 3,175 ft 65 B10
Clover Lick Knob 2,329 ft 30 B3
Cloyds Mountain 2,718 ft 65 D7
Coalpit Knob 2,844 ft 37 B9
Coates Mountain 2,539 ft 50 B4
Coby Knob 2,820 ft 84 E5
Coe Knob 2,408 ft 82 D5
Cole Mountain 3,927 ft 50 B5
Coleman Mountain 2,687 ft 50 C4
Coles Knob 2,884 ft 66 F2
Coles Mountain 2,910 ft 36 E2
Comers Rock 4,080 ft 84 C1
Compton Mountain 2,655 ft 62 C3
Compton Peak 2,920 ft 24 F2
Cooper Mountain 2,080 ft 30 D2
Coopers Knob 3,156 ft 37 F7
Copper Creek Knobs 1,919 ft 80 E4
Copper Ridge 80 D5;80 F1; 81 B9
Couchs Knob 3,570 ft 83 E9
Cove Mountain 3,319 ft 64 F3
Cove Mountain 3,050 ft 66 A3
Cow Knob 4,039 ft 30 B1
Coyner Mountain 2,080 ft 67 A7
Craig Mountain 2,580 ft 66 E2
Crawford Knob 3,728 ft 37 B9
Crawford Knob 3,028 ft 38 F4
Crawford Mountain 3,760 ft 37 B9
Crawford Mountain 2,272 ft 49 D7
Crockett Knob 3,104 ft 84 A5
Cross Mountain 2,182 ft 30 C3
Cubbage Mountain 2,030 ft 31 D8
Cumberland Mountain 78 E4;F1

D

Dale Mountain 3,251 ft 37 F6
Dameron Mountain 2,895 ft 48 C3
Davis Knob 2,960 ft 84 F4
Davis Mountain 2,126 ft 38 C5
Davis Mountain 2,590 ft 62 D2
Dead Pine Mountain 3,448 ft 85 A7
Dee Cee Hill 2,000 ft 66 D2
DeHart Mountain 2,697 ft 85 A9
Deisher Mountain 2,418 ft 49 C6
Den Hill 2,254 ft 66 D2
Deskin Mountain 3,766 ft 63 E6
Devils Den 3,160 ft 84 C3
Devils Knob 3,851 ft 38 F3
Devils Tanyard 2,835 ft 31 D8
Dial Rock 3,766 ft 63 D8
Dickey Hill 2,444 ft 24 F2
Dickey Knob 3,649 ft 83 D8
Dickey Mountain 2,609 ft 81 E8
Dicks Knob 3,050 ft 85 E6
Dismal Mountain 2,816 ft 51 B6
Dobie Mountain 2,712 ft 38 E4
Doe Hill 3,970 ft 29 F6
Doe Mountain 3,973 ft 65 B8
Doefoot Mountain 3,040 ft 51 B6
Donald Fauber Mountain 3,058 ft 38 E2
Double Mountain 2,880 ft 64 D5
Double Ridge Knob 3,080 ft 66 B2
Double Top 4,534 ft 83 D7
Doubletop Mountain 3,455 ft 31 D10
Dovel Mountain 2,441 ft 31 D8
Draper Mountain 3,360 ft 65 F6
Dry Pond Mountain 2,880 ft 85 B6
Duncan Knob 2,803 ft 31 B8
Duncan Knob 3,839 ft 36 C4
Dundore Mountain 4,101 ft 30 D1
Dusenberry Knob 2,594 ft 65 F6
Dyers Knob 4,080 ft 29 E9

E

Eagle Rock 2,600 ft 23 B9
East Knob 3,209 ft 85 D10
East River Mountain 63 D8; 64 B4;C1
Edwards Hill 2,700 ft 84 F4
Edwards Knob 3,166 ft 85 D6
Elephant Mountain 2,101 ft 50 C4
Eliza Knob 2,644 ft 79 D10
Elk Knob 2,880 ft 79 D10
Elk Mountain 2,566 ft 38 E4
Elkhorn Mountain 2,810 ft 29 F10
Elliott Knob 4,463 ft 37 C9
Enoch Knob 2,965 ft 84 E5
Epperly Knob 2,726 ft 66 F2
Ewing Mountain 3,066 ft 84 C3

F

Farmers Mountain 3,023 ft 84 C4
Felt Knob 3,162 ft 85 E6
First Mountain 2,646 ft 31 E6;D7
First Mountain 2,841 ft 65 F7
First Peak 4,610 ft 83 E8
Fisher Peak 3,580 ft 85 F6
Fishers View Mountain 2,699 ft 66 E2
Fivemile Mountain 2,660 ft 66 F4
Flagg Knob 2,998 ft 36 C2
Flagpole Knob 4,380 ft 29 D10
Flat Top Mountain 3,994 ft 50 F1
Flat Top Mountain 3,920 ft 64 C5
Flat Top 4,400 ft 83 D7
Flattop Mountain 3,323 ft 39 A7
Flattop Mountain 4,528 ft 82 A4
Fleming Mountain 2,111 ft 50 F4
Fletcher Mountain 2,940 ft 50 C5
Flint Mountain 3,451 ft 38 F2
Floyds Mountain 3,485 ft 50 B5
Fodder House 3,625 ft 36 B3
Fore Mountain 2,926 ft 49 B6
Fork Mountain 3,845 ft 31 E10
Fork Mountain 2,064 ft 32 B1
Fork Mountain 2,574 ft 50 C5
Fork Mountain 3,251 ft 51 A7
Fork Mountain 3,918 ft 64 A3
Fork Mountain 3,522 ft 82 E5
Fort Lewis Mountain 3,251 ft 66 B3
Fossil Point 2,323 ft 84 B5
Foster Knob 2,880 ft 65 A8
Fosters Falls Mountain 2,702 ft 85 B6
Fox Knob 3,175 ft 83 F10
Fox Mountain 39 B7
Fries Knob 4,049 ft 83 E10
Fulk Mountain 3,468 ft 30 B2
Fuller Mountain 2,800 ft 62 E2
Fullhart Knob 2,291 ft 67 A7
Furnace Mountain 2,657 ft 38 B5

G

Gabes Knob 2,980 ft 86 D3
Gap Mountain 2,973 ft 65 C9
Garden Mountain 3,200 ft 49 D9
Garden Mountain 4,354 ft 63 D9;F9
Garrisons Knob 3,840 ft 63 F6
Gate Mountain 2,473 ft 30 C2
Ghost Knob 4,080 ft 63 E9
Gibson Knob 3,020 ft 85 D9
Gibson Mountain 2,491 ft 39 B7
Ginseng Mountain 3,221 ft 29 E6
Glade Mountain 4,093 ft 83 B9
Glade Valley 38 A2
Gleaves Knob 2,827 ft 84 B2
Goat Knob 3,173 ft 63 F7
Goat Knob 2,830 ft 82 B5
Goat Knob 3,173 ft 83 A8
Gobble Mountain 2,648 ft 30 A2
Gobbler Knob 2,720 ft 63 E7
Goods Mountain 3,576 ft 30 D1
Gordons Peak 3,915 ft 29 F9
Gose Knob 4,084 ft 63 E10
Grassy Knob 3,040 ft 83 E9
Grassy Knob 2,480 ft 86 E2
Grassy Knoll 3,480 ft 86 C1
Grassy Mountain 3,345 ft 49 C9
Grave Mountain 4,640 ft 83 D6
Great Knobs 32 E2
Great North Mountain 23 C7
Great North Mountain 37 D8
Green Hill 3,281 ft 49 B10
Green Mountain 23 F9
Green Mountain 2,149 ft 31 E8
Greens Knob 2,523 ft 67 B8
Griffith Knob 2,715 ft 36 F4
Griffith Knob 3,782 ft 64 F1
Grindstone Knob 2,040 ft 67 A8
Grindstone Mountain 2,702 ft 29 F10
Grindstone Mountain 2,850 ft 31 E8
Grosses Mountain 3,840 ft 82 D5
Groundhog Hill 3,180 ft 83 A9
Groundhog Mountain 3,035 ft 85 E9
Grubbs Knob 3,200 ft 31 E6
Guest Mountain 2,805 ft 81 A6
Guinea Mountain 2,280 ft 65 B7
Gulf Mountain 3,325 ft 29 D6
Gully Mountain 3,494 ft 49 D9
Gum Tree Mountain 3,105 ft 36 C4
Gwin Mountain 3,770 ft 37 A7

H

Half Acre of Rocks 2,470 ft 66 C2
Hall Knob 2,605 ft 82 C3
Hall Mountain 2,771 ft 38 B5
Hamilton Knob 3,140 ft 84 A5
Hampton Knob 2,820 ft 84 E4
Hanging Rock 3,720 ft 48 E3
Hankey Mountain 3,450 ft 37 A10
Hanks Knob 3,032 ft 84 E5
Hanse Mountain 2,153 ft 31 F7
Hardscrabble Knob 4,282 ft 29 F9
Harkening Hill 3,372 ft 49 F10
Harles Hill 2,500 ft 66 A1
Harvey Knob 3,340 ft 83 C10
Hawthorne Knob 2,365 ft 82 D5
Haycock Knob 2,821 ft 37 C8
Hayes Knob 3,393 ft 65 A9
Hazel Mountain 2,880 ft 32 C1
Headforemost Mountain 3,730 ft 50 F1
Heard Mountain 2,385 ft 39 F6
Hematite Mountain 2,390 ft 84 B5
Hemppatch Mountain 3,068 ft 66 D5
Henley Mountain 3,255 ft 84 B2
Hickory Hill 2,051 ft 48 C4
Hickory Knob 3,309 ft 48 A3
High Knob 2,388 ft 24 E3
High Knob 4,090 ft 29 C10
High Knob 2,382 ft 66 D1
High Knob 4,160 ft 83 D10
High Knob 3,784 ft 84 D2
High Knoll Mountain 3,261 ft 85 A8
High Point 4,040 ft 83 D8
High Rock 3,798 ft 64 E4
High Rocks 3,653 ft 84 A3
High Top Mountain 2,369 ft 39 B
High Top Mountain 2,224 ft 51 B97
Highco Mountain 2,848 ft 50 C4
Highcock Knob 3,073 ft 50 E2
Hightop Mountain 2,619 ft 66 D2
Hog Mountain 3,574 ft 86 C1
Hogback Mountain 3,474 ft 32 A1
Hogback Mountain 2,542 ft 37 F7
Hogback 4,447 ft 37 C9
Hogpen Mountain 2,825 ft 30 C2
Horne Knob 3,507 ft 83 C10
Horse Heaven 3,873 ft 84 C2
Horse Knob 3,523 ft 85 F6
Horse Mountain 2,627 ft 49 B6
Horsehead Mountain 2,078 ft 38 B5
Horseshoe Mountain 2,438 ft 51 A8
Hot Mountain 2,523 ft 32 C1
House And Barn Mountain 3,574 ft 62 F3
House Rock 3,781 ft 36 D4
Howard Knob 2,930 ft 49 B6
Hubble Hill 2,651 ft 63 D7
Huckleberry Knob 2,440 ft 66 A2
Huckleberry Knob 3,327 ft 83 C10
Huckleberry Mountain 2,158 ft 31 F8
Huffman Knob 2,900 ft 85 C7
Hulls Hill 3,040 ft 29 F7
Humpback Mountain 3,615 ft 38 F4
Hurricane Knob 3,100 ft 85 D10
Hurricane Mountain 4,445 ft 83 D7
Hussy Mountain 3,150 ft 84 C2
Hutchinson Rock 4,480 ft 63 E9

I

Indian Grave Mountain 2,247 ft 86 E2
Indian Mountain 2,608 ft 60 F4
Indian Ridge 85 C8
Ingles Mountain 2,300 ft 65 E9
Irish Mountain 2,865 ft 85 A7
Iron Mountains 84 C1
Iron Ore Knob 2,117 ft 49 C6

J

Jack Mountain 3,917 ft 29 E7; 36 B4
Jackson Knob 2,840 ft 85 D9
Jenkins Mountain 2,028 ft 32 A2
Jenny Knob 3,031 ft 64 D4
Jesses Knob 3,811 ft 64 B4
Jingling Rocks 3,520 ft 48 C4
JJJ Mountain 2,105 ft 38 E3
Joes Knob 2,780 ft 86 E1
Johnnies Knob 2,639 ft 23 C9
Johns Creek Mountain 3,693 ft 48 F2; 65 B9; 66 A1
Johnson Mountain 3,002 ft 49 B7
Jones Knob 3,123 ft 83 E9
Jones Knob 3,816 ft 84 C3
Jones Mountain 3,482 ft 31 E9
Jones Mountain 3,547 ft 86 C1
Julian Knob 3,160 ft 65 B10
Jump Mountain 2,451 ft 37 F7
Jump Rock 3,149 ft 37 F8

K

Keister Hill 2,480 ft 65 B10
Kelley Mountain 3,291 ft 38 F2
Kelly Knob 3,742 ft 65 A10
Kennedy Peak 2,566 ft 31 A9
Kerns Mountain 2,569 ft 31 B7
Kindrick Mountain 3,800 ft 83 E9
Kingery Hill 2,769 ft 66 F2
Kire Mountain 3,400 ft 64 A2
Kirtley Mountain 2,593 ft 31 F9
Knob Mountain 2,861 ft 31 A10; 32 A1
Knob Mountain 37 E7
Knob Mountain 4,230 ft 63 E6
Knob of Rocks 3,192 ft 38 F2
Kretchie Mountain 3,035 ft 30 B2

L

Lairds Knob 3,282 ft 31 E6
Lands Run Gap 24 F2
Lantz Mountain 3,939 ft 28 F4
Laurel Mountain 3,816 ft 82 E5
Lawson Knob 2,760 ft 36 A4
Lewis Mountain 3,573 ft 31 E9
Lewis Mountain 2,554 ft 39 A6
Lewis Mountain 2,945 ft 48 B3
Lewis Peak 2,760 ft 39 A6
Lick Mountain 2,930 ft 48 A5
Lick Mountain 3,520 ft 84 B3
Lighted Top 2,697 ft 31 F9
Lina Rocks 3,816 ft 83 D10
Little Apple Mountain 2,762 ft 50 D3
Little Bald Knob 4,351 ft 29 F9
Little Brushy Mountain 3,456 ft 36 E3
Little Brushy Mountain 2,874 ft 63 F8
Little Brush Mountain 2,540 ft 64 F4
Little Brushy Mountain 2,940 ft 82 B5
Little Brushy Mountain 3,005 ft 83 B8
Little Butt 3,113 ft 37 F7
Little Camp Mountain 3,174 ft 49 C9
Little Crease Mountain 2,265 ft 23 E10
Little Doe Hill 3,242 ft 29 F6
Little Doubles 3,490 ft 63 F7
Little Flat Mountain 3,150 ft 39 B7
Little Friar 2,930 ft 51 B6
Little Harkening Hill 2,962 ft 49 F10
Little Horse Heaven 3,025 ft 84 C2
Little Huckleberry Knob 3,040 ft 83 C10
Little Irish Mountain 2,611 ft 85 A7
Little Mare Mountain 3,445 ft 36 E3
Little Mountain 2,336 ft 30 A3
Little Mountain 3,228 ft 36 B4;C2
Little Mountain 3,480 ft 36 A4
Little Mountain 2,340 ft 36 C3;E3;F2
Little Mountain 80 C3; 82 B3
Little Mountain 2,340 ft 48 D5
Little Mountain 3,200 ft 48 D4
Little Mountain 3,012 ft 48 E2
Little Mountain 2,403 ft 48 E4
Little Mountain 3,317 ft 49 B6
Little Mountain 2,345 ft 49 B7
Little Mountain 2,543 ft 65 F6
Little Mountain 3,707 ft 80 B4
Little Mountain 2,484 ft 82 C2
Little Mountain 2,800 ft 83 A8
Little Mountain 3,660 ft 83 B9
Little Mountain 3,800 ft 83 C9
Little Mountain 3,360 ft 83 D6
Little Mountain 2,661 ft 84 C4
Little Mt Pleasant 3,104 ft 51 B6
Little North Mountain 23 D9
Little North Mountain 24 B1
Little North Mountain 2,240 ft 30 C3
Little North Mountain 2,345 ft 37 A10
Little North Mountain 2,963 ft 37 E8
Little Priest 3,733 ft 51 B7
Little Rock 3,200 ft 82 A1
Little Rocky Mountain 3,402 ft 50 B5
Little Rocky Row 2,448 ft 50 D2
Little Schloss 2,624 ft 23 E7
Little Sluice Mountain 3,113 ft 23 D7
Little Spy Mountain 2,658 ft 38 F1
Little Stone Mountain 3,040 ft 85 D10
Little Stony Man 3,560 ft 31 C10
Little Turkey Knob 3,180 ft 83 A10
Little Valley 83 A6
Little Walker Mountain 3,235 ft 64 F2; 65 E6
Locust Knob 2,776 ft 63 C8
Locust Knob 3,493 ft 64 A1
Locust Mountain 3,904 ft 83 C9
Locust Thicket Mountain 3,110 ft 85 A8
Lone Mountain 2,280 ft 79 C9
Lone Pine Peak 4,054 ft 65 A10
Long Arm Mountain 39 F6
Long Drive Mountain 3,327 ft 38 F1
Long Mountain 2,205 ft 50 C4
Long Mountain 3,400 ft 85 C10
Lookoff Rock 4,120 ft 65 A8
Lookout Mountain 2,864 ft 29 F10
Lost Mountain 3,592 ft 83 E6
Lugar Hill 2,503 ft 66 A1
Lundy Knob 3,030 ft 84 D3
Lunsford Hill 2,042 ft 37 F9
Lusk Hill 2,010 ft 37 F9
Lynn Camp Mountain 3,160 ft 63 F8
Lynville Mountain 1,335 ft 67 D7

M

Macks Mountain 3,363 ft 85 A8
Mad Sheep 4,225 ft 36 B2
Maintop Mountain 4,040 ft 51 A6
Maple Knob 3,120 ft 29 F7
Martins Mountain 2,089 ft 39 B7
Marys Rock 3,514 ft 32 B1
Masons Knob 3,170 ft 66 D5
Massanutten Mountain 23 F9; 30 F5; 31 A8;D6
Massanutten Peak 2,922 ft 30 F5
Massies Mountain 2,168 ft 38 F5
Mayo Mountain 2,056 ft 86 E1
Mays Mountain 2,687 ft 36 D4
Mays Mountain 2,751 ft 30 A2
Mays Mountain 3,216 ft 49 D9
McClung Mountain 2,798 ft 50 A5
McClure Peak 2,757 ft 50 B4
McFalls Mountain 2,770 ft 49 F10
McQueen Knob 3,858 ft 82 E5
Meadow Knob 3,894 ft 30 D1
Meadow Mountain 3,196 ft 38 F3
Medley Valley 63 E9
Meneka Peak 2,393 ft 23 D10
Mertins Rock 2,280 ft 31 A8
Middle Knob 2,846 ft 36 D4
Middle Knob 4,208 ft 82 B2
Middle Mountain 2,480 ft 23 E6
Middle Mountain 3,941 ft 28 D5
Middle Mountain 2,924 ft 29 F10
Middle Mountain 2,800 ft 30 C2
Middle Mountain 2,800 ft 31 B8
Middle Mountain 3,187 ft 36 F3
Middle Mountain 2,057 ft 39 C6
Middle Mountain 3,148 ft 48 E3
Middle Mountain 2,832 ft 49 B10
Middle Mountain 3,042 ft 49 C6
Milford Gap 23 F10
Mill Knob 2,077 ft 66 D2
Mill Mountain 3,297 ft 23 D7
Mill Mountain 2,523 ft 36 F5; 37 E6
Miller Knob 2,283 ft 81 E7
Millers Head 3,484 ft 31 C10
Mine Bank Mountain 3,488 ft 38 F1
Minie Ball Hill 3,947 ft 65 A9
Mitchell Knob 3,224 ft 85 E7
Moccasin Ridge 80 E4; 81 C8;D6
Mock Knob 2,240 ft 82 E1
Mollys Knob 3,270 ft 83 B7
Monterey Mountain 4,062 ft 28 F5
Montgomery Knob 3,560 ft 49 C6
Moore Knob 3,241 ft 80 B5
Moore Mountain 2,605 ft 50 C3
Morning Knob 3,400 ft 48 C4
Morris Hill 2,136 ft 36 F1
Morris Knob 4,455 ft 63 F6
Moses Mountain 2,020 ft 39 F6
Mottesheard Mountain 3,727 ft 48 F1
Mt Carlyle 2,298 ft 37 A6
Mt Pleasant 4,021 ft 50 B5
Mt Rogers 5,729 ft 83 E7
Mud Run Mountain 3,514 ft 49 C6
Mullins Mountain 2,560 ft 62 B3

N

Naked Mountain 2,000 ft 51 B10
Narrow Back Mountain 2,485 ft 30 F1
Neighbor Mountain 2,736 ft 31 B10
Nettle Mountain 3,330 ft 50 A5
Nicholls Knob 3,561 ft 48 C5
No Business Mountain 2,760 ft 50 F3
No Business Mountain 1,978 ft 86 E3
North Mountain 48 F5
North Mountain 49 C9
North Mountain 66 A4
North Sister Knob 3,292 ft 37 C6
Northeast Peak 3,811 ft 37 C6
Nutters Mountain 2,813 ft 48 E4

O

Oak Knob 3,217 ft 85 D10
Oak Knob 3,501 ft 30 D1
Old Rag Mountain 3,268 ft 32 D1
Oliver Mountain 3,565 ft 48 B2
Onion Mountain 3,812 ft 50 F1
Onyx Hill 1,583 ft 30 E3
Opechee Peak 2,621 ft 23 F9
Ore Knob 2,680 ft 85 B7
Orebank Mountain 3,450 ft 49 D9
Osborne Mountain 2,825 ft 62 D3
Oventop Mountain 2,468 ft 32 B1

P

Paddy Mountain 3,013 ft 23 C8
Page Valley 31 B9;C8
Paint Lick Mountain 62 F5
Paint Rock 3,412 ft 62 F5
Painter Mountain 2,800 ft 49 C9
Painter Mountain 3,305 ft 50 A5
Panther Knob 3,232 ft 86 B1
Panther Mountain 2,251 ft 50 C5
Paris Mountain 3,000 ft 66 C2
Pass Mountain 3,052 ft 32 B1
Pats Knob 2,168 ft 51 B8
Patterson Mountain 2,250 ft 49 D6
Pearis Mountain 3,770 ft 65 B6
Peavine Mountain 2,226 ft 50 D3
Penitentiary Hill 2,680 ft 84 F1
Periwinkle Mountain 2,660 ft 85 B6
Perkins Knob 3,852 ft 84 C2
Peters Hill 2,045 ft 48 F3
Peters Mountain 48 D3
Peters Mountain 64 A1; 65 A6
Peters Point 2,288 ft 31 E9
Pickem Mountain 3,420 ft 80 A4
Pierce Mountain 2,037 ft 51 C6
Pike Knob 3,187 ft 85 D6
Pikes Mountain 2,090 ft 86 F1
Pilgrim Knob 2,200 ft 62 C3
Pilot Knob 2,497 ft 61 E7
Pilot Mountain 2,947 ft 66 F1
Pine Hill 2,067 ft 80 E1
Pine Mountain 2,017 ft 31 E8
Pine Mountain 3,341 ft 49 C6
Pine Mountain 2,760 ft 50 E1
Pine Mountain 2,795 ft 60 E3; 61 C6
Pine Mountain 5,526 ft 83 E7
Pine Ridge 80 E2
Pinestand Mountain 2,979 ft 39 B6
Piney Mountain 2,789 ft 31 D8
Piney Mountain 2,778 ft 38 F3
Piney Mountain 2,376 ft 51 C6
Pinnacle Rock 2,107 ft 23 B9
Pinnacle 2,844 ft 23 B9
Pinnacles Of Dan 2,663 ft 85 E10
Piny Knob 2,375 ft 49 C10
Pisgah Hill 2,189 ft 37 E9
PJs Mound 2,258 ft 38 F3
Point Lookout 2,800 ft 85 D10
Pompey Mountain 4,032 ft 51 B6
Pond Hill 2,067 ft 66 E2
Pond Knob 3,586 ft 30 D1
Pond Mountain 3,380 ft 83 C7
Pond Mountains 25 F8
Poor Knob 3,092 ft 84 D2
Poor Mountain 3,920 ft 66 D3
Poor Mountain 3,560 ft 82 B3
Poor Valley Ridge 79 D7
Poor Valley 82 C2
Poorhouse Knob 2,403 ft 66 E1
Pope Knob 3,000 ft 84 E5
Poplar Camp Mountain 2,996 ft 84 C5; 85 B6
Poplar Hollow 23 C9
Poplar Knob 3,080 ft 84 E5
Porter Mountain 3,220 ft 49 B6
Porter Mountain 3,455 ft 84 C1
Potato Hill Knob 3,800 ft 82 B2
Potato Hill 3,684 ft 80 B1
Potts Arm 3,282 ft 48 E4
Potts Mountain 48 E3;F1
Powell Mountain 79 E9;F6
Powell Mountain 2,676 ft 31 E9
Powell Mountain 2,381 ft 65 A6
Powell Mountain 80 B2; D1
Price Mountain 2,710 ft 49 E6
Price Mountain 2,480 ft 65 D10
Prisehouse Mountain 2,720 ft 49 C9
Privett Knob 2,840 ft 84 F1
Prospect Knob 2,540 ft 30 D2
Pt Lookout Mountain 4,550 ft 84 E2
Puckett Knob 2,300 ft 82 E1
Punchbowl Mountain 2,840 ft 50 C3
Purgatory Mountain 2,995 ft 49 E9

QR

Queens Knob 3,205 ft 64 F2
Rader Knob 3,343 ft 30 B2
Raffety Knob 3,186 ft 82 D5
Ragged Mountain 3,320 ft 37 F6
Ragged Mountain 3,300 ft 64 B4
Rakes Knob 2,931 ft 86 B2
Ramsey Mountain 2,150 ft 38 D5
Ramsay Mountain 2,520 ft 84 A4
Ratcliff Knob 2,440 ft 82 D1
Rathole Mountain 2,008 ft 49 D8
Read Mountain 2,353 ft 67 B7
Red Oak Knob 4,229 ft 28 E5
Reddish Knob 4,397 ft 29 E10
Redrock Mountain 4,413 ft 82 A4
Rice Mountain 2,208 ft 50 C4
Rich Hill 2,285 ft 65 C7
Rich Hill 3,026 ft 85 D9
Rich Hills 3,320 ft 29 E6
Rich Mountain 63 E8; 64 D1
Rich Mountain 3,480 ft 82 B3
Rich Mountain 3,627 ft 83 C7
Rich Mountain 3,540 ft 85 F6
Rich Patch Mountains 3,704 ft 49 C6
Rich Valley 81 E8; 82 D1; 83 B6
Richland Mountain 3,373 ft 29 D10
Richwood Knob 3,211 ft 86 D3
Riven Rock Mountain 2,880 ft 30 D1
River Mountain 3,160 ft 82 A1
Roanoke Mountain 2,193 ft 67 D6
Roaring Hill 3,205 ft 83 D10
Robinson Knob 3,300 ft 80 B5
Rock House Mountain 4,000 ft 82 A4
Rock Mountain 2,908 ft 86 E1
Rockfish Valley 38 F4
Rocks Mountain 2,945 ft 38 C5
Rocky Knob 3,572 ft 86 C1
Rocky Mount 2,746 ft 39 A7
Rocky Mountain 2,864 ft 39 A6
Rocky Mountain 2,359 ft 50 F3
Rocky Mountain 3,380 ft 65 A9
Rockytop 2,856 ft 39 A6
Rose Hill 2,540 ft 66 E1
Ross Knob 3,694 ft 83 E9
Rough Mountain 36 F4
Round Hill 2,444 ft 36 B5
Round Knob 2,700 ft 85 B6
Round Mountain 3,448 ft 38 F1
Round Mountain 2,096 ft 49 D9
Round Mountain 2,042 ft 50 F3
Round Mountain 3,952 ft 64 D1
Round Mountain 2,923 ft 64 F5
Round Mountain 3,284 ft 84 C4
Round Top Knob 3,220 ft 83 B6
Round Top 3,986 ft 83 D7
Round Top 3,085 ft 84 C4
Roundhead Mountain 2,160 ft 31 D8
Roundtop 2,969 ft 39 A7
Rowe Mountain 2,334 ft 62 C1
Russell Knob 3,629 ft 83 E10

S

Saddleback Mountain 3,375 ft 31 F8
Sag Top 2,208 ft 31 E10
Sams Knob 3,080 ft 85 F6
Sand Mountain 3,721 ft 84 A2
Sand Mountain 3,040 ft 84 B2
Sand Spring Mountain 3,737 ft 29 E10
Sanders Hill 2,146 ft 82 B5
Sandy Ridge 81 A7
Scott Knob 3,133 ft 63 C9
Scott Mountain 2,762 ft 38 D5
Scott Mountain 2,430 ft 51 C6
Scurff Mountain 2,511 ft 49 C8
Second Mountain 3,566 ft 30 D2
Second Peak 4,857 ft 83 E8
Sells Knob 3,606 ft 83 D9
Seng Mountain 3,629 ft 83 D7
Sentinel Point 3,444 ft 65 B6
Sevenmile Mountain 2,780 ft 48 F1
Seybert Hills 3,173 ft 29 E6
Shady Mountain 2,726 ft 50 C4
Shady Mountain 2,250 ft 51 D6
Sharp Top Mountain 3,852 ft 49 F10
Sharp Top 4,320 ft 83 D6
Shaver Mountain 2,640 ft 30 A2
Sheets Mountain 2,684 ft 49 C8
Shenandoah Mountain 29 F9; 30 C1; 37 C6
Shoal Hill 2,680 ft 84 F1
Shoemaker Knob 2,429 ft 49 C6
Short Hill 25 A8
Short Hill 2,360 ft 84 C4
Short Hills 49 D10
Short Mountain 2,164 ft 23 B9
Short Mountain 2,811 ft 31 A8
Short Mountain 2,337 ft 32 C1
Short Mountain 2,442 ft 36 F4
Short Mountain 3,980 ft 62 F5
Short Mountain 4,200 ft 63 D8
Short Mountain 4,085 ft 82 A4
Short Mountain 2,848 ft 82 E5
Short Mountain 3,000 ft 83 D7
Shortts Knob 2,907 ft 86 A2
Sideling Hill 3,095 ft 37 D6
Signal Corps Knob 3,906 ft 37 A8
Signal Knob 2,106 ft 24 D1
Silas Knob 2,966 ft 50 D3
Silver Peak 2,117 ft 50 B3
Sindion Point 3,018 ft 84 C1
Sinking Creek Mountain 48 F3; 65 B10; 66 B1
Sittlington Hill 2,815 ft 37 A7
Slate Mountain 3,520 ft 86 C1
Slaty Mountain 2,969 ft 48 C2
Smith Hill 2,867 ft 66 F2
Smith Knob 3,080 ft 82 A2
Smith Mountain 2,664 ft 31 D8
Snake Den Mountain 3,660 ft 83 C10
Snake Hollow Mountain 2,904 ft 30 A2
Sounding Knob 4,377 ft 28 F5
Sourwood Mountain 2,595 ft 61 F10
South Mountain 2,800 ft 50 A4
South Sister Knob 3,088 ft 37 C6
Southwest Mountains 39 D10; 40 C1
Spesard Knob 2,034 ft 48 F4
Spitler Hill 3,720 ft 31 D10
Spoon Mountain 3,088 ft 86 D2
Spring Knob 3,356 ft 64 B4
Spruce Run Mountain 3,180 ft 65 B9
Spy Rock 3,701 ft 51 A6
Staley Knob 2,780 ft 83 C7
Stamping Ground Mountain 2,771 ft 49 C9
Steer Knob 3,400 ft 63 F8
Stevens Knob 3,200 ft 84 D3
Stocker Knob 2,887 ft 80 C1
Stockers Knob 2,820 ft 86 B2
Stone Mountain 2,920 ft 62 E3
Stone Mountain 79 D9; 80 C1
Stone Mountain 4,931 ft 83 E8
Stone Mountain 3,164 ft 85 D10
Stoneman Hill 2,510 ft 84 D4
Stony Mountain 3,600 ft 31 D10
Stony Mountain 2,464 ft 85 A7
Stony Ridge 63 D8
Straight Mountain 4,045 ft 83 D6
Straight Mountain 4,160 ft 83 D8
Strickler Knob 2,780 ft 31 B7
Striped Rock 3,400 ft 84 E1
Stuart Mountain 3,280 ft 84 B2
Suck Mountain 2,182 ft 50 F1
Sugar Cove Mountain 2,920 ft 62 C3
Sugar Knob 3,216 ft 23 D7
Sugar Run Mountain 4,087 ft 64 C5
Sugarloaf Knob 2,125 ft 37 C6
Sugarloaf Mountain 3,629 ft 49 D9
Sugarloaf Mountain 2,268 ft 51 B10
Sugarloaf Mountain 2,961 ft 86 B2
Sugarloaf 3,240 ft 32 A1
Sugarloaf 2,217 ft 37 D10
Sugarloaf 3,029 ft 85 E6
Summers Mountain 2,545 ft 37 B6
Sunset Hill 2,044 ft 49 F10
Supin Lick Mountain 2,026 ft 30 A4
Swecker Mountain 3,031 ft 84 B3
Sweet Springs Mountain 3,181 ft 48 C3
Switzer Mountain 2,720 ft 49 E7

T

Tanbark Flat 2,913 ft 31 C10
Target Hill 2,400 ft 50 C3
Tater Knob 2,922 ft 63 E7
Taylor Knob 2,080 ft 82 F1
Tea Mountain 2,391 ft 23 D8
Tearjacket Knob 4,229 ft 29 F9
Terrapin Mountain 3,506 ft 50 E2
Texas Knob 2,620 ft 66 B3
The Bump 3,634 ft 37 B7
The Butt 4,020 ft 81 C10
The Doubles 2,814 ft 60 D5
The Doubles 2,960 ft 82 A2
The Friar 3,357 ft 51 B6
The Haycocks 3,140 ft 86 B2
The Jumps 2,200 ft 63 D6
The Knob 2,600 ft 31 A7
The Knob 2,240 ft 37 E7
The Knob 2,675 ft 49 D10
The Knob 3,163 ft 86 D1
The Loop 2,880 ft 82 A2
The Peak 2,925 ft 32 A2
The Peak 3,674 ft 37 A8
The Pilot 2,760 ft 84 D3
The Pinnacle 3,841 ft 37 A9
The Pinnacle 4,550 ft 84 E1
The Priest 4,063 ft 51 A7
The Rocks 3,120 ft 38 E4
The Stamp 4,115 ft 28 D5
Third Peak 4,928 ft 83 E8
Thomas Mountain 2,250 ft 50 E1
Three Sisters Knobs 2,206 ft 50 D2
Three Sisters 2,086 ft 31 B10
Three Top Mountain 23 E10
Threemile Mountain 2,060 ft 23 E6
Tibbet Knob 2,926 ft 23 E6
Tims Knob 2,966 ft 84 D2
Tinker Mountain 2,980 ft 49 F6
Tinsley Knob 3,220 ft 86 C1
Tobacco Knob 2,521 ft 86 D1
Tobacco Row Mountain 2,932 ft 50 E5
Toby Knob 2,360 ft 84 D4
Toms Knob 3,386 ft 48 D4
Tower Hill Mountain 3,245 ft 36 C5
Tract Mountain 2,713 ft 64 E5
Trayfoot Mountain 3,374 ft 38 B5
Trimble Knob 3,123 ft 28 F5
Trimble Mountain 2,760 ft 29 F10
Turk Mountain 2,946 ft 38 C5
Turkey Knob 3,640 ft 82 B1
Turkey Knob 3,030 ft 84 D3
Turkey Nest Knob 3,240 ft 85 D10
Turners Knob 2,503 ft 86 B3
Turnhole Knob 2,280 ft 65 B6
Twelve O'clock Knob 2,660 ft 66 C4
Twelve O'Clock Knob 2,842 ft 86 C2

UV

Upper Sharp Knob 3,809 ft 83 D9
Utz Hightop 2,140 ft 31 E10

W

Waits Mountain 3,216 ft 49 B7
Walker Knob 2,960 ft 84 D5
Walker Mountain 3,218 ft 37 D7
Walker Mountain 3,494 ft 64 E3;F1
Walker Mountain 64 E3
WALKER MOUNTAIN 65 D6
Walker Mountain 81 E9; 82 C3; 83 A7
Wallace Peak 3,795 ft 37 C6
Wallen Ridge 79 E9;F6; 80 C1
Walnut Knob 4,049 ft 83 F7
Waonaze Peak 2,707 ft 23 F8
Ward Knob 2,980 ft 84 E5
Warm Springs Mountain 3,801 ft 36 F2
Warwick Mountain 2,766 ft 36 C3
Waterfall Mountain 2,780 ft 31 B7
Weaver Mountain 2,864 ft 39 A7
Weavers Knob 2,686 ft 30 A4
Webb Mountain 3,040 ft 82 A2
Well Hill 2,526 ft 66 A1
Wetzel Knob 2,910 ft 30 A3
Wheeler Knob 2,050 ft 85 F7
White Grass Knob 3,261 ft 30 A2
White Rock Mountain 3,200 ft 36 B4
White Rock Mountain 3,286 ft 37 F6
White Rock Mountain 3,341 ft 65 A8
White Rock Mountain 3,380 ft 83 C10
White Rocks 3,580 ft 36 D3
White Rocks 3,380 ft 78 E4
Whiterock Mountain 4,000 ft 82 A4
Whites Peak 2,896 ft 50 B4
Whitetop Mountain 5,525 ft 83 E6
Wigwam Mountain 3,200 ft 50 A5
Wildcat Knob 2,460 ft 86 E1
Wildcat Mountain 3,000 ft 49 C9
Wildcat Mountain 2,695 ft 50 E1
Willie Knob 3,018 ft 84 F3
Willoughby Hill 2,160 ft 82 E2
Wilson Knob 2,805 ft 84 E5
Wilson Mountain 3,095 ft 36 C4
Wilson Mountain 2,044 ft 50 E1
Wind Rock 4,128 ft 65 A9
Witcher Knob 2,871 ft 85 C8
Wolf Creek Mountain 3,724 ft 64 C3
Wolf Knob 2,600 ft 65 B10
Wolf Mountain 2,288 ft 37 F7
Wolfpen Knob 2,840 ft 62 D3
Wrights Valley 63 C8
Wylie Mountain 2,220 ft 65 A6
Wynne Peak 4,273 ft 63 E8

Introduction

The US state of Virginia, officially the Commonwealth of Virginia and nicknamed the Old Dominion, has a diverse environment in its history and physical geographically. Situated in the Mid-Atlantic region, the state borders Maryland and Washington, DC to the north, the Atlantic Ocean to the east, North Carolina and Tennessee to the south, with Kentucky and West Virginia to the west. The coastal plain, or Tidewater region, includes the major estuaries of the Chesapeake Bay and is dominated by marsh and swamplands. The higher elevations in the area provide rich farmland evidenced by extensive agricultural estates. Between this Tidewater and the Appalachian Mountains in the west sit the Piedmont region and the infamous Blue Ridge.

Virginia's varied landscapes supply outdoor enthusiasts with almost endless recreational opportunites. From paddling the James River or surfing at Virginia Beach in the east to horseback riding on one of the numerous multi-use trails or exploring an stalagmite filled cavern in the mountains of the west, the Old Dominion will never disappoint.

Towns arose in the early 1500s as Algonquian peoples farmed and settled in the Tidewater. Vast native trade networks led to the rise of Chief Powhatan, father of Pocahontas. He was the leading military and politcal leader of the regions' native tribes at the time of the first english settlement in North America at Jamestown in 1607. Jamestown is the first corner of what is known as America's Historic Triangle. Williamsburg, the states second capital, forms the next corner and Yorktown, the location of General Cornwallis' surrender to George Washington in 1781 is the third.

Steeped in colonial, Revolutionary and Civil War history, Virginia offers visitors historical sites, museums and living history attractions. Touring Thomas Jefferson's home at Monticello or taking in a Civil War reenactment at New Market Battlefield State Historical Park are only two of the many historical attractions that await.

Also known as the Mother of Presidents for being the birthplace to eight US presidents, Virginia has a major role in the country's government. Arlington is home to the Pentagon, headquarters of the US Department of Defense in the largest office building in the world. Washington, DC is just across the Potomac River where government operations, buildings, monuments and federal parks abound.

Not to be mistaken as frozen in time, Virginia is a vibrant place for art, science and music. Fine art and science museums can be found in most major cities and several music festivals showcase the state's rich variety of musical genres. Winemaking has a long tradition in the Commonwealth and several wineries, as well as breweries and distilleries, are open to the public for tasings and tours.

As a starting point, the Gazetteer features a selection of activities for all interests. For a more comprehensive list of destinations, contact the following state and federal agencies.

TRAVEL

The Virginia Department of Transportation (VDOT) is a comprehensive information source for travelling in the Old Dominion. Through its Travel Center, VDOT provides information on construction projects, traffic and road conditions. VDOT hosts 13 welcome centers providing information to travelers entering the state on interstates and maintains a network of rest areas along the highways.

VDOT is also a source for information on Virginia's scenic highways and byways, which include the famous Blue Ridge Parkway. From maps to travel tips to commuter information VDOT is a one-stop source for the commonwealth's motorists. To obtain up-to-the-minute information on traffic, weather and road conditions in Virginia, visitors and residents can use the VDOT call line at 511 Virginia.

Virginia Department of Transportation
www.virginiadot.org

511 Virginia
www.511virginia.org

STATE FACTS

Admitted to Union:
June 25, 1788; 10th state
Capital: Richmond
Size: 42,775 square miles
Population: 8,535,519 (2019 estimate)
Nickname: Old Dominion
Motto: "Sic Semper Tyrannis–Thus Always to Tyrants"
Song: "Carry Me Back to Old Virginny" by James A. Bland
Bird: Cardinal
Dog: American Foxhound
Insect: Tiger Swallowtail Butterfly
Fish: Brook Trout
Shell: Oyster
Fossil: Chesapecten jeffersonius
Tree: Dogwood
Boat: Chesapeake Bay Deadrise
Major Industries: Healthcare, tourism, government and manufacturing

Major Cities (with Population)
Virginia Beach 449,974
Chesapeake 244,835
Norfolk 242,742
Arlington 236,842
Richmond 230,436
Major Mountains
Mount Rogers ....5,729 feet
Whitetop Mountain ....5,525 feet
Beartown Mountain ....4,689 feet
Elliot's Knob ....4,463 feet
Major Rivers
James ....410 miles
Potomac ....383 miles
Rappahannock ....184 miles
Shenandoah ....150 miles
Roanoke ....410 miles

RECREATION

Virginia Tourism, well known for their slogan, "Virginia is for Lovers," produces a comprehensive guide to travelling in the Commonwealth of Virginia. Before you even depart, they provide information for how to get to the state and put places to stay at your fingertips. Whether you are looking for a campground, a bed & breakfast, a luxury resort or anything in between, Virginia Tourism has you covered.

Within the Old Dominion, Virginia Tourism is the one-stop source for all types of liesurely interests. From historical sites and museums to theme parks, zoos, wineries and gardens, all the notable attractions are accessible. The website highlights the state's endless outdoor activities too, pointing visitors to golf courses, winter sports, bicycle routes and water-sports. They cover hiking trails in the Shenandoah and shopping and nightlife in Richmond. All manner of recreation can be found through Virginia Tourism, including festivals, performances and other annual events.

Virginia Tourism Corporation
www.virginia.org
(800) 847-4882

Virginia's 37 state parks provide a wide variety of recreational activities in all corners of the state. Visitors can paddle and hike where the first English settlers lived at First Landing State Park. They can camp on the Potomac River in the shadow of Washington and Lee at Westmoreland State Park. They can tour a battlefield where the Old Dominion's youngest soldiers held a bridge of critical importance. Visitors to Virginia state parks will find opportunities to bike across soaring bridges, delve into expansive caverns and watch bald eagles nesting. There is boating, fishing and swimming on a variety of lakes and rivers. Trails allow hikers, bikers and horseback riders to ascend peaks, follow old railroad lines and access the Appalachian National Scenic Trail. From the Chesapeake to the heart of Appalachia, there are recreational opportunities waiting at any Virginia state park.

Virginia Department of Conservation & Recreation
www.dcr.virginia.gov/state-parks
(800) 933-PARK (7275)

Further opportunities to recreate exist in Virginia's national parks. A variety of recreational areas and historic sites in the Old Dominion are administered by the National Park Service. Shenandoah National Park features Skyline Drive; a road far above the valley floor with countless scenic overlooks. A museum explores the mountains and valley that was once the "breadbasket of the Confederacy." A network of trails offering true wilderness is just a step from Washington.

Colonial National Historical Park preserves the colonial and revolutionary spirit of early Virginians in two corners of the state's Historic Triangle. The museums, exhibits of living history and reenactments of Yorktown and Jamestown are linked by the Colonial Parkway.

There are sites of a startling variety along the George Washington Memorial Parkway, the route from Washington's home of Mount Vernon to the nation's capital. Great Falls Park offers the chance to step out of civilization. Sites dedicated to historical figures like Clara Barton and Robert E. Lee abound. Bike routes depart from the parkway at every turn, offering cyclists the chance to explore northern Virginia and Washington, DC.

Elsewhere, national historic sites preserve the major battles between the Union and the Confederacy. At Fredericksburg, Manassas and numerous other sites, memories of that tragic period teach visitors lessons of history.

Many other historic sites memorialize important Virginians such as Booker T. Washington and Maggie L. Walker. Assateague Island National Seashore on the far flung Virginia Tidelands is famous for its wild ponies.

Virginia also boasts two national forests. Jefferson and George Washington National Forests, named for two of the state's favorite sons, support recreation in the forested mountains of western Virginia. Visitors have opportunities to fish, hunt, hike, camp and view Appalachian wildlife. Between the forests, parks and historic points, Virginia's federal lands offer unlimited recreation opportunities.

National Park Service
www.nps.gov

USDA Forest Service
www.fs.fed.us/r8/gwj

FISHING AND HUNTING

Virginia's wild spaces provide uncountable opportunities for hunting and fishing. The Gazetteer provides locations and species information for hunting on Wildlife Management Areas and other state facilities. A selection of choice fishing waters is also listed in the Gazetteer. To locate these in the atlas, look on the appropriate map page for the fishing symbol and corresponding four-digit number.

It is important to be familiar with local rules, regulations and restrictions before fishing or hunting in any area. For comprehensive guides and licensing information contact the following agency.

Department of Game & Inland Fisheries
www.dgif.virginia.gov/wildlife
(804) 367-1000

CAMPGROUNDS

Campgrounds with a variety of different facilities are located on state, federal and private lands. The public campground symbol, as shown in the Legend (see inside front cover), identifies campgrounds located within national forests and parks. For all information on fees, services and reservations at public campgrounds, contact one of the state or federal agencies listed above.

The Gazetteer also lists information on a selection of privately owned and operated campgrounds. To locate campgrounds listed in the Gazetteer on the maps, look on the given page for the purple campground symbol and corresponding four-digit number.

Hunting

NAME, LOCATION	PAGE & GRID	ACREAGE	DEER	BEAR	SQUIRREL	RABBIT	FOX	RACCOON	TURKEY	DOVE	GROUSE	RUFFLED GROUSE	QUAIL	WOODCOCK	RAIL	WATERFOWL
Amelia WMA, Amelia	54 F1	2,217	•		•	•	•		•	•			•		•	•
Appomattox–Buckingham State Forest, Appomattox	52 F2	19,808							•							
Big Survey WMA, West Piney	84 B3	7,500	•	•					•	•		•				
Briery Creek WMA, Farmville	70 D4	3,164	•		•	•	•	•	•	•						
Browne SF, Center Cross	56 B4	129	•													
Cavalier WMA, Cornland	95 F10	3,800	•		•				•							
CF Phelps WMA, Remington	33 E7	4,539	•		•	•	•		•	•			•			•
Chickahominy WMA, Williamsburg	74 B2	5,217	•		•				•							•
Chincoteague NWR, Birch Town	47 F6	14,000	•											•		•
Clinch Mountain WMA, Saltville	82 A3	25,477	•	•	•				•		•					•
Conway Robinson SF, Gainesville	25 F9	444	•													
Crooked Creek WMA, Galax	85 E6	1,796	•		•	•			•	•						
Cumberland State Forest, Cumberland	53 E6	16,233	•						•							
Dick Cross WMA, South Hill	91 E6	1,400			•	•				•						
Dragon Run SF, West Point	56 C4	9,562	•													
Eastern Shore of Virginia NWR, Kiptopeke	76 E4	1,127														
Fairystone Farms WMA, Martinsville	86 C4	5,321	•		•	•			•					•		
Featherfin WMA, Beazley Ford	70 A3	2,800	•		•	•								•		
Game Farm Marsh WMA, Windsor Shades	74 A1	429														•
Gathright WMA, Covington	36 E1	13,428	•	•					•							
George Washington National Forest, Luray	31 B7	956,222	•	•	•	•		•	•	•	•	•		•		
Goshen WMA, Craigsville	37 E7	16,125	•						•							
GR Thompson WMA, Front Royal	24 D4	4,084	•		•				•		•					
Great Dismal Swamp NWR, Wallaceton	95 D7	111,000	•	•												
Hardware River WMA, Scottsville	52 B4	1,034	•		•	•			•					•		•
Havens WMA, Roanoke	66 B4	7,190	•		•				•		•					
Hidden Valley WMA, Lebanon	82 B1	6,400	•	•	•				•							

NAME, LOCATION	PAGE & GRID	ACREAGE	DEER	BEAR	SQUIRREL	RABBIT	FOX	RACCOON	TURKEY	DOVE	GROUSE	RUFFLED GROUSE	QUAIL	WOODCOCK	RAIL	WATERFOWL
Highland WMA, McDowell	36 B5	14,283	•	•	•	•			•			•				
Hog Island WMA, Surry	74 D5	3,908	•		•				•					•		•
Horsepen Lake WMA, Buckingham	52 E3	2,910	•		•	•	•	•	•	•			•			
James River NWR, Blairs	73 C10	4,200	•													
James River WMA, Lovingston	52 C1	1,213	•		•	•			•	•						•
Jefferson National Forest, Sugar Grove	83 C8	690,106	•	•	•	•		•	•		•	•		•		
Little North Mountain WMA, Estaline	37 D8	17,572	•						•		•					
Mason Neck NWR, Lorton	34 B4	2,277														
Mattaponi WMA, Bowling Green	42 D2	2,552	•		•				•					•		•
Merrimac Farm WMA, Aden	33 C10	301														
Mockhorn Island WMA, Cape Charles	76 C5	7,356													•	
Pettigrew WMA, Port Royal	42 B3	934			•		•		•	•						
Powhatan WMA, Powhatan	53 E9	4,462	•		•	•	•		•	•			•			•
Presquile NWR, Presque Isle	73 A8	1,329	•													
Prince Edward–Gallion State Forest, Burkeville	71 D6	6,496							•							
Princess Anne WMA, Virginia Beach	96 F4	1,546														•
Ragged Island WMA, Smithfield	95 A7	1,537	•		•											•
Rapidan WMA, Culpepper	31 E10	10,362	•	•	•				•			•		•		
Rappahannock River Valley NWR, Richmond Beach	43 F9	7,711														
Sandy Point SF, King William	56 C2	2,000									•	•	•			
Saxis WMA, Saxis	46 F2	5,678			•	•	•									
Short Hills WMA, Lexington	49 C10	4,232	•	•	•				•	•						
Stewart's Creek WMA, Galax	85 F6	1,087	•		•				•							
Turkeycock Mountain WMA, Martinsville	87 C9	2,679	•		•	•										
White Oak Mountain WMA, Chatham	88 C4	2,748	•						•	•						•

GAME & INLAND FISHERIES REGIONAL OFFICES

Region 1
Charles City Office
3801 John Tyler Hwy
Charles City, VA 23030
(804) 829-6580

Region 2
Forest Office
1132 Thomas Jefferson Rd.
Forest, VA 24551
(434) 525-7522

Region 3
Marion Office
1796 Highway Sixteen
Marion, VA 24354
(276) 783-4860

Region 4
Verona Office
517 Lee Hwy (physical)
P.O. Box 996 (mailing)
Verona, VA 24482
(540) 248-9360

● VDGIF Headquarters
7870 Villa Park Dr. Suite 400 (physical)
P.O. Box 90778 (mailing)
Henrico, VA 23228
(804) 367-1000   ◆ VDGIF Regional Office

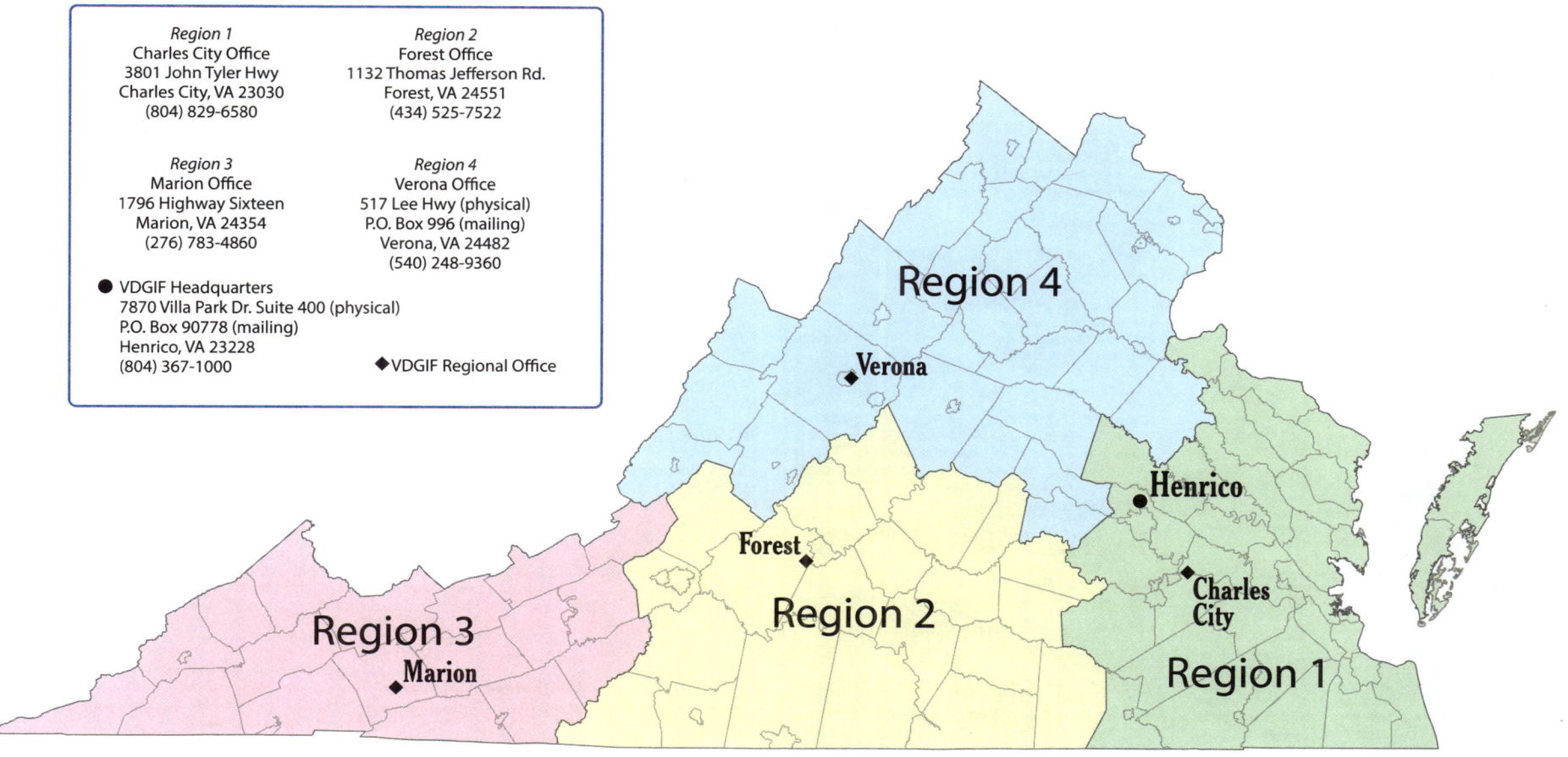

Family Outings

AGECROFT HALL & GARDENS – Richmond – 54 E5 15th-century Tudor house disassembled in England and shipped to Virginia in 1925. Furnished with historical pieces. Elizabethan-style gardens containing 16th- and 17th-century varieties. Herbal knot garden. Fragrance garden. 1920s-style sunken garden.

ALDIE MILL HISTORIC PARK – Aldie – 25 D9 Working mill presents a vision of life in the old rural south by offering milling demonstrations daily. Gristmill at Aldie Mill once served as an important part of the local economy.

THE AMERICAN CIVIL WAR MUSEUM – Richmond – 55 E6 Nation's largest collection of Confederate memorabilia. Exhibits include personal belongings of Confederate President Jefferson Davis, documents, uniforms and other military items. Paintings. Features the White House of Confederacy, a Neoclassical John Brockenbrough house that served as the residence of Jefferson Davis, first and only president of Confederate States of America from 1861 to 1865. Original furnishings.

AMERICAN REVOLUTION MUSEUM AT YORKTOWN – Yorktown – 75 C7 Museum-theater re-creates the crucial sea battle on Virginia coast and siege of Yorktown leading to British surrender in the Revolutionary War. Actors in re-created Continental Army camp portray 18th-century soldiers relating stories of camp life. Multi-media presentations and rotating gallery include documentary film "The Road to Yorktown."

ARLINGTON HOUSE–ROBERT E LEE MEMORIAL – Arlington – 27 E6 Memorial to Confederate General Robert E. Lee and his home from 1831 to 1861. Greek revival-style home built in 1802 by George Washington Parke Custis. Estate commemorates three Virginia families: Lee, Washington and Custis.

ARLINGTON NATIONAL CEMETERY – Arlington – 27 E6 Famous national cemetery with more than 400,000 veterans and their families buried on 624 acres. Tomb of the Unknown Soldier contains three unknown servicemen from World Wars I and II and the Korean Conflict. Memorials to President John F. Kennedy, *USS Maine* sailors and space shuttle *Challenger* astronauts.

ASH LAWN–HIGHLAND – Charlottesville – 39 E9 Former home of fifth US President James Monroe welcomes visitors to a working plantation. Built in 1799 on a 535-acre estate. Family possessions and artifacts. Boxwood gardens.

THE ATHENAEUM – Alexandria – 27 F6 Art gallery housed in restored 1850 Greek Revival building. Varied, temporary exhibits may include painting, sculpture, prints or ceramics. Architecture exhibits.

BACON'S CASTLE – Surry – 74 E5 1665 home built in then-current European style with 18th-century furnishings and an English-style garden. Period herbs, flowers, vegetables and fruit.

BERKELEY PLANTATION – Charles City – 73 B9 1726 Georgian mansion built on site of first official English Thanksgiving in 1619. Costumed guides interpret the history of the birthplace of Benjamin Harrison, signer of the Declaration of Independence and William Henry Harrison, ninth US president. Terraced gardens and period furnishings.

BLANDY EXPERIMENTAL FARM – White Post – 24 C4 700-acre agricultural research facility includes over 8,000 trees. Herb, perennial, boxwood and azalea display gardens. Self-guided interpretive trails. Features the State Arboretum of Virginia and the Boxwood Society's Memorial Garden, a grove of Chinese Ginkgo trees.

BLUE BIRD GAP FARM – Hampton – 75 F9 15-acre working farm and zoo. Farm livestock. Exotic, colorful poultry. Native wildlife including black bears, deer and wolf. Exhibits include antique and modern farm equipment, and artifacts common to Virginia homes.

BLUE RIDGE PARKWAY – Afton – 38 E4 Famed route along the spine of the Blue Ridge Mountains winds through Virginia and North Carolina to Great Smoky Mountains National Park. Elevations range from 649 to 6,053 feet above sea level, offering panoramic views of the Southern Highlands. Visitor centers at Humpback Rocks, James River, Peaks of Otter, Explore Park, Rocky Knob and Blue Ridge Music Center. 217 miles in Virginia.

BOOKER T WASHINGTON NATIONAL MONUMENT – Hardy – 67 E9 Reconstructed Burroughs Plantation, where former slave and educator Booker T. Washington lived during childhood. Audio-visual presentation and exhibits at visitor center. Buildings include tobacco barn, smokehouse, birthplace and kitchen cabin. Self-guided tour follows Plantation Trail.

BUSCH GARDENS WILLIAMSBURG – Williamsburg – 75 C6 Theme park features areas replicating six European countries with rides, shows and exquisite landscapes. Five coasters including Griffon, which plunges downward into a French village from 205 feet at a ninety degree angle. The Curse of DarKastle offers four dimensional frights in an old German castle.

CARLYLE HOUSE HISTORIC PARK – Alexandria – 27 F6 Georgian stone mansion built in 1753 by John Carlyle and patterned after a Scottish country house. Site where British General Braddock held a meeting in 1755 with royal governors to plan early campaigns of the French and Indian War. Period-style garden.

CEDAR CREEK & BELLE GROVE NATIONAL HISTORICAL PARK – Middletown – 24 C1 Belle Grove Plantation served as Union General Sheridan's headquarters during 1864 Battle of Cedar Creek. Stone house built in 1794 with guidance from Thomas Jefferson. Tours of estate and extensive gardens. Auto tour of Cedar Creek Battlefield.

CHESAPEAKE BAY BRIDGE–TUNNEL – Virginia Beach – 96 A2 World's largest bridge–tunnel complex crosses Chesapeake Bay and connects Virginia Beach with Virginia's eastern peninsula. Twelve miles of trestled roadway, two mile-long tunnels and two bridges. Views of Navy and commercial ships using busy shipping channel. Restaurant, gift shop and fishing pier on first island.

CHILDREN'S MUSEUM OF RICHMOND – Richmond – 55 E6 Hands-on exhibits for young children encourage imagination and curiosity. Exhibits include art studio, performing arts area, grocery store, water play area, limestone cave, climbing trees and inventor's lab. Infant/toddler activity area.

CHILDREN'S MUSEUM OF VIRGINIA – Portsmouth – 95 B10 Hands-on exhibits exploring science and everyday experiences. Bubble exhibit. Displays exploring health and the urban environment. Planetarium.

CHINCOTEAGUE NATIONAL WILDLIFE REFUGE – Chincoteague Island – 47 F6 Refuge famous for herd of wild ponies descended from domesticated stock of 17th-century settlers. Coastal habitat on Assateague Island home to many migratory and nesting birds. Network of trails departs from visitor center to explore the habitat and offer views of the wild ponies.

CHIPPOKES PLANTATION STATE PARK – Surry – 74 D5 1,403-acre plantation uses living history exhibits to maintain a working farm. In operation since 1619, producing soy beans, peanuts, corn and beef cattle.

CHRYSLER MUSEUM OF ART – Norfolk – 95 B10 Expansive museum includes works spanning the history of art from ancient Greece, Rome, Asia and pre-Columbian America. European and American art, including works by Rubens, Cézanne, Rodin, Matisse, Cassatt and Homer. Contemporary paintings and sculpture. Extensive glass collection. Photography. Changing exhibits.

CLAUDE MOORE COLONIAL FARM – McLean – 26 D5 Living history farm features period-costumed interpreters demonstrating family life on a small, low-income farm in northern Virginia in 1771. Activities include cultivation of period crops, livestock management and food preparation on an open hearth.

COLONIAL PARKWAY – Williamsburg – 74 C4 Scenic and historic route traverses all the points of Virginia's Historic Triangle. Begins at Jamestown, site of the first English settlement and continues through Colonial Williamsburg to Yorktown, a key site of the Revolution. History is preserved and interpreted at every corner in the Historic Triangle; further opportunities for exploration include a driving tour of the famous battlefields and forts at Yorktown. 23 miles.

COLONIAL WILLIAMSBURG – Williamsburg – 74 C5 Expansive living history project preserves over 500 restored and reconstructed buildings, houses, taverns and shops. Full immersion into 18th-century living in the former capital of Virginia. Live interpretation of our colonial history all year long. Theatrical productions bring to life the events that led to the revolution. Museums of folk art and decorative arts maintain collections of period arts and artifacts.

CUMBERLAND GAP NATIONAL HISTORICAL PARK – Ewing – 78 E2 Historic mountain pass through Appalachian Mountains from Virginia to Kentucky and Tennessee. Preserved settlements, including high altitude cabins and overlooks can be reached by the park's 70 miles of hiking trails. Ranger-led tours of underground caverns. Visitor center with museum exhibits.

DANVILLE MUSEUM OF FINE ARTS & HISTORY – Danville – 88 F3 Five art galleries exhibit work by professional artists and local craftspeople. Research center and rose garden. Historic rooms and local memorabilia on display. Located in 19th-century Italianate mansion.

DINOSAUR LAND – White Post – 24 C3 Life size replicas of various dinosaurs and other ancient beasts. Visitors are greeted by stegosaurus, triceratops and woolly mammoth. 60-foot shark.

EDGAR ALLAN POE MUSEUM – Richmond – 55 E6 Museum presents life and career of poet Edgar Allan Poe. Impressive collection of pictures, relics and verse. Collection includes Poe's trunk, walking stick and wife's trinket box. Poe's handwritten autobiography.

FORT MONROE NATIONAL MONUMENT – Fort Monroe – 75 F10 Fort construction completed in 1834 for protection of Hampton Roads. Decommissioned in 2011. Headquarters of defenses of Chesapeake Bay during World War II. Casemate Museum features cell where Jefferson Davis, President of the Confederacy, was held prisoner.

THE FRALIN MUSEUM OF ART – Charlottesville – 39 D8 Museum at the university founded by Thomas Jefferson boasts an impressive collection of art from the age of Jefferson, both American and international. Also holds a large collection of art from Asia, the ancient Mediterranean and the 20th century, as well as changing exhibits.

FRONTIER CULTURE MUSEUM – Staunton – 38 C2 Living history museum on 78-acre site in the Shenandoah Valley. Farmsteads from the 16th-18th centuries represent different cultures that settled in Virginia. Farms from Native American, US, England, Ireland, Germany and West Africa.

GEORGE C MARSHALL MUSEUM & RESEARCH LIBRARY – Lexington – 50 B2 Museum commemorates the political and military careers of General George C. Marshall, 1953 Noble Peace Prize recipient and author of post–World War II Marshall Plan. Displays include photomurals, electronic World War II map and audio-visual presentations.

GEORGE MASON'S GUNSTON HALL – Lorton – 34 B5 Former colonial plantation home of George Mason, leading anti-federalist and author of the Virginia Bill of Rights, precursor of the Constitution's Bill of Rights. Georgian house features many American Chippendale-style furnishings. Formal gardens and outbuildings.

GEORGE WASHINGTON BIRTHPLACE NATIONAL MONUMENT – Colonial Beach – 43 B7 Birthplace and early childhood home of first US President George Washington. Period furnishings, buildings, flower gardens and crops. Originally Pope's Creek Plantation, later named Wakefield.

GEORGE WASHINGTON MASONIC MEMORIAL – Alexandria – 27 F6 Classic Greek building, 333 feet-high was built from 1922 to 1932 by Freemasons of America to honor president and prominent mason George Washington. Exhibits feature Washington relics, including Washington family bible, as well as paintings, prints and historical documents. Observation deck offers views of the Potomac River and Washington, DC from vantage point on Shooters Hill.

GEORGE WASHINGTON MEMORIAL PARKWAY – Alexandria – 34 A5 Parkway along the Potomac River begins at Mount Vernon, home of first US president, and follows river to Great Falls Park in the capital. Scenic 25-mile route passes through idyllic wooded settings.

GEORGE WASHINGTON'S MOUNT VERNON ESTATE & GARDENS – Alexandria – 34 B5 Historic estate was the home of first US President George Washington. Built in 1735 and restored to 18th-century appearance. Authentically painted and decorated with Washington's original furnishings. 500-acre estate includes tomb of Martha and George Washington, numerous outbuildings and period gardens. Museum on Washington's life. Authentic working gristmill and distillery, built by Washington. Tours of mansion and gardens.

HAMPTON UNIVERSITY MUSEUM – Hampton – 75 F9 Oldest African American museum in the country holds an extensive collection of ethnic art. Traditional art objects from African, Asian, Pacific islands and American Indian cultures. Fine arts collection include paintings by most major 20th-century Black artists. Sculptures and graphics.

HERMITAGE MUSEUM & GARDENS – Norfolk – 95 A10 Collection of Asian and Western art housed in Tudor-style mansion. Paintings, ivories, cloissonné, glass, ceramics, tapestries, furniture and sculpture in marble, bronze and wood. 12 acres of gardens.

HIGHLAND SCENIC TOUR – Lexington – 36 F5 Route through George Washington National Forest explores the ways in which the forest service manages the land. Numerous scenic views on this trip through forested uplands. Passes historic sites in a former mining community. 44 miles.

HISTORIC CRAB ORCHARD MUSEUM & PIONEER PARK – Tazewell – 63 E7 Museum exhibits artifacts from early pioneer families, American Revolution and Civil War periods, and Late Woodland Indians. Exhibits include geology, native plants and animals, and industrialization of Southwest Virginia. Located on 110-acre archaeological site.

HISTORIC JAMESTOWNE – Williamsburg – 74 C4 First permanent English settlement in North America, colonized in 1607. Capital of Virginia from 1607 to 1699. Reconstructed 1608 glasshouse and original Old Church Tower. Excavated foundations and interpretive signs along automobile and walking routes.

HISTORIC KENMORE – Fredericksburg – 42 A1 Colonial mansion of patriot and member of Virginia House of Burgesses Colonel Fielding Lewis. Built for his wife Betty, George Washington's only sister. House noted for plaster decorations. Nearby Ferry Farm is the boyhood home of George Washington and draws visitors with nature trails and archaeology site.

HISTORIC SMITHFIELD PLANTATION – Blacksburg – 65 C10 Costumed guides lead tours of 1772 home built by Colonel William Preston after his uncle, James Patton, was granted 120,000 acres by the King of England. Home of three Virginia governors. Demonstration garden.

HUNTER HOUSE VICTORIAN MUSEUM – Norfolk – 95 B10 Richardsonian Romanesque-style home built in 1894 houses Victorian furnishings and decorative pieces of the James Hunter family. Period reproductions of floor and wall coverings, lighting fixtures and draperies. Open April to December.

JAMES MADISON MUSEUM – Orange – 40 B3 Museum exhibits life and times of fourth US President James Madison. Furnishings from Madison's residence, Montpelier, books, correspondence and women's clothing. Hall of Agriculture features early farm machinery.

JAMES MADISON'S MONTPELIER – Orange – 40 B2 2,700-acre estate, home of fourth US President James Madison. Exhibits on Madison and his role in writing the Constitution. Madison Temple and family cemetery. Formal gardens. Guided tour includes 55-room mansion, stables and extensive gardens.

JAMES MONROE MUSEUM & MEMORIAL LIBRARY – Fredericksburg – 42 A1 Museum houses extensive collection of artifacts that belonged to fifth US President James Monroe and members of his family. Includes fine and decorative arts, furniture, portraits, jewelry, costumes, books and documents. Monroe practiced law on same town lot from 1786 to 1789.

JAMESTOWN SETTLEMENT – Williamsburg – 74 C4 Living history site re-creates the lives of the first 17th-century settlers with demonstrations, reproductions and exhibits. Full-scale replicas of the English sailing ships that brought the first permanent colonists to Virginia. Re-created Powhatan Peoples village. Recon-

HISTORIC CIVIL WAR SITES

APPOMATTOX COURT HOUSE NATIONAL HISTORICAL PARK – Appomattox – 69 A10 Former village of Appomattox Court House restored to 1865 appearance. Commemorates surrender of Confederate General Robert E. Lee's Army of Northern Virginia to General Ulysses S. Grant, General-in Chief of all Union forces, marking the end of the War Between the States. Visitor center in courthouse offers living history programs and museum exhibits. Buildings include McLean House, site of the surrender.

BALL'S BLUFF BATTLEFIELD REGIONAL PARK – Leesburg – 25 B10 Park preserves site of the Battle of Ball's Bluff, Confederate victory that took place on October 21, 1861. Surrounds Ball's Bluff National Cemetery, containing graves of 54 soldiers who died in battle. Interpretive trail. Guided tours.

THE CAPITOL – Richmond – 55 E6 Built in 1788. Designed by Thomas Jefferson to resemble a French temple, Maison Carrée. Famous for Aaron Burr's treason trial. Officially made Capitol of Confederacy May 21, 1861. Statue of Robert E. Lee in Hall of Delegates. Busts of Confederate heroes include Stonewall Jackson, J.E.B. Stuart, Joseph E. Johnston and Fitzhugh Lee. Guided and self-guided tours.

FORT WARD MUSEUM & HISTORIC SITE – Alexandria – 26 F5 Reconstructed, 36-gun Union fort built to defend Washington, DC, against Confederate attack. Fifth largest fort of a group called Defenses of Washington. Museum houses large collection of Civil War artifacts. Living history exhibits interpret Alexandria as an occupied city.

FORT WOOL – Fort Monroe – 75 F10 Fort built on 15-acre island, artificially created by placing stone slabs on top of Rip Raps Shoal. Fort construction began in 1819 and continued through early 1900s. Fort supported Union fleet during battle of ironclad ships *Monitor* and *Virginia (Merrimack)*. Accessible by boat only.

FREDERICKSBURG & SPOTSYLVANIA NATIONAL MILITARY PARK – Fredericksburg – 42 A1 6,500-acre park commemorating four major Civil War battles—Fredericksburg, Chancellorsville, Wilderness and Spotsylvania. Main visitor center in Fredericksburg. Museums located in Fredericksburg and Chancellorsville. Audio-visual presentations describing troop movements. Seasonal living-history programs. Sites include Stonewall Jackson Shrine, Salem Church and Chatham Manor. Self-guided automobile tour.

MANASSAS NATIONAL BATTLEFIELD PARK – Manassas – 25 F10 3,800-acre battlefield park commemorates the two battles of Manassas (Bull Run). The first major battle between the Union and the Confederacy occurred here in July 1861. A second battle took place on the same field in August 1862. A Confederate victory led to the pinnacle of Southern power and chances for independence. Visitor center displays slide and map program describing troop movements of opposing armies. Interpretive trails. Sites include Stone Bridge, Stone House and Unfinished Railroad.

MORVEN PARK – Leesburg – 25 B10 Turn of the 20th-century mansion evolved from fieldstone farmhouse, located in Virginia's hunt country. Rooms and furnishings of various styles and times. Museum of Hounds & Hunting. Winmill Carriage Museum. International Equestrian Center. Expansive gardens.

PETERSBURG NATIONAL BATTLEFIELD – Fort Lee – 73 C7 2,740-acre park preserving largest battlefield and site of longest siege of the Civil War, from June 18, 1864, to April 2, 1865. During battle, crater was forged by Pennsylvanian regiment of coal miners who tunneled 510 feet and exploded four tons of gun powder beneath Confederate line. Entrance to tunnel and crater among exhibits. Petersburg National Cemetery. Self-guided tour and living history programs. Visitor center.

RICHMOND NATIONAL BATTLEFIELD PARK – Richmond – 55 E6 Battle for former supply depot and Confederate capital memorialized in several park units east and south of Richmond. Visitor center at Tredegar Iron Works. Civil War exhibits, battlefield diagrams, audio-visual presentation and living history programs.

SAILOR'S CREEK BATTLEFIELD STATE PARK – Jetersville – 71 B7 Park preserves battlefield of last major battle of the Civil War. The Confederate defeat on April 6, 1865, forced Lee's surrender of the Army of Northern Virginia at Appomattox three days later. Annual reenactments.

STAUNTON RIVER BATTLEFIELD STATE PARK – Randolph – 90 B1 Site where, in June 1864, a relatively small group of Confederate soldiers, mostly old men, young boys and local citizens, defended a railroad bridge and important supply line against 5,000 Union cavalry forces. Well-preserved earthwork fort, rifle trenches and other battle remnants. Multi-use trail passes through battlefield. Two visitor centers with exhibits.

structed James Fort contains 18 wattle and daub buildings, similar to first homes of colonists.

JOHN TYLER'S SHERWOOD FOREST – Charles City – 74 B1 Working plantation built in 1680 and owned continuously by family of tenth US President John Tyler. At 300 feet, longest frame house in US. Furnished with 18th- and 19th-century Tyler family heirlooms. 25 acre grounds.

KINGS DOMINION – Doswell – 55 A6 Theme park boasts 13 roller coasters of both wooden and steel varieties on 400 acres. Kidzville area has many attractions for the young. Water Works area includes a wave pool and numerous water slides.

LEE CHAPEL & MUSEUM – Lexington – 50 B2 Victorian gothic brick building built in 1867. Commemorates Robert E. Lee's service as president of Washington College from 1865 to 1870. Exhibits include Peale portrait of George Washington, Edward Valentine statue of Lee and Lee's office. Lee's burial place.

LIGHTSHIP MUSEUM – Portsmouth – 95 B10 Museum housed in *Lightship Portsmouth*, commissioned in 1915. Traces history of Lightship Service beginning in 1820. Ship restored to original condition. Galley, quarters and large windlass room on display.

LONGWOOD CENTER FOR THE VISUAL ARTS – Farmville – 70 B5 Art museum of Longwood University. Permanent collections include works of contemporary Virginia artists and 19th-century American art. Changing exhibitions.

LURAY ZOO – Luray – 31 B9 Rescue zoo provides a home for over 250 former exotic pets. Tigers, wallabies and kookaburras. Opportunities for up-close experiences with numerous animals. Large snake collection.

MACARTHUR MEMORIAL – Norfolk – 95 B10 City square of four buildings commemorates life of US Army General Douglas MacArthur. Theater contains displays and news reels on MacArthur's career. Library and archives house over two million items of correspondence, photographs, messages and maps.

MAGGIE L WALKER NATIONAL HISTORIC SITE – Richmond – 55 E6 Restored home of prominent African American community leader and first woman in US to charter and serve as president of a bank. Original furnishings. Guided tours.

MAGNOLIA GRANGE HOUSE & MUSEUM – Chesterfield – 72 A5 Federal-style plantation house built in 1822 by William Winfree. Noted for distinctive architecture including sophisticated carvings and ceiling medallions. Period wallpaper and carpeting. Living history exhibits interpret the lifestyle of the plantation's 19th century inhabitants.

THE MARINERS' MUSEUM – Newport News – 75 F8 Maritime historical museum features figureheads, model ships and nautical instruments. International small craft collection. *USS Monitor* Center explores multiple facets of the first armored gunboat and its famous battle with the *CSS Virginia*. 17th-century paintings. Extensive photograph collection.

MARTINSVILLE SPEEDWAY – Ridgeway – 87 E7 Oval racetrack built in 1947 features two NASCAR Sprint Cup races annually. The shortest track used in the Sprint Cup is also a part of NASCAR's modified racing tour and truck series.

MAYMONT – Richmond – 55 E6 Country estate of James Dooley preserves 25 historic buildings among gardens and wildlife. Carriage house with collection of period carriages. Children's farm features domestic Virginia livestock. Nature Center preserves the wildlife of the James River in a series of aquariums. A wildlife park provides natural habitats for larger animals including bison and bears. Variety of specialized gardens.

MEADOW FARM MUSEUM – Glen Allen – 54 C5 Living history museum and 19th-century farm. 150 acres of pasture and woodland provide a setting for costumed interpreters of the rural south. Historic fruit orchard. Farm animals and native wildlife. Audio-visual presentation and rotating exhibits.

MEADOWLARK BOTANICAL GARDENS REGIONAL PARK – Vienna – 26 D3 Former private farm is now a 95-acre park. Herb garden. Azalea and lilac garden. Korean Bell garden. Collection of flowering cherry trees. Spring-blooming bulbs. Walking trails.

MILL MOUNTAIN ZOO – Roanoke – 67 C6 Mountain-top zoo overlooking Roanoke Valley. 29 species of native and exotic animal. Bald eagle, python, mountain lions, spider monkeys and prairie dogs. Domestic hoofstock and small mammals.

MUSEUM OF THE SHENANDOAH VALLEY – Winchester – 24 A2 Museum explores the art, history and culture of the valley. Authentic, 18th-century home furnished with period art and artifacts. Six-acre garden. Permanent and changing exhibits on various elements of the Shenandoah Valley through several time periods.

NASA VISITOR CENTER – New Church – 46 F5 Exhibits at launch facility on Wallops Island chronicle the history of flight. Hands-on displays include rocket and satellite models. Moon rock and space suit.

NATIONAL AIR & SPACE MUSEUM – Chantilly – 26 E1 Smithsonian Institution facility displays over 200 historic aircraft and large space artifacts, several aircraft engines and more than 1,000 smaller artifacts. Highlights include space shuttle *Enterprise*, Lockheed SR-71 Blackbird, Boeing 367-80 (Boeing 707 prototype), B-29 Superfortress *Enola Gay* and Concorde. Observation tower. Flight simulator. IMAX theater.

NATIONAL INVENTORS HALL OF FAME MUSEUM – Alexandria – 27 F6 Exhibits highlight achievements of over 200 inventors. Includes workshops and educational programs.

NAUTICUS – Norfolk – 95 B10 Museum explores maritime activities, both military accomplishments and peaceful commercial relations. The battleship *Wisconsin*, docked at Nauticus, can be toured or explored. Exhibits on the launching of the 1907 American fleet and deep sea exploration among other permanent and changing exhibits. 3-D movies.

NORFOLK BOTANICAL GARDENS – Norfolk – 96 B1 155-acre public gardens. Azalea garden containing 200,000 specimens. Bicentennial Rose garden. Rhododendron, Japanese and perennial gardens. Fragrance garden for the blind. Tropical Display House containing tropical plants and orchids. Flowering arboretum. 12 miles of walking trails. Train and boat tours.

NORTH ANNA NUCLEAR INFORMATION CENTER – Mineral – 41 D7 Hands-on, electronic displays and films illustrate nuclear power generation and other modern power systems. Bicycle generator, fiber optics display and computer quiz.

OATLANDS HISTORIC HOUSE & GARDENS – Leesburg – 25 C9 Three-story, Greek Revival-style mansion built in 1804 by George Carter. Interior decorated in Greek Revival-style with molded plaster designs and flanking staircases. Formal terraced gardens. Guided and self-guided tours.

PAMPLIN HISTORICAL PARK & THE NATIONAL MUSEUM OF THE CIVIL WAR SOLDIER – Petersburg – 73 D6 Battlefield Center illustrates battle through artifacts and interactive displays. Breakthrough trail details events on the April 2, 1865 battlefield. The National Museum of the Civil War Soldier explores soldier life during the War Between the States. Living history demonstrations. Restored 1810 Tudor Hall Plantation.

PATRICK HENRY'S SCOTCHTOWN – Beaverdam – 54 A4 Home of American statesman and orator Patrick Henry during his period of orations from 1771–1778. Restored manor house furnished with 18th-century antiques.

THE PENTAGON – Arlington – 27 E6 One of the largest office buildings in the world houses US Department of Defense. 17.5 miles of corridors. Built during early years of World War II. Guided tours.

POPLAR FOREST – Lynchburg – 68 B4 Brick octagonal villa, built 1806-1816, is one of only two houses that Thomas Jefferson designed for himself. Served as a retreat when visiting his nearby plantations. Guided tours explain on-going restoration process.

PORTSMOUTH NAVAL SHIPYARD MUSEUM – Portsmouth – 95 B10 Museum houses models of first shipyard, established in 1767, and first dry-docked ship in US history. Displays interpret battle preparations for Confederate ironclad *Virginia* with Union's ironclad *Monitor*. Exhibits include flags, swords, weaponry and regional maps.

PRESTWOULD PLANTATION – Clarksville – 90 E3 Built in 1795 by American-born baronet Sir Peyton Skipwith. House noted for scenic wallpapers and Lady Skipwith's library.

RED HILL – Brookneal – 69 F9 National Memorial and burial place of American statesman and orator Patrick Henry. Includes museum, reconstructed home and original law office. Exhibits include Henry's furnishings and other memorabilia.

RIVER FARM – Alexandria – 35 A6 Headquarters of American Horticultural Society features collection of test and display gardens. Wildflower meadow. Orchard with a varity of fruit trees. Sunken wall garden and Wildlife Garden with ponds and plants that attract birds, turtles and frogs.

SCIENCE MUSEUM OF VIRGINIA – Richmond – 55 E6 Hands-on exhibits housed in Richmond's original train station. Electricity and computer displays. Aerospace and crystal exhibits. Aquarium and planetarium. IMAX theater.

SCIENCE MUSEUM OF WESTERN VIRGINIA – Roanoke – 67 C6 Hands-on exhibits covering natural history, oceanography, weather and energy. Computer displays. Planetarium.

SHENANDOAH CAVERNS – Quicksburg – 31 A6 Underground caverns can be toured along a one-mile route. Elevator service brings visitors to a level cave surface that showcases spectacular underground formations. Aboveground Yellow Barn holds various exhibits on agriculture. Children's attraction, Main Street of Yesteryear, re-creates mid-20th-century department store window displays.

SHIRLEY PLANTATION – Charles City – 73 B8 Georgian mansion built 1723–1738 on the site of the first Virginia plantation. Outbuildings form unique Queen Anne forecourt. Original interiors feature carved staircase, window panes and paneling. Birthplace of Anne Hill Carter, mother of Confederate General Robert E. Lee. Guided tours.

SHOT TOWER HISTORIC STATE PARK – Max Meadows – 84 B5 Shot tower used for lead manufacturing, built in 1807 by Thomas Jackson. Lead was dropped the height of the tower, from a sieve into a kettle.

SKYLINE DRIVE – Front Royal – 24 E2 Popular, scenic route through Shenandoah National Park follows ridge tops of the Blue Ridge Mountains. Numerous overlooks offer outstanding views of surrounding mountains and valleys. Two visitor centers, five campgrounds and numerous picnic areas. Joins Blue Ridge Parkway at southern end. 105 miles.

SMITH'S FORT PLANTATION – Surry – 74 D4 1765 colonial house on land given by Chief Powhatan as a wedding gift to John Rolfe and his daughter Pocahontas in 1614. House noted for original woodwork and period furnishings. Small English garden.

SOUTHWEST VIRGINIA MUSEUM HISTORICAL STATE PARK – Big Stone Gap – 80 B2 Museum displays depict history and culture of southwest Virginia. Exhibits include antique firearms, weaponry, Native American artifacts and early frontier tools. Local mountain crafts.

STONEWALL JACKSON HOUSE – Lexington – 50 B2 Former home of Confederate General Thomas Jonathan "Stonewall" Jackson. Furnishings include Jackson's personal belongings and furniture. Restored garden. Audio-visual presentation and guided tour.

STRATFORD HALL – Montross – 43 C8 Birthplace of Confederate General Robert E. Lee and home to the Lee family, including Revolutionary war hero Light Horse Harry Lee. Georgian manor house was built 1730–1738 by Thomas Lee and features an elaborately paneled Great Hall. Rebuilt grist mill. Formal gardens and nature trails.

TEMPLE HALL FARM REGIONAL PARK – Leesburg – 25 A10 Working farm allows for animal encounters in an educational experience. Alpacas and miniature horses alongside traditional barnyard creatures. Guided and unguided tours. Corn maze.

THOMAS JEFFERSON'S MONTICELLO – Charlottesville – 39 E9 Mountaintop estate designed and built by Declaration of Independence author Thomas Jefferson. Residence and burial place. Original furnishings. Re-created gardens. Guided tours of entire estate.

US ARMY TRANSPORTATION MUSEUM – Fort Eustis – 75 D7 Museum examines US Army transportation vehicles from American Revolution to present. Exhibits include experimental vehicles, helicopters, amphibious craft, and overland transport and supply vehicles.

US ARMY WOMEN'S MUSEUM – Fort Lee – 73 C7 Museum interprets history of women in US Army. Exhibits feature uniforms, military insignia and photographs, highlight current achievements. Located at Fort Lee, home of Women's Army Corps Training Center from 1948 to 1954.

VIRGINIA AIR & SPACE CENTER – Hampton – 75 F9 Visitor center for NASA Langley Research Center presents more than 40 exhibits outlining achievements in air and space travel highlighting current NASA research. Interactive exhibits include scale models of NASA rockets and space shuttle, space suit and *Viking Mars Lander*. Guided tours.

VIRGINIA AQUARIUM & MARINE SCIENCE CENTER – Virginia Beach – 96 C4 Aquarium features animal life of Chesapeake Bay and the Atlantic Ocean as well as that of a saltwater marsh. Science center presents hands-on exhibits interpreting Virginia's marine environments. Bird aviary. IMAX theater.

VIRGINIA BEACH SURF & RESCUE MUSEUM – Virginia Beach – 96 B4 Museum housed in former US Life-Saving/Coast Guard Station built in 1903. Depicts history of the US Life-Saving and Coast Guard services and shipwrecks off Virginia coast. Interactive and changing exhibits.

VIRGINIA DISCOVERY MUSEUM – Charlottesville – 39 E9 Hands-on displays explore science, history and art. Exhibit topics include space and design, colors, music, optics, and spinning and weaving.

VIRGINIA LIVING MUSEUM – Newport News – 75 E8 Zoological park and museum presents the native animals of Virginia in their natural habitats. Elevated boardwalk traverses forests and wetland, offering views of wolves, foxes, deer and other Virginia animals. Museum exhibits the life of Virginia's mountains and coastal plains. Two-story glass aviary. Planetarium. Observatory.

VIRGINIA MILITARY INSTITUTE MUSEUM – Lexington – 50 B2 Collection of military memorabilia includes belongings of General Stonewall Jackson, former VMI professor, and George C. Marshall. Civil War art collection.

VIRGINIA MUSEUM OF FINE ARTS – Richmond – 55 E6 State's chief art museum features ancient to modern art including paintings, sculpture and decorative arts. African art collection. Russian Imperial jewels including Faberge Easter eggs. Artifacts from India, Tibet and Nepal. Works by Monet, Renoir and van Gogh.

VIRGINIA MUSEUM OF NATURAL HISTORY – Martinsville – 87 D7 Museum explores Virginia's natural heritage through visual and hands-on exhibits. 22-million-item collection includes a complete fossil of 500 million year old stromatolite. Includes rocks and minerals, Native American stone tools and solar system exhibits.

VIRGINIA MUSEUM OF THE CIVIL WAR – New Market – 31 B6 300-acre grounds memorializing 1864 Battle of New Market where 6,300 Union and 4,100 Confederate soldiers, including 257 cadets from Virginia Military Institute, clashed to Southern victory. Hall of Valor Civil War Museum chronicles the war through exhibits including the Emmy-award-winning film *Field of Lost Shoes*.

VIRGINIA MUSEUM OF TRANSPORTATION – Roanoke – 67 C6 Restored railway freight station holds diverse collection of historical vehicles. Features steam, electric and diesel locomotives. Caboose and railway post office cars. Auto collection holds cars from every decade, freight trucks, fire engines and carriages.

THE VIRGINIA WAR MUSEUM – Newport News – 75 F8 Museum documents US military history from 1775 to the present. More than 50,000 artifacts include uniforms, weapons, accoutrements and propaganda posters. Exhibits include 1883 brass Gatling Gun and early American light tank.

VIRGINIA ZOO – Norfolk – 95 B10 Growing zoological park with a variety of exotic and native animals. Featured areas include the African Okavango Delta where giraffes and elephants roam a naturalistic setting. North America exhibit includes a Virginia Barnyard and an expansive prairie dog town.

WATER COUNTRY USA – Williamsburg – 75 C6 Water park themed around the 1950s features a variety of rides, slides and shows. Speed slides, tube slides, family raft rides. Watercoaster accelerates riders up hills and around curves. Two lazy river rides including the Hubba Hubba Highway, a high current trip around a 1,500 foot loop with no tube necessary. Wave pool. High-diving show.

WILTON HOUSE MUSEUM – Richmond – 54 E5 Georgian house built in 1753 by William Randolph III. Moved in 1933 from Richmond to present site overlooking the James River. Queen Anne and Chippendale-style furniture. Original paneling and window panes. Once headquarters of French general and American Revolution supporter Marquis de Lafayette. Guided tours.

WOODROW WILSON PRESIDENTIAL LIBRARY & MUSEUM – Staunton – 38 C2 Greek Revival townhouse built in 1846 was the birthplace of 28th US President Thomas Woodrow Wilson. Many original Wilson family furnishings. Wilson's 1919 PierceArrow limousine. Adjacent museum explores numerous facets of the *14 Points Plan* author's life.

YORKTOWN BATTLEFIELD – Yorktown – 75 C7 Site commemorates George Washington's victory over British General Lord Cornwallis and the last major battle of the American Revolution. Reconstructed earthworks of army batteries. French and American encampments and headquarters. Old town with buildings and homes of British officers. Visitor center and self-guided tours.

WASHINGTON, DC OUTINGS

FREDERICK DOUGLASS NATIONAL HISTORIC SITE – Washington – 27 E7 Home of the noted 19th-century abolitionist preserved with period furnishings. Visitor center contains museum exhibit and film on Douglass' life and work. Guided tours.

INTERNATIONAL SPY MUSEUM – Washington – 27 E6 Large collection of spy-related artifacts in museum dedicated to exhibiting the role of espionage throughout world history. Interactive exhibits and programs engage visitors thoroughly. Programs for kids and adults include scavenger hunts and mission simulations.

NATIONAL GALLERY OF ART – Washington – 27 E6 Extensive collection of western art, including paintings, sculpture, decorative arts and photographs. Permanent collection features French and Italian paintings and sculpture of the 14th-17th centuries. Regularly changing exhibits. Concert series September to May.

SMITHSONIAN MUSEUMS – Washington – 27 E6 Smithsonian Institution maintains a series of national museums on the National Mall. Museum of Natural History. National Museum of American History. National Air and Space Museum. American Art Museum. National Museum of the American Indian. National Portrait Gallery. National Postal Museum. Hirshhorn Museum and Sculpture Garden. Museum of African Art.

SMITHSONIAN NATIONAL ZOO – Washington – 27 E6 Zoological park houses over 1,500 animals of 300 species, including its famous giant pandas. Animals from all over the world include big cats and gorillas. South American bears, Amazonian frogs, Asian elephant and farm animals.

THOMAS JEFFERSON MEMORIAL – Washington – 27 E6 Memorial to the Virginia statesman is designed to recall the Parthenon of ancient Greece. The inside of the memorial, dedicated to the author of The Declaration of Independence and lifelong devotee of liberty, is inscribed with his own words. Completed in 1943.

WASHINGTON MONUMENT – Washington – 27 E6 World's tallest obelisk memorializes the "Father of His Country," Virginia general and statesman George Washington. Obelisk is notably mirrored in the reflecting pool that lies at its foot. Completed in 1884.

Recreation Areas

NAME, LOCATION	PAGE & GRID	ACREAGE	AGENCY	EQUESTRIAN CAMPING	CAMPING	CABINS	SWIMMING	HIKING	HORSEBACK RIDING	BIKING	PICNICKING	BOATING	COMMENTS
Algonkian Regional Park, Sterling	26 C2	838	NVRPA			•	•	•			•	•	Day-use park along Potomac River. Volcano Island Waterpark with slides and 500-gallon dumping bucket. Golf course. Boat ramp. Mini-golf.
Appomattox–Buckingham State Forest, Appomattox	52 F2	19,808	VDOF					•	•	•	•		Hardwood and pine forest surrounding Holliday Lake State Park. Rolling terrain.
Assateague Island National Seashore, Chincoteague	47 F6	15,616	NPS		•		•	•	•				The park's wild horses roam freely on both sides of the state line. Trails offer hikers chances to watch them from a moderate distance.
Barbours Creek Wilderness, Jefferson National Forest	48 D4	5,382	USFS		•			•					Forested terrain in a remote valley. Wildflowers.
Bear Creek Lake State Park, Cumberland	53 E6	329	VDCR		•	•	•	•			•	•	40-acre lake surrounded by gently rolling, wooded terrain. Fishing pier.
Beartown Wilderness, George Washington National Forest	63 E8	5,613	USFS					•					Diverse forest with a rugged landscape, far from the well-travelled areas of the National Forest.
Belle Isle State Park, Lancaster	57 B6	892	VDCR		•			•	•	•	•	•	Diverse landscapes feature 8 miles of river frontage on the lower Rappahannock.
Bourassa State Forest, Graves Store	68 E1	288	VDOF					•	•				Mixed hardwood forest is used for various purposes.
Breaks Interstate Park, Breaks	61 B8	4,600	BIPC		•	•	•	•	•		•	•	Park in Virginia and Kentucky. Scenic overlooks of Breaks Canyon, a deep gorge along the Russell Fork River, known as "The Grand Canyon of the South". Rock climbing, zipline and water park. Visitor Center.
Bull Run Regional Park, Centreville	26 F1	1,500	NVRPA		•		•	•	•		•		Atlantis Waterpark. Skeet and trap shooting center with indoor archery range. Disc golf. Access to Occoquan Water Trail.
Caledon State Park, King George	42 A5	2,587	VDCR					•	•		•		Forested area offers hikers the chance to spot bald eagles in their natural habitat.
Carvins Cove Natural Reserve, Roanoke	66 A5	12,700	RPR					•	•	•		•	Second largest municipal park in US. Over 60 miles of trails with varying degrees of difficulty. Scenic overlooks.
Claytor Lake State Park, Dublin	65 E8	472	VDCR		•	•	•	•			•	•	21-mile-long lake supports a sandy swimming beach, a marina and a boat ramp. Historic Howe house.
Conway Robinson State Forest, Gainesville	25 F9	444	VDOF					•	•		•		Old-growth forest offers a natural setting for recreation close by important historic sites.
Crawfords State Forest, Providence Forge	56 F1	258	VDOF					•	•				Hardwood forest is used for education and demonstration of forestry techniques.
Cumberland State Forest, Cumberland	53 E6	16,233	VDOF					•	•	•	•		Hardwood and pine forest in Virginia's piedmont territory.
Douthat State Park, Millboro	36 F3	4,545	VDCR		•	•	•	•		•	•	•	Sandy swimming beach on a high altitude lake with Alleghany Mountain scenery.
Fairy Stone State Park, Stuart	86 C4	4,741	VDCR		•	•	•	•	•	•	•	•	Sandy swimming beach on 168-acre lake. Named for unusual staurolite crystals.
False Cape State Park, Virginia Beach	96 E5	3,844	VDCR		•			•		•			Access on foot or bicycle through Back Bay National Wildlife Refuge or by boat.
First Landing State Park, Virginia Beach	96 A3	2,888	VDCR		•	•	•	•		•	•		Site of English colonists' first arrival. One of Virginia's most visited parks. Chesapeake Bay frontage and diverse natural landscape with 20 miles of trails.
Fountainhead Regional Park, Fairfax Station	34 A3	2,000	NVRPA					•		•	•	•	Scenic views of Occoquan Lake. Boat ramp and access to Occoquan Water Trail. Mini golf.
George Washington National Forest, Luray	31 B7	956,222	USFS	•	•	•	•	•	•	•	•	•	Mountains and valleys in northwestern Virginia and West Virginia. Hiking trails including Appalachian National Scenic Trail.
Grayson Highlands State Park, Volney	83 E8	4,502	VDCR	•	•			•	•				Rugged mountain scenery with views of Mount Rogers. Access to Appalachian National Scenic Trail.
Great Falls Park, Great Falls	26 D3	800	NPS					•	•	•	•		Quiet spot on the George Washington Memorial Parkway where the Potomac tumbles through Mather Gorge. Museum exhibits on local history.
Hawks State Forest, Lambsburg	85 F6	121	VDOF					•					Demonstrates forest management and protects wildlife in a unique natural area.
Hemlock Overlook Regional Park, Clifton	34 A2	890	NVRPA		•			•	•		•		Outdoor education center with obstacles and group programs is available by reservation. Hiking and bridle trails open to public.
Holliday Lake State Park, Appomattox	70 A2	560	VDCR		•		•	•	•	•	•	•	Aquatic recreation on a 150-acre lake. Idyllic forest setting for a swimming beach and boat launch.
Hungry Mother State Park, Marion	83 B7	3,334	VDCR		•	•	•	•			•	•	Sandy swimming beach on 108-acre boating lake. Park surrounds Molly's Knob.
James River Face Wilderness, Jefferson National Forest	50 D2	8,907	USFS		•			•	•				The area south of the James River offers some high peaks and the descents of the James River Gorge.
James River State Park, Gladstone	51 D10	1,561	VDCR		•	•	•	•	•	•	•	•	Rolling hills, fishing ponds and meadows alongside three miles of frontage on the James River.
Jefferson National Forest, Marion	83 C8	690,106	USFS	•	•		•	•	•	•	•	•	Wooded mountains and valleys extending nearly to the western tip of Virginia from James River. 950 miles of hiking trails including Appalachian National Scenic Trail.
John H Kerr Dam & Reservoir Project, Boydton	91 F6	105,000	USACE		•		•	•			•	•	Day-use and overnight facilities at an extraordinary fishing lake. Largest man-made lake in the state.
John W Flannagan Dam & Reservoir Project, Haysi	61 C7	8,600	USACE		•		•				•	•	1,145-acre lake nestled in the Cumberland Mountains. Visitor Center. Marina.
Kimberling Creek Wilderness, Jefferson National Forest	64 D3	6,277	USFS					•					Hardwood forest has no maintained trails and steep, difficult terrain.
Kiptopeke State Park, Cape Charles	76 D4	562	VDCR		•	•	•	•		•	•	•	Chesapeake Bay setting is a major flyway for migratory birds. Rare animal species and a coastal dune environment.
Lake Anna State Park, Bells Crossroad	41 C6	3,127	VDCR		•	•	•	•	•	•	•	•	Day-use park with 8.5 miles of lakeshore. Visitor center on site of old gold mine features mining and wildlife exhibits.
Leesylvania State Park, Woodbridge	34 C3	543	VDCR					•		•	•	•	A blend of historic, natural and recreational features at the birthplace of Revolutionary War hero Light-horse Harry Lee.
Lesesne State Forest, Tyro	51 A8	422	VDOF					•					Wildlife sanctuary is used for research and recreation.
Lewis Fork Wilderness, Jefferson National Forest	83 E7	6,072	USFS	•				•	•				Popular wilderness area boasts Mount Rogers, the highest peak in the state at 5,729 feet.
Little Dry Run Wilderness, Jefferson National Forest	84 C1	2,845	USFS					•	•				Easily accessible area that remains lightly travelled.
Little Wilson Creek Wilderness, Jefferson National Forest	83 E8	5,461	USFS					•	•				Hardwood forest in high elevation portion of Mount Rogers National Recreation Area.
Mason Neck State Park, Lorton	34 B4	1,856	VDCR					•		•	•	•	Day-use park along the Potomac River. Woodlands, swamp and shoreline attract variety of birds including great blue heron and bald eagle.
Matthews State Forest, Galax	84 E4	556	VDOF					•	•	•			Nature trails explore forest where white pine dominates the landscape. American chestnut orchard on site for reintroduction of species.
Mount Pleasant National Scenic Area, George Washington National Forest	50 C5	7,695	USFS					•	•				Popular destination for hikers. Wildflowers and alpine meadows. Towering ridges.
Mount Rogers National Recreation Area, Jefferson National Forest	83 E6	200,000	USFS	•	•	•		•	•	•	•		Recreation area surrounds Virginia's highest mountain. Auto road to Whitetop Mountain. Over 60 miles of the Appalachian National Scenic Trail run through area.
Mountain Lake Wilderness, Jefferson National Forest	65 A10	16,525	USFS		•			•					Scenic overlooks in this high altitude spot. Wilderness extends into West Virginia.
Natural Tunnel State Park, Duffield	80 D3	909	VDCR		•	•	•	•			•		Park highlight is 850-foot-long tunnel worn through limestone ridge. Amphitheater. Visitor center.
Niday Place State Forest, Simmonsville	66 A1	254	VDOF					•					Mountainous terrain and hardwood forests.
Occoneechee State Park, Clarksville	90 E3	2,698	VDCR	•	•	•	•	•	•	•	•	•	On shores of state's largest man-made lake. Trails interpret the history of local Native Americans and settlers.
Occoquan Regional Park, Lorton	34 B3	350	NVRPA								•	•	350-acre day-use park along Occoquan River. Boat ramp. Picnic area. Visitor center.
Paul State Forest, Ottobine	30 E2	173	VDOF					•	•				Hardwood forest of varied species allows for research and education alongside recreational opportunities.
Peters Mountain Wilderness, Jefferson National Forest	65 A8	4,512	USFS		•			•					Appalachian National Scenic Trail cross the wilderness, intersecting with the two other trails that offer access to the area.
Philpott Lake Project, Bassett	86 C5	9,326	USACE		•		•	•			•	•	Clear lake in the Blue Ridge Mountains.
Pocahontas State Park, Chesterfield	72 A5	7,919	VDCR		•	•	•	•	•	•	•	•	Water recreation on Swift Creek just a step from Metro Richmond.

Recreation Areas, continued

NAME, LOCATION	PAGE & GRID	ACREAGE	AGENCY	EQUESTRIAN CAMPING	CAMPING	CABINS	SWIMMING	HIKING	HORSEBACK RIDING	BIKING	PICNICKING	BOATING	COMMENTS
Pohick Bay Regional Park, Lorton	34 B4	1,000	NVRPA	●			●	●		●	●	●	Golf course. Mini golf. Disc golf. Swimming pool with water playground. Observation deck overlooking Potomac River. Boat ramp.
Potomac Overlook Regional Park, Arlington	26 E5	67	NVRPA					●			●		Natural area in the Potomac palisades. Nature center features wildlife and archaeological displays. Interpretive garden.
Prince Edward–Gallion State Forest, Burkeville	71 D6	6,461	VDOF					●	●	●			Hardwood and pine forest. Rolling terrain.
Prince William Forest Park, Triangle	34 D2	15,000	NPS	●	●			●		●	●		Wooded site along Quantico Creek is just outside the Washington, DC area. Nature center.
Ramseys Draft Wilderness, George Washington National Forest	29 F9	6,577	USFS	●				●					Old-growth forest punctuated by eight trails.
Red Rock Wilderness Overlook Regional Park, Leesburg	25 B10	67	NVRPA					●					Wilderness park serves as nature sanctuary. Views of Potomac River.
Rich Hole Wilderness, George Washington National Forest	49 A10	6,532	USFS	●				●					Old mining area still bears plentiful evidence of its formal usage.
Rough Mountain Wilderness, George Washington National Forest	36 F5	9,326	USFS										Rugged terrain of ridges and mountain creeks.
Sandy Point State Forest, West Point	56 C2	2,043	VDOF					●		●	●		Hardwood forest offers education and demonstration programs.
Shawvers Run Wilderness, Jefferson National Forest	48 D3	5,784	USFS	●									Remote mountainous area maintains no trails.
Shenandoah National Park, Front Royal	24 E2	197,439	NPS	●		●		●	●	●	●		Scenic park located east of the Shenandoah River Valley in Blue Ridge Mountains. Over 500 miles of hiking trails including 95-mile stretch of Appalachian National Scenic Trail. 105-mile Skyline Drive with scenic overlooks.
Sky Meadows State Park, Delaplane	24 D5	1,860	VDCR					●	●	●	●		Rolling terrain on eastern slope of Blue Ridge Mountains. Access to aa National Scenic Trail. Historic Mount Bleak House.
Smith Mountain Lake State Park, Huddleston	67 E10	1,148	VDCR	●		●	●	●		●	●	●	Water recreation on one of the largest lakes in Virginia. 16 miles of shoreline. Interpretive programs.
Saint Mary's Wilderness, George Washington National Forest	38 F1	9,826	USFS					●					Rugged terrain surrounding the Saint Mary's River. 17 miles of trails.
Staunton River State Park, Scottsburg	90 D2	2,336	VDCR	●	●	●	●	●		●	●	●	Woodlands, meadows and lakeshore. Tennis courts and amphitheater.
Three Ridges Wilderness, George Washington National Forest	51 A8	4,612	USFS	●				●					Remote area of mixed forest and vegetation.
Thunder Ridge Wilderness, Jefferson National Forest	50 E2	2,428	USFS					●					Mixed forest adjacent to the Blue Ridge Parkway offers the pristine namesake ridge.
Twin Lakes State Park, Burkeville	71 D6	548	VDCR				●	●	●		●	●	Two freshwater lakes and pine and hardwood forests. Sandy swimming beach.
Westmoreland State Park, Montross	43 C8	1,321	VDCR			●	●	●		●	●	●	Nearby several historic sites. Fossils found on beaches and at base of Horsehead Cliffs. Outsanding views of the Potomac.
Whitney State Forest, Warrenton	33 B7	147	VDOF					●	●				Wildlife sanctuary also provides research and demonstration.
Wilderness Road State Park, Ewing	78 E3	327	VDCR					●	●	●	●		Living history park straddling historic 8.5-mile Wilderness Road Trail, part of road carved by Daniel Boone in 1775. Trail connects with Cumberland Gap National Historical Park. Amphitheater. Visitor center.
York River State Park, Williamsburg	74 A5	2,531	VDCR					●	●	●	●		Day-use park of forest, marshland and river frontage. Delicate estuarine habitat with abundant wildlife.
Zoar State Forest, Aylett	55 B10	378	VDOF					●		●	●		Hardwood and pine forest. Riverside terrain.

Campgrounds

NUMBER, NAME, LOCATION	PAGE & GRID	RV SITES	TENTING
2010 Amelia Family Campground, Amelia Court House	72 B1	80	●
2020 Americamps Lake Gaston, Bracey	91 F9	120	●
2030 Americamps RV Resort: Richmond, Ashland	55 C6	198	●
2040 Anvil Campground, Williamsburg	74 B5	57	●
2050 Aquia Pines Camp Resort, Stafford	34 E2	124	●
2070 Bethpage Camp-Resort, Urbanna	57 D6	700	●
2080 Charlottesville KOA, Charlottesville	39 F8	90	●
2090 Cherrystone Family Camping & RV Resort, Cape Charles	76 B3	700	●
2100 Chesapeake Bay Camp Ground, Reedville	44 F5	82	●
2110 Chesapeake Bay RV Resort, Gloucester	57 E7	365	●
2120 Chincoteague Island KOA, Chincoteague Island	47 F6	550	●
2130 Christopher Run Campground, Mineral	41 D6	200	●
2140 Country Inn, Big Stone Gap	80 B2	10	●
2150 Cozy Acres Family Campground, Powhatan	53 E9	115	●
2160 Davis Mobile Home & RV Park, Newport News	75 F8	20	●
2170 Dixie Caverns Campground, Salem	66 C3	50	●
2180 Ed Allen's Campground & Cottages, Lanexa	74 A2	250	●
2190 Endless Caverns Campground, New Market	31 C6	141	●
2200 Fredericksburg VA/Washington DC South KOA, Fredericksburg	42 C1	79	●
2210 Goose Dam Campground, Rocky Mount	87 B7	25	●
2220 Greenville Farm Family Campground, Haymarket	25 E9	165	●
2230 Harrisonburg/Shenandoah Valley KOA, Broadway	31 D6	59	●
2240 Holiday Trav-L-Park, Virginia Beach	96 C4	700	●
2250 Interstate Overnight Park, Christiansburg	66 D1	32	●
2260 Misty Mountain Camp Resort, Greenwood	39 D6	90	●
2270 Monroe Bay Marina & Campground, Colonial Beach	43 B7	300	●
2280 New Point Campground, New Point	75 B10	321	●
2290 New River Campground Canoe & Kayak, Independence	84 F2	80	●
2300 Prince William Forest RV Campground, Dumfries	34 C2	76	●
2310 Richmond North/Kings Dominion KOA, Doswell	55 A6	195	●
2320 Riverside Campground, Abingdon	82 C1	94	●
2330 Shenandoah Acres Family Campground, Stuarts Draft	38 E2	98	●
2340 Shenandoah Hills Campground, Madison	32 F1	67	●
2350 Shenandoah Valley Campground, Verona	38 B2	132	●
2360 The Cove Campground, Gore	23 A10	100	●
2370 Thor's Hollow Retreat, Cross Junction	19 D8	30	●
2380 Toms Cove Park, Chincoteague Island	47 F6	900	●
2390 Virginia Beach KOA, Virginia Beach	96 C4	750	●
2400 Walnut Hills Campground & RV Park, Staunton	38 D1	150	●
2410 Williamsburg Campark, Williamsburg	74 B5	550	●
2420 Wytheville KOA, Wytheville	84 A3	106	●
2430 Yogi Bear's Jellystone Park at Emporia, Emporia	93 D6	83	●
2440 Yogi Bear's Jellystone Park at Luray, Luray	31 B10	145	●
2450 Yogi Bear's Jellystone Park at Natural Bridge, Natural Bridge Station	50 D2	105	●

Freshwater Fishing

NUMBER	NAME	PAGE & GRID	BROOK TROUT	BROWN TROUT	RAINBOW TROUT	SMALLMOUTH BASS	LARGEMOUTH BASS	MUSKELLUNGE	NORTHERN PIKE	WALLEYE	BLUEGILL	CRAPPIE	CATFISH
3003	Abel Lake	34 F1					•				•	•	•
3006	Airfield Pond	94 B1					•				•	•	•
3012	Amelia Lake	53 F10					•				•	•	•
3015	Appomattox River	73 B8				•	•				•	•	•
3018	Ararat River	85 F9	•	•	•								
3021	Back Creek	19 F8		•	•								
3024	Back Creek	28 F4	•		•								
3027	Back Creek	36 C2	•										
3030	Back Creek	37 D10			•								
3033	Banister Lake	89 C8					•				•	•	•
3036	Barbours Creek	48 D4	•										
3039	Bark Camp Lake	80 B5		•	•		•				•	•	•
3042	Bear Creek Lake	53 E6					•				•	•	•
3045	Beaver Creek Reservoir	39 D7					•				•	•	•
3048	Beaverdam Reservoir	25 C10					•				•	•	•
3051	Beaverdam Swamp Reservoir	57 F7					•				•	•	•
3054	Big Cedar Creek	82 A1		•	•								
3057	Big Ivy Creek	86 D1	•										
3060	Blackwater River	94 D2					•				•	•	•
3063	Braley Pond	37 A9					•				•	•	
3066	Briery Branch	30 E1	•										
3069	Brumley Creek	82 B1		•	•								
3072	Brunswick County Lake	92 C3					•				•	•	•
3075	Buffalo Branch	37 B10	•										
3078	Bullpasture River	37 A7	•	•	•								
3081	Burke Lake	34 A3					•	•		•	•	•	•
3084	Burks Fork	85 C9			•								
3087	Burns Creek	80 A5			•								
3090	Carvins Cove Reservoir	67 A6				•	•				•	•	
3093	Cedar Creek	23 B10		•	•								
3096	Cedar Creek	23 D8	•	•									
3099	Chandlers Millpond	43 D8					•				•	•	•
3102	Chickahominy Lake	74 A2					•				•	•	•
3105	Chickahominy River	74 A3					•				•	•	•
3108	Claytor Lake	65 F8				•	•			•	•	•	•
3111	Clear Creek	80 A4		•	•								
3114	Clifton Forge Reservoir	49 A7			•		•				•	•	•
3117	Clinch River	80 E3		•	•	•	•	•		•	•	•	•
3120	Comers Creek	83 D8			•								
3123	Cove Branch	48 E4	•	•									
3126	Cove Creek	63 D10	•										
3129	Cowpasture River	37 A7		•	•								
3132	Cowpasture River	49 A9		•	•								
3135	Craig Creek	66 B1		•	•								
3138	Cressy Creek	83 D9		•	•								
3141	Crooked Creek	84 D5		•									
3144	Cub Run	31 D7							•				
3147	Dan River	85 E10	•	•	•	•					•	•	•
3150	Dan River	86 E1				•					•	•	•
3153	Davis Mill Creek	50 B5					•				•	•	
3156	Diascund Creek Reservoir	74 A3					•				•	•	•
3159	Dickey Creek	83 D8		•	•								
3162	Dismal Creek	62 C4			•								
3165	Dismal Creek	64 D5			•								
3168	Dry River	30 E3	•		•								
3171	Elk Creek	84 D1			•								
3174	Elkhorn Lake	37 A10	•								•	•	
3177	Emporia Reservoir	92 D5					•					•	•
3180	Fairy Stone Lake	86 C4					•				•	•	•
3183	Fluvanna Ruritan Lake	39 F10					•		•		•	•	•
3186	Fort Pickett Lakes	71 F10					•				•	•	•
3189	Fox Creek	83 D8		•	•								
3192	Francis Mill Creek	84 C2		•									
3195	Fryingpan Creek	61 E9		•									
3198	Game Refuge Lake	73 F9					•				•	•	•
3201	Garth Run	31 F10	•										
3204	Gatewood Reservoir	64 F5					•					•	•
3207	German River	30 A3	•		•								
3210	Germantown Lake	33 C8					•				•		
3213	Glade Creek	67 B7		•	•								
3216	Goose Creek	66 E3	•	•	•		•		•		•	•	
3219	Green Cove Creek	82 E5	•	•									
3222	Gullion Fork	63 F10			•								
3225	Harrison Lake	73 B9					•				•	•	•
3228	Hearthstone Lake	30 F1			•								
3231	Helton Creek	83 E7		•	•								
3234	Hidden Valley Lake	82 B1		•	•								
3237	Hoge Run	24 B2	•										
3240	Holliday Lake	70 A2					•				•	•	•

NUMBER	NAME	PAGE & GRID	BROOK TROUT	BROWN TROUT	RAINBOW TROUT	SMALLMOUTH BASS	LARGEMOUTH BASS	MUSKELLUNGE	NORTHERN PIKE	WALLEYE	BLUEGILL	CRAPPIE	CATFISH
3243	Holston River, Middle Fork	83 B9				•					•		•
3246	Holston River, North Fork	82 B4			•	•							•
3249	Holston River, South Fork	83 D6		•	•								
3252	Holston River, South Fork	83 C8		•	•								
3255	Hone Quarry Run	30 E1	•										
3258	Horsepen Lake	52 F3					•				•	•	•
3261	Howell Creek	86 B1	•										
3264	Hughes River	32 C1	•	•	•								
3267	Hunting Creek	50 E2	•										
3270	Hunting Run Reservoir	33 F9					•				•	•	•
3273	Hurricane Creek	83 D7			•								
3276	Irish Creek	50 A5	•										
3279	Jackson River	36 D3	•	•	•								
3282	James River, Lower	74 C3				•	•				•	•	•
3285	James River, Upper	49 E10				•	•				•	•	•
3288	Jennings Creek	49 F10	•	•									
3291	Jerrys Run	48 B3	•										
3294	John H Kerr Reservoir (Buggs Island Lake)	90 F5					•			•	•	•	•
3297	John W Flannagan Reservoir	61 C7					•	•		•	•	•	•
3299	Lake Albemarle	39 D7					•				•	•	•
3300	Lake Anna	41 E8					•			•	•	•	•
3303	Lake Arrowhead	31 B10					•				•		
3306	Lake Biggins	75 F8					•					•	
3309	Lake Brittle	33 A8					•				•	•	•
3315	Lake Burnt Mills	95 B6					•				•	•	•
3318	Lake Burton	88 B1					•				•	•	•
3321	Lake Chesdin	72 C5					•				•	•	•
3324	Lake Cohoon	95 D6					•				•	•	•
3327	Lake Conner	89 A10					•				•	•	•
3330	Lake Curtis	33 E10					•				•	•	•
3333	Lake Frederick	24 C3					•				•	•	•
3336	Lake Gaston	91 F9					•			•	•	•	•
3339	Lake Gordon	91 D7					•				•	•	•
3342	Lake Gordonsville	40 D2					•				•	•	•
3345	Lake Keokee	80 B1					•				•	•	
3348	Lake Kilby	95 D6					•				•	•	•
3351	Lake Laura	22 F5					•				•		
3354	Lake Maury	75 F8					•						
3357	Lake Meade	95 D6					•				•	•	•
3360	Lake Moomaw	36 E1	•	•	•		•				•	•	
3363	Lake Nottoway	71 D10					•				•	•	•
3366	Lake Orange	40 B4					•				•	•	•
3367	Lake Pelham	32 E4					•				•	•	•
3369	Lake Prince	95 C6					•				•	•	•
3372	Lake Robertson	49 B10					•				•	•	•
3375	Lake Shenandoah	30 F4					•				•	•	
3378	Lake Smith	96 B2					•				•	•	•
3381	Lake Whitehurst	96 B1					•				•	•	•
3384	Lake Witten	63 D7		•	•		•				•		
3387	Laurel Creek	63 F7	•		•								
3390	Laurel Creek	64 C1	•		•								
3393	Laurel Fork	85 D8			•							•	
3396	Lee Hall Reservoir	75 D7					•				•	•	•
3399	Leesville Lake	68 F2					•				•	•	•
3402	Lick Creek	63 F9	•		•								
3405	Lick Creek	83 A8			•								
3408	Little Indian Creek	85 A9	•										
3411	Little Irish Creek	50 C4	•										
3414	Little Passage Creek	23 D10			•								
3417	Little Reed Island Creek	85 C6		•									
3420	Little River	66 F1				•	•				•	•	
3423	Little River, West Fork	86 B1	•										
3426	Little Stony Creek	81 B6	•										
3429	Little Stony Creek	81 B6	•										
3432	Little Tumbling Creek	82 A5	•										
3435	Lone Star Lakes	95 B7					•						
3438	Lovills Creek	85 F8				•							
3441	Lynch River	39 A7				•							
3444	Maggodee Creek	67 E7											•
3447	Martin Creek	78 E5											•
3450	Martinsville Reservoir	87 D7					•				•	•	•
3453	Mattaponi River	56 C1					•				•	•	•
3456	Maury River	37 F7				•					•		•
3459	McFalls Creek	49 F10				•							
3462	Meherrin River	92 D4					•				•	•	•
3465	Middle Creek	49 E10			•								
3468	Middle Fox Creek	83 D10	•										
3471	Mill Creek	30 A5											•
3474	Mill Creek	37 E6	•										

12

Freshwater Fishing, continued

NUMBER, NAME		PAGE AND GRID	BROOK TROUT	BROWN TROUT	RAINBOW TROUT	SMALLMOUTH BASS	LARGEMOUTH BASS	MUSKELLUNGE	NORTHERN PIKE	WALLEYE	BLUEGILL	CRAPPIE	CATFISH
3477	Mills Creek	38 F2	•										
3480	Mira Fork	85 B9	•	•									
3483	Moormans River, South Fork	38 C5	•										
3486	Moormans River, North Fork	39 C6	•										
3489	Mossy Creek	30 F2	•	•	•								
3492	Motts Run Reservoir	41 A10					•			•	•	•	•
3495	Nelson Lake	51 C9					•				•	•	•
3498	New River	84 B5		•	•	•	•			•	•	•	•
3501	Ni Reservoir	41 A9					•				•	•	
3504	North Creek	50 E1	•		•								
3507	North Landing River	96 E3					•				•	•	•
3510	North River	29 F10	•	•									
3513	North River	29 F10	•										
3516	Northwest River	96 F1					•				•	•	•
3519	Nottaway River, Lower	94 F2				•	•				•	•	•
3522	Nottaway River, Upper	93 C10				•	•				•	•	•
3525	Occoquan Reservoir	34 A3					•		•	•	•	•	•
3528	Occoquan River	34 B3				•	•				•	•	•
3531	Otter Lake	50 E3				•	•				•	•	
3534	Paddy Run	23 C9		•	•						•	•	
3537	Pads Creek	36 F4											
3540	Pamunkey River	55 C9				•	•						•
3543	Passage Creek	23 F9	•	•	•								
3546	Passage Creek	31 A8	•	•	•								
3549	Pauls Creek	85 F7											
3552	Peak Creek	64 F5											
3555	Pedlar River	50 B4	•		•	•						•	•
3558	Pedlar River	50 D4		•	•								
3564	Peters Mill Run	23 E9											
3567	Phelps Pond	33 E7					•			•			•
3570	Philpott Reservoir	86 C5				•	•			•	•	•	•
3573	Piankatank River	57 E8											
3576	Piney River	51 B7	•	•	•								
3579	Piney River, South Fork	51 B6	•										
3582	Poorhouse Creek	86 E2	•										
3585	Poorhouse Creek, North Fork	86 E2	•										
3588	Potomac River, South Branch	29 D6	•		•	•							
3591	Potts Creek	48 E2		•	•					•			
3594	Pound River	60 D5		•	•								
3597	Pounding Mill Creek	49 B6				•							
3600	Poverty Creek	65 C9											
3603	Powell River	80 A4				•	•	•		•	•	•	
3606	Powell River, North Fork	79 C9		•		•		•		•			
3609	Powhatan Lakes	53 E10					•				•	•	•
3612	Rapidan River	31 E10											
3615	Rappahannock River	42 A1											
3618	Reed Creek	83 A10											
3621	Rivanna Reservoir	39 D9					•				•	•	•
3624	Roanoke River	67 C7	•	•	•					•			
3627	Roanoke River, South Fork	66 C3		•	•								
3630	Roaring Fork	63 F8	•		•								
3633	Roaring Run	49 C7	•		•								
3636	Robinson River	32 F2	•		•								
3639	Rock Castle Creek	86 C2	•										
3642	Rockfish River, South Fork	51 A9	•		•		•						

NUMBER, NAME		PAGE AND GRID	BROOK TROUT	BROWN TROUT	RAINBOW TROUT	SMALLMOUTH BASS	LARGEMOUTH BASS	MUSKELLUNGE	NORTHERN PIKE	WALLEYE	BLUEGILL	CRAPPIE	CATFISH
3645	Rose River	32 D1	•		•								
3648	Round Meadow Creek	85 D10	•		•								
3651	Runnet Bag Creek	86 A4											
3654	Rural Retreat Lake	83 B10					•	•	•		•	•	
3657	Rush Fork	86 C1	•										
3660	Russell Fork	61 C8		•	•	•					•		•
3663	Russell Fork	61 D8		•	•	•							
3664	Saint Mary's River	38 F1	•		•								
3666	Sandy River Reservoir	71 C6					•				•	•	•
3669	Shenandoah River, Main Stem	24 C5				•		•		•			•
3672	Shenandoah River, North Fork	31 B6				•		•					•
3675	Shenandoah River, South Fork	38 A5				•		•					•
3678	Shields Lake	55 E6		•	•								
3681	Shoemaker River	30 C3	•										
3684	Silver Lake	30 E3	•										
3687	Skidmore Reservoir	30 C1	•										
3690	Smith Creek	49 A7		•									
3693	Smith Mountain Lake	67 F10					•			•	•	•	•
3696	Smith River	86 C5		•	•								
3699	Smith River	87 D7				•		•					•
3702	South Fork Rivanna River Reservoir	39 D9					•				•	•	•
3705	South Holston Lake	82 E2				•	•			•	•	•	•
3708	South Mayo River	86 E2		•	•								
3711	South River	31 F9	•	•	•								
3714	South River	50 A4											•
3717	Spring Run	36 B3	•	•									
3723	Staley Creek	83 C8											
3726	Staunton River	69 E6				•		•		•			•
3729	Stewarts Creek	85 F6	•										
3732	Stock Creek	80 D3											
3735	Stonehouse Lake	51 C6					•				•	•	
3738	Stony Creek	23 E6											
3741	Stony Creek	65 A8	•										
3744	Stony Creek	80 B4	•										
3747	Stony Fork	64 F1	•										
3750	Straight Branch	82 E5											
3753	Straight Fork	80 C4											
3756	Swift Creek Lake	72 A5					•				•	•	
3759	Thrasher Lake	51 C6					•				•	•	
3762	Tinker Creek	67 B6											
3765	Toms Creek	65 C10	•		•								
3768	Totier Creek Reservoir	52 B3					•				•	•	•
3771	Trashmore Lake	96 C2					•						
3774	Tumbling Creek	82 A3											
3777	Tye River	51 D9	•	•	•							•	
3780	Tye River, North Fork	38 F1	•										
3783	Valley Creek	82 E5											
3786	Waller Mill Reservoir	74 B5					•				•	•	•
3789	Western Branch Reservoir	95 C6					•	•					
3792	Whitetop Laurel Creek	82 E5											
3795	Wilkins Lake	24 A3					•				•	•	
3798	Wilson Creek	83 E8	•										
3801	Wolf Creek	63 D9		•	•						•		
3804	Wolf Creek	64 C3				•					•		
3807	Woodstock Pond	74 A5					•				•	•	

Saltwater Fishing

NUMBER, NAME		PAGE & GRID	SPOT	CROAKER	BLUEFISH	FLOUNDER	GRAY TROUT	COBIA	STRIPED BASS	KINGFISH	SPANISH MACKEREL	DRUM
3810	Back Bay	96 E4		•	•	•	•		•			•
3813	Cape Charles Fishing Pier	76 C3										
3816	James River Bridge	75 F8										
3819	James T Wilson Fishing Pier	75 F10										
3822	Little Island Park	96 D4										

NUMBER, NAME		PAGE & GRID	SPOT	CROAKER	BLUEFISH	FLOUNDER	GRAY TROUT	COBIA	STRIPED BASS	KINGFISH	SPANISH MACKEREL	DRUM
3825	Ocean View Fishing Pier	95 A10	•	•	•	•	•	•	•	•	•	•
3828	Sea Gull	96 A2	•	•	•	•	•					
3831	Virginia Beach	96 B4										
3834	Willoughby Bay	95 A10										
3837	Yorktown Fishing Pier	75 C7										

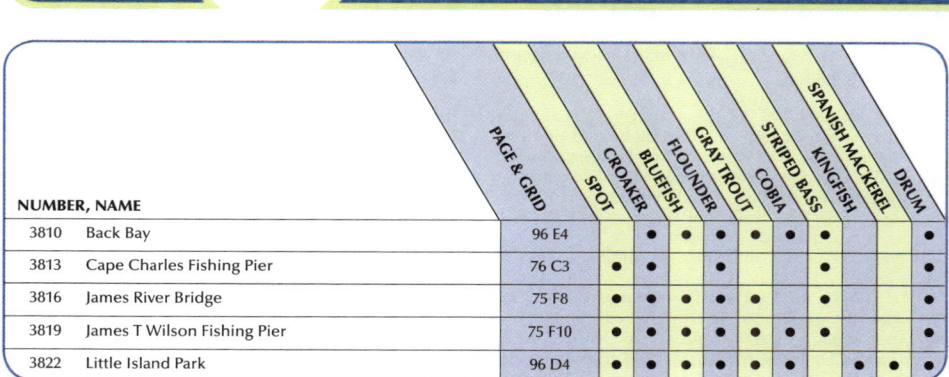

Outdoor Adventures

BIKING

ATLANTIC COAST ROUTE – Arlington – 27 E6 Portion of bicycle route from Bar Harbor, Maine, to Fort Meyers Beach, Florida. Enters state across Arlington Memorial Bridge from Washington, DC, travels along US 1 and runs to North Carolina border near John H. Kerr Reservoir.

BACK BAY–FALSE CAPE BICYCLE TRAILS – False Cape State Park – 96 E5 Network of trails through False Cape State Park offers views of dunes, marshes and ocean. 15 miles of gravel surface. Seasonally, riders may continue into Back Bay National Wildlife Refuge, riding parallel to the sea to visitor center and back.

BLACKWATER CREEK BIKEWAY – Blackwater Creek Natural Area – 68 A5 Trail along abandoned railroad right-of-way. Overlooks creek. 12-mile route passes natural and historic sites before terminating in downtown Lynchburg.

CAPE HENRY TRAIL – First Landing State Park – 96 A3 Bicycling and hiking trail extends 7 miles through First Landing State Park. Trail begins at visitor center and travels south through center of park to 64th Street. Turns west along Broad Bay to boat ramp.

COLONIAL PARKWAY – Colonial National Historical Park – 75 C7 Scenic drive from Yorktown to Williamsburg is open to bicyclists as well as autos. 23-mile route passes assorted historic sites from the colonial and revolutionary periods, ending at Virginia's former capital.

HEART OF APPALACHIA BIKE ROUTE – Tazewell – 63 E9 Signed route crosses 128 miles of scenic Appalachia on a variety of road types. Often an extremely isolated route, utilizing untraveled roads, trails, and rail-trails. Moderately difficult, but challenging for its length alone. From Guest River Gorge to Burkes's Garden.

HIGH BRIDGE TRAIL STATE PARK – High Bridge Trail State Park – 70 C2 Old railroad grade open for hikers, bikers and equestrians. Highlight of the trail is High Bridge, a thin, former railroad bridge that extends 2,400 feet over the Appomattox River. 31 miles.

NEW RIVER TRAIL STATE PARK – New River Trail State Park – 84 E4 Abandoned rail line parallels the New River for 39 of its 57 miles. Two tunnels and three major bridges. Five campgrounds. Multiple access points. Open to hiking, bicycling and horseback riding.

NORTHERN VIRGINIA TRAIL NETWORK – Vienna – 26 E3 Extensive network of trails and bicycle lanes offers over 600 miles of bicycling in northern Virginia. A variety of routes are possible in relatively flat Arlington and Fairfax Counties. Numerous access points, including junctions with major trails.

POTOMAC OVERLOOK TOUR – Potomac Overlook Regional Park – 26 E5 Bicycle loop follows 6.3 miles of bike lanes and trails over the challenging hills of historic and scenic Arlington. Stunning vistas of the Potomac River.

PRINCE EDWARD–GALLION MULTI-USE TRAIL – Prince Edward-Gallion State Forest – 71 D6 Trail traverses forest over unpaved roads and trails. Shared use trail is relatively flat with easy hiking. Trailhead at parking lot on SSR 689. Open to biking and horseback riding. 8 miles.

TOBACCO HERITAGE TRAIL – Lawrenceville – 92 D1 70-mile route through flat, tobacco growing country on rail beds and bicycle lanes. More stages will eventually lengthen trail.

TRANSAMERICA BICYCLE TRAIL – Yorktown – 75 C7 Final portion of 4,228 mile transcontinental bicycle route beginning in Astoria, Oregon. Enters Virginia at Kentucky border near Breaks Interstate Park and ends in Yorktown.

WASHINGTON & OLD DOMINION RAILROAD REGIONAL PARK – Arlington – 26 F5 Paved trail on old railroad grade provides 44 miles of biking and pedestrian travel. Numerous access points in between termini at Shirlington and Purcellville. Parallel, 32-mile bridle trail begins in Vienna.

WASHINGTON DITCH TRAIL – Suffolk – 95 E7 Unpaved road through Great Dismal Swamp National Wildlife Refuge leads 4 miles to Lake Drummond. Over 140 miles of other unpaved roads in extensive refuge are open to bicycling and hiking.

WILDLIFE LOOP – Assateague Island National Seashore – 47 F6 Loop for hikers and bikers circles refuge, offering outstanding wildlife viewing opportunities. Paved loop totals 3 miles, but offshoot trails lead to beaches and additional wildlife.

YORK RIVER STATE PARK TRAILS – York River State Park – 74 A5 Two singletrack mountain bike trails. Marl Ravine Trail is a difficult 6-mile trek for experienced bikers. Laurel Glen Trail provides beginners with a 2-mile singletrack experience. Other trails in park are shared between hikers, bikers and horses.

HIKING

APPALACHIAN NATIONAL SCENIC TRAIL – Shenandoah National Park – 31 C10 Virginia portion of long-range trail follows ridgelines of eastern mountains. Roughly parallels Skyline Drive and Blue Ridge Parkway, passing through Jefferson and George Washington National Forests and Shenandoah National Park. 548 miles in state.

APPLE ORCHARD FALLS–CORNELIUS CREEK LOOP – Jefferson National Forest – 50 E1 Rugged but popular hike in Jefferson National Forest encounters stunning views of namesake waterfall. Trailhead and parking at end of FR 59. Cornelius Creek Trail is a difficult uphill climb, but return along Apple Orchard Falls Trail is refreshingly downhill. At Apple Orchard Falls, a viewing platform offers the best vista. 6 miles.

BALCONY FALLS TRAIL – Jefferson National Forest – 50 D2 Trail follows switchbacks up a ridge to James River Face Wilderness. Scenic views of James River Gorge. Trailhead at end of FR 3093 in Jefferson National Forest. 6-mile trail open to horseback riding.

BARK CAMP LAKE LOOP TRAIL – Jefferson National Forest – 80 B5 Easy, flat trail around Bark Camp Lake in Jefferson National Forest. 3.7-mile route circles lake and passes through marsh habitat at upper end of lake. Trailhead at dam.

BIG DEVILS STAIRS TRAIL – Shenandoah National Park – 32 A2 Trail to scenic canyon in Shenandoah National Park. Relatively easy to steep along canyon. Hike offers views of the Shenandoah Valley and distant mountains from a high vantage point. Trailhead at Gravel Springs Gap Parking area on Skyline Drive. 5.5 miles.

BIG SCHLOSS HIKE – George Washington National Forest – 23 E6 Trail ascends the peak of Big Schloss on the West Virginia border. Relatively easy hike for a peak, but includes a somewhat steep climb to the rock outcrops. Panoramic views from top. Trailhead at Wolf Gap Campground. 2 miles.

BLUE RIDGE PARKWAY – Lyndhurst – 38 E4 Parkway runs along crests of Southern Appalachians and extends into North Carolina for total length of 470 miles. Bicycling is permitted on paved road surfaces and parking areas. Many steep grades as parkway ranges in elevation from 600 to 6,000 feet. Long distances between access points.

CASCADES TRAIL – Jefferson National Forest – 65 B8 Moderately difficult trail leads to fantastic 60-foot waterfall. Mostly uphill on trail to falls. Alternate route leads back to trailhead following Little Stony Creek. Trailhead at Cascades Recreation Area. 2 Miles.

CHESSIE NATURE TRAIL – Lexington – 50 B2 Trail along old railroad grade between Lexington and Buena Vista. Follows Maury River, passing several locks and historic sites. Steep cliffs, pastures and woodlands. Large variety of birds and wildflowers in spring. 7 miles.

CHIEF BENGE SCOUT TRAIL – Jefferson National Forest – 80 B4 Difficult trail on uneven mountainous terrain within Jefferson National Forest. 16-mile route descends High Knob through forest to High Knob Lake. Skirts along Mountain Fork of Big Stony Creek and continues to Edith Gap. Reaches Bark Camp Lake, then follows Little Stony Creek to Little Stony Trail. Trailhead at High Knob Tower parking area. Ends at parking lot on FR 701.

CRABTREE FALLS TRAIL – George Washington National Forest – 51 A7 Scenic trail in George Washington National Forest featuring series of five major cascades and several smaller falls. Route follows creek south across a wooden bridge and past four overlooks. Trailhead at paved parking lot along SR 56. 3-mile trail ends at parking lot on SSR 826.

CRAWFORD MOUNTAIN TRAIL – George Washington National Forest – 37 B9 Rugged trail in George Washington National Forest begins by climbing steep grade to knob at 3,012 feet. 8-mile route crosses varied terrain including broad ridge crests, narrow hollows and sharp, rocky ridges. Trailhead across from parking area at Dry Branch Gap on SR 688. Steep descent to end of trail at US 250.

CUMBERLAND MULTI-USE TRAIL – Cumberland State Forest – 53 E6 Multi-use loop trail winds 14 miles through Cumberland State Forest along FRs and trails. Trailhead at Cumberland State Forest Office. Open to biking and horseback riding.

DARK HOLLOW FALLS – Shenandoah National Park – 31 D9 Short hike to waterfall closest to Skyline Drive. Trail descends along Hogcamp Branch to foot of falls offering views of 70-foot-high cascade. Return by same route. Trailhead at Dark Hollow Falls parking area.

DEVILS FORK TRAIL – Jefferson National Forest – 80 C4 Moderately difficult loop along Devils Fork in Jefferson National Forest. 7-mile route passes through scenic area, crossing stream ten times. Passes small waterfall. Trailhead at parking lot on SSR 619.

FLAT PETER LOOP – Jefferson National Forest – 65 A9 8-mile loop follows North Fork Creek through woodlands, into a clearing and across a bridge. Continues on Dixon Branch Trail, crossing stream several times. Crosses saddle to Dismal Branch Trail and follows stream down the mountain. Trail becomes old logging road, then joins Laurel Branch Trail for return to trailhead at gate across from Glenn Alton Rd.

FLAT TOP–FALLINGWATER CASCADES – Blue Ridge Parkway 50 F1 Moderately difficult climb as trail makes numerous switchbacks and ascends peak of Flat Top at 3,999 feet. Peak offers panoramic views of the Peaks of Otter area. Trail descends to Peaks of Otter Lake. Or take a small loop to reach Fallingwater Cascades. Trailhead at Fallingwater Parking Area on Blue Ridge Parkway. 6 miles.

GREAT NORTH MOUNTAIN TRAIL – George Washington National Forest – 37 B9 15-mile route begins on old logging road and ascends to follow ridge crest. Rugged terrain varies from narrow, rocky ridges to broad ridge crests. Trail passes just below Elliott Knob, one of the highest points in George Washington National Forest at 4,463 feet. Panoramic views.

GUEST RIVER GORGE TRAIL – Jefferson National Forest – 81 A6 Multi-use trail along old railroad grade follows scenic river. Passes through 1922 Swede Tunnel and over several trestles. Trailhead at parking lot off of SR 72. 6-mile trail is open to biking.

HAWKSBILL MOUNTAIN TRAIL – Shenandoah National Park – 31 D10 Short, steep climb to Hawksbill Mountain, highest peak in Shenandoah National Park at 4,050 feet. Panoramic views from observation platform at summit. Trailhead at Hawksbill Gap parking area on Skyline Drive. 1.7 miles.

HENRY LANUM MEMORIAL TRAIL – George Washington National Forest – 50 B5 5-mile loop offers panoramic views of the Blue Ridge Mountains. Climbs slowly to Pompey Mountain summit (4,032 feet), then follows ridge to Mount Pleasant (4,021 feet). Crosses two creeks on return to trailhead at parking area off of FR 51.

HIDDEN VALLEY TRAIL – George Washington National Forest – 36 D3 Trail runs parallel to the Jackson River on both sides, as it crosses the river before looping back to the trailhead. 6-mile route traverses pristine terrain that remains untouched for a century. Climbs to ledge offering a fantastic vista overlooking the river. Trailhead at Hidden Valley Campground.

JAMESTOWN SCENIC LOOP – Colonial National Historical Park – 74 C4 5-mile loop around historic Jamestown Island explores the land found by the first English settlers. Parking at Historic Jamestowne. Paved.

JOHNS CREEK MOUNTAIN TRAIL – Jefferson National Forest – 66 A1 Easy, 4-mile trail along ridge crossing peaks and several saddles. Several vistas with panoramic views. Abundant wildlife. Trail intersects Appalachian Trail and continues down steep slope to parking area on SR 601. Trailhead on Johns Creek Mountain Road.

LEWIS SPRING FALLS TRAIL – Shenandoah National Park – 31 D9 Loop trail past scenic waterfall in Shenandoah National Park. Trail proceeds south to falls and returns via Appalachian National Scenic Trail. Some steep, rugged stretches. Trailhead at amphitheater parking area in Big Meadows complex. 3.3 miles.

LITTLE STONY TRAIL – Jefferson National Forest – 81 B6 3-mile trail follows former narrow-gauge railroad bed north and west along Little Stony Creek. Passes through deep, scenic gorge. Two waterfalls, numerous cascades and large pools. Marked trail, moderate level of difficulty. Trailhead at Hanging Rock picnic area. Ends at parking lot on FR 701.

MASON NECK STATE PARK TRAILS – Mason Neck State Park – 34 B4 Multiple trails overlooking Belmont Bay in Mason Neck State Park. From a sandy beach to boardwalk traversing a marsh. Inland trails through hardwood forest and offers several observation blinds for wildlife viewing. 7.5 miles.

MASSANUTTEN MOUNTAIN TRAIL – George Washington National Forest – 23 F9 71-mile loop trail encircles Massanutten Mountain, more of a range than a single peak. Partially used by mountain bikers and equestrians as well.

MOUNT ROGERS TRAIL – Jefferson National Forest – 83 D7 Rugged, 4-mile climb to Mount Rogers, the state's highest peak. Route ascends to junction with Appalachian Trail then heads east to join Summit Spur Trail to peak. Trailhead at Grindstone Campground.

MOUNT VERNON TRAIL – George Washington Memorial Parkway – 34 A5 Trail running along Potomac River and George Washington Memorial Parkway. Begins at Mount Vernon, historic home of George Washington. Points of interest along 18-mile route include parks, Dyke Marsh, Jones Point Lighthouse and historic Alexandria. Crosses the Potomac River, ends at Theodore Roosevelt Island. Hiking and jogging.

NORTH MOUNTAIN TRAIL – George Washington National Forest – 49 B9 Trail follows ridge of North Mountain in George Washington National Forest. Winds through dense forests, by streams and around rocky ledges. Several overlooks including panoramic views of Peaks of Otter from Top Drive Overlook. Trailhead at Longdale Recreation Area. Ends at intersection with Cocks Comb Trail. 12.5 miles.

NORTH RIVER GORGE TRAIL – George Washington National Forest – 29 F10 Scenic trail winding 4 miles between Lookout and Trimble Mountains in George Washington National Forest. Marked trail over level terrain crosses river nine times. Several wildlife clearings. Trailhead at parking area on FR 95. Ends at North River Campground.

PINE MOUNTAIN TRAIL – Jefferson National Forest – 60 D4 Steep, rocky trail along Pine Mountain parallels Virginia–Kentucky border. Sheer drops towards Kentucky offer panoramic views. Several access points. Trailhead at Pound Gap on US 23. Ends at Breaks Interstate Park. Open to horseback riding. 23 miles.

POCAHONTAS STATE PARK TRAILS – Pocahontas State Park – 72 A5 Over 64 miles of multi-use trails. Network connects points of interest within park. Crushed stone surfaces.

PONY TRAIL – Assateague Island National Seashore – 47 F6 Loop trail offers views of grazing wild ponies. 1.5-mile trail leads through marshes to observation platform and returns. Coastal vegetation. Trailhead on Beach Road.

POTOMAC HERITAGE NATIONAL SCENIC TRAIL – George Washington Memorial Parkway – 27 E6 Network of trails explores region around the Potomac River in several states. Mostly flat trails and roadways accessible to bicyclists. Steep sections and scenic overlooks along Potomac Palisades.

PROSPECTORS' TRAIL – Jefferson National Forest – 61 B8 Blazed trail along top of cliffs in Breaks Interstate Park. Moderate grade follows contours of the land, 350 feet below overlooks. Views of canyon and rock cliffs. Trailhead at Tower Tunnel Overlook. Ends at intersection with Laurel Branch Trail. 1.5 miles.

RAMSEYS DRAFT TRAIL – George Washington National Forest – 37 A8 Trail through Ramseys Draft Wilderness in George Washington National Forest. Trailhead at picnic area off of US 250. Route zigzags northeast along stream on abandoned roadway. Passes rare stands of virgin hemlock. Follows steep footpath along right prong. Side trail to Hardscrabble Knob at 4,281 feet. 6.5-mile trail ends at intersection with Shenandoah Mountain Trail.

RIBBLE TRAIL – Jefferson National Forest – 64 C5 Steep trail ascends Flat Top Mountain. Blazed, 2-mile trail heads north up slope ending just below crest at Honey Springs Cabin. Terrain varies from flat ridgetops to steep side slopes. Intersects with Appalachian Trail. Trailhead at end of Dismal Creek Rd.

RIDGE TRAIL – Cumberland Gap National Historical Park – 78 F2 Strenuous, 16-mile trail traverses ridge in Cumberland Gap National Historical Park. Ridge offers views of both sides of the Virginia–Kentucky border. Several side trails along first 5 miles offer alternate loop routes. Four primitive campgrounds. Trailhead at Pinnacle Overlook.

RIVER BANK TRAIL – Staunton River State Park – 90 D2 Loop trail circles Staunton River State Park. Follows scenic shoreline along Dan and Staunton Rivers. Trailhead at parking area for boat ramp. 8.5 miles.

RIVER TRAIL – Great Falls – 26 D3 Scenic trail along Mather Gorge on the Potomac River. Moderately strenuous, occasionally climbs over rocks. Trailhead at picnic area in Great Falls Park. Ends at Cow Hoof Rock with spectacular views of gorge. 2.5 miles.

ROCK CASTLE GORGE TRAIL – Blue Ridge Parkway – 86 C2 Rugged loop trail through a deep gorge then a severe climb leads to ridgetop portion of trail offering stunning vistas. Trailhead at end of SSR 605. 11 miles. Multiple access points along Blue Ridge Parkway.

SHENANDOAH MOUNTAIN TRAIL – George Washington National Forest – 37 A8 Trail winds through ridges of Shenandoah Mountain Range. Traverses moderately difficult terrain, passing springs and wildlife water holes. Views of remote valleys and peaks. Trailhead at road across from Confederate Breastworks on SR 250. 24-mile route ends at SR 678.

SIGNAL KNOB LOOP TRAIL – George Washington National Forest – 24 D1 Marked, loop hike leads to several scenic overlooks en route to Signal Knob at 2,106 feet. Panoramic vistas. Trailhead at parking lot along SSR 678 north of Elizabeth Furnace Recreation Area. 10 miles.

SPOTSYLVANIA BATTLEFIELD HISTORY TRAIL – Fredericksburg & Spotsylvania National Military Park – 41 B9 Trail connecting important sites of 1864 Battle of Spotsylvania. Points of interest include monuments, remains of battle trenches and ruins of historic houses. 7-mile trail begins at exhibit shelter. Open to horseback riding.

STONE MOUNTAIN TRAIL – Jefferson National Forest – 79 C10 Rugged trail crossing Stone Mountain begins by crossing several miles of rocky terrain. At Olinger Gap, a side trail heads north to Keokee Lake. Main trail crosses High Butte, large rock outcrop with panoramic views of valley and traverses Roaring Branch, passing rock formations and small cascades. Trailhead at Cave Springs Recreation Area. Rock stairs lead to end of trail on US 23. 14 miles.

STONY MAN NATURE TRAIL – Shenandoah National Park – 31 C10 Self-guided trail to Stony Man Mountain, the second highest peak in Shenandoah National Park at 4,011 feet. Panoramic views from outlooks near summit. Trailhead at parking area at north entrance to Skyland resort. Return by same route. 1.5 miles.

VIRGINIA CAPITAL TRAIL – Williamsburg – 74 C4 Multi-use trail links Virginia's current capital with its original. Follows James River for most of 52-mile

Outdoor Adventures, *continued*

route. Encounters numerous historical attractions in Williamsburg and Jamestown.

VIRGINIA CREEPER TRAIL – Abingdon – 82 D2 Former railroad grade converted to 34-mile, multi-use trail. Traverses the Blue Ridge Mountains and descends into the state's low-lying valleys for a truly scenic ride.

WAR SPUR & CHESTNUT TRAIL – Jefferson National Forest – 65 A9 Short loop trails in Mountain Lake Wilderness of Jefferson National Forest. Trails cross gentle terrain in old-growth forest, beginning on Chestnut Trail. War Spur Overlook offers optional loop to reach a grand overlook. Trailhead on SSR 613.

WHITE OAK CANYON TRAIL – Shenandoah National Park – 31 C10 4.5-mile trail leads to the first of six waterfalls in a steep gorge, deep in Shenandoah National Park. Passes through swampy area and grove of 400-year-old hemlocks. Encounters pools and cascades en route to 86-foot-high waterfall. Overlook offers an unforgettable view. Return by same route or continue through the gorge to find five additional waterfalls. Trailhead at White Oak Canyon parking area.

WILD OAK TRAIL – George Washington National Forest – 29 F10 Loop trail follows ridgetops in George Washington National Forest. Climbs Little Bald Knob (4,351 feet) over steep, rocky terrain. Crosses Big Bald Knob (4,120 feet), passing wildlife clearings. Final segment is steep and rocky, offering several scenic overlooks. Trailhead on FR 95. Open to horseback riding. 25.5 miles.

WOODMARSH TRAIL – Elizabeth Hartwell Mason Neck NWR – 34 B5 Loop trail borders Great Marsh, the largest freshwater marsh in northern Virginia, and passes through hickory, oak and maple forest. Two side trails cut across loop. Interpretive brochures available at trail entrance. 3 miles.

PADDLING

APPOMATTOX RIVER – Petersburg – 72 C5 Flatwater stretch to dam portage features Class II rapids and rock gardens. After portage, flows through a network of channels through islands and features several Class III rapids at remains of dams and canals. Intermediate level trip. Put-in at canoe launch at Chesdin Dam. Take-out 6.5 miles downstream at SR 36 in Petersburg.

AQUIA CREEK – Stafford – 34 D1 Intermediate trip flows through a hazardous gorge with Class II rapids, rock walls and evergreens. Portage around dam precedes section of flatwater paddling. Put-in on SR 610. Take-out 10.5 miles downstream at SR 1.

BACK BAY – Virginia Beach – 96 E4 Vast expanse of open water, extensive marshes and undeveloped wooded islands allows paddling on network of small coves, islands, canals and inlets. Large waves possible in open water. Common put-in at a boat ramp on Redhead Bay. Take-out at boat ramp in Trojan Wildlife Management Area.

BLACKWATER RIVER – Zuni – 94 C3 Flatwater river features slow-moving, often practically still, water. Canoe trip features abundant wildlife on a scenic, secluded river, lined with trees, lending a swampy feel to the river. Several access points allow for a variety of trips. Excellent fishing. Common put-in on SSR 603/Unity Rd.

CLINCH RIVER – Gate City – 80 D4 Fairly easy, 17-mile run of Class I–II rapids and numerous ledges is accompanied by exceptional mountain scenery and vistas. Put-in at Craft's Mill Bridge. Take-out at boat ramp downstream from SSR 625 on Tennessee border.

CLINCH RIVER – Honaker – 62 F2 Class I–III rapids on expert level river through a scenic, undeveloped gorge. Put-in at boat ramp upstream from Blackford Bridge on SSR 641. Take-out upstream from SSR 645 at Nash's Ford. 18 miles.

DIFFICULT RUN – McLean – 26 D4 Short, 1-mile run for experts only. Requires paddling Class III–IV rapids. Portage possible around Class VI–VII waterfalls. Put-in at Route 193. Route follows left channel around island and enters Potomac River. Take-out downstream on Potomac River. Seasonal.

GREAT DISMAL SWAMP – Chesapeake – 95 F9 Flatwater route follows Feeder Ditch 8 miles to Lake Drummond in the center of Great Dismal Swamp National Wildlife Refuge. Put-in at boat launch site on Dismal Swamp Canal on SR 17. Portage around spillway to enter lake. Abundant wildlife. Return by same route.

JAMES RIVER – Buchanan – 49 E9 River cuts through Blue Ridge Mountains with Class I–II rapids amidst wilderness scenery. Class IV Balcony Falls at Glasgow. Portaging the falls allows beginners to paddle river. Put-in at Springwood access. Take-out 32 miles downstream at US 501/SR 130 bridge.

JAMES RIVER – James River Park – 55 E6 Whitewater stretch for experts only through an urban area, encountering numerous Class II–IV rapids. Hazards include broken dams, debris, dams and heavy rapids. Put-in at Riverside Drive and Hillcrest Rd. Take-out 2 miles downstream at US 360 (14th Street).

JAMES RIVER – Scottsville – 52 B4 Scenic channel braided by dozens of islands. Put-in at Scottsville Landing. First segment traverses Class I–II riffles upstream from Bremo Bluff. Predominately flat stretch from there to take-out at Columbia bridge. 22.5 miles.

MATTAPONI RIVER – Aylett – 55 B10 Scenic, slow-moving river is suitable for beginning paddlers. Abundant wildlife. Put-in at Zoar Nature Trail near Herring Creek. Take-out 5 miles downstream at SGOF boat landing in Aylett.

MAURY RIVER – Goshen–Little Mountain WMA – 37 F7 Expert level river flows through a steep mountain pass over Class II-IV rapids, including Devil's Kitchen, where river drops 20 feet over a 50-yard stretch. Ledges and rock gardens. Put-in on SR 39 above Goshen Pass. Take-out 6 miles downstream on SR 39 at Rockbridge Baths.

NORTH BAY LOOP – Virginia Beach – 96 D4 Put-in at Lotus Gardens canoe access site. Flatwater route follows Ashville Bridge Creek to Muddy Creek. Enters North Bay and follows the shoreline to Hell Point Creek, then follows creek north to Ashville Bridge Creek. Returns to Lotus Gardens. Meandering streams, marshlands, dense woodlands and open expanse of water on North Bay. 5.4 miles.

NORTH LANDING RIVER – Chesapeake – 96 E2 Put-in at canoe access site on Pocaty River at Blackwater Road. Flatwater route on popular recreational waterway follows creek east to North Landing River. Continues south on the river to Seneca Campground on east shore, north of the North Carolina border. Hardwood swamps and extensive marshlands. 12 miles.

NOTTOWAY RIVER – McKenney – 92 B3 Moderately difficult river meanders through secluded region, offering some difficult rapids amidst peaceful stretches of water. Put-in at Cut Bank access point. Take-out 11 miles downstream at Purdy.

OCCOQUAN WATER TRAIL – Bull Run Regional Park – 26 F1 Put-in at Bull Run Regional Park. First half of trip is on Bull Run. River widens into Occoquan Lake. Trips of varied lengths are made possible by access points at eight Northern Virginia Regional Parks. Generally acceptable difficulty for beginning paddlers. Last take-out 40 miles downstream at Pohick Bay Regional Park.

PAMUNKEY RIVER – Hanover – 55 B7 Popular trip amidst rustic scenery is entirely suitable for beginners. Follows coastal river with no rapids. Put-in at US 301. Take-out at US 360. 35 miles.

PASSAGE CREEK – George Washington National Forest – 24 E1 Scenic route through mountain valley for expert canoeists. Gravel bars, ledges, rock gardens and Class II–IV rapids. Dam portage at fish hatchery. Put-in at Elizabeth Furnace Recreation Area in George Washington National Forest. Take-out 7 miles downstream at SR 55 east of Waterlick.

POHICK CREEK – Pohick Stream Valley Park – 34 A4 Small, rocky stream. During high water, suitable only for expert canoeists. Class II–IV rapids downstream from confluence with Middle Run. Put-in at Hooes Road. Take-out 6 miles downstream at US 1 in Lorton.

POTOMAC RIVER – Great Falls – 26 D3 Put-in at Rocky Cove access in Maryland. Flows through the high rock walls of Mather Gorge. Several Class II rapids above SR 495, before the river widens and islands form many channels. Take-out on Maryland shore across from Sycamore Island. 7 miles.

RAPIDAN RIVER – Locust Grove – 33 F7 Put-in at Germanna Ford on SR 3. Section above Ely Ford is suitable for beginners with few riffles or ledges. A few Class II rapids above take-out at confluence with Rappahannock River. 12 miles.

RAPPAHANNOCK RIVER – Remington – 33 E7 Put-in at bridge on SR 620 at Kelly's Ford. Numerous Class I–II rapids to confluence with Rapidan River. Remains of canal locks and dams create some difficult stretches. Campsites along route. Take-out at Motts Run Landing. 25 miles.

SHENANDOAH RIVER – Boyce – 24 C5 Scenic, slow-moving section of river with views of Blue Ridge Mountains is suitable for beginners. Put-in at Berry's Ferry Landing. Take-out 10 miles downstream at Locke's Landing.

SHENANDOAH RIVER; SOUTH FORK – Elkton – 31 F6 Spectacular Blue Ridge Mountain scenery along popular river. Ledges, some flatwater paddling and two dam portages. Suitable for novices. Put-in at boat ramp at Island Ford. take-out 23 miles downstream at Whitehouse Landing.

SHENANDOAH RIVER; SOUTH FORK – Luray – 31 A9 Class II rapids along intermediate route include many staircase ledges and long horseshoe bends. Scenic views of Blue Ridge Mountains. Portage at low bridge, then continue for flatwater paddling above Karo. Scenery of last segment includes woodlands, pastures and high, limestone cliffs. Put-in at Foster's Landing boat ramp off of South Page Valley Rd. Take-out at Simpson's Landing. 26.5 miles.

THORNTON RIVER – Woodville – 32 B2 Scenic route suitable for experienced canoeists features Class II–III rapids. Downed trees and fences may require portaging. Boulders, rock cliffs and overhanging trees. Put-in at SSR 620. Take-out 7 miles downstream at SSR 626 at Rock Mills.

TYE RIVER – George Washington National Forest – 51 A7 Spectacular mountain scenery along route suitable for experienced paddlers. Continuous Class II–IV rapids. Rock formations, cliffs and steep, wooded slopes line river. Put-in on SR 56. Take-out 8.5 miles downstream at SR 56 at Massies Mill.

UPPER NEW RIVER – Mouth of Wilson – 83 F10 Northern flowing route through mountain scenery. Upper stretches include numerous riffles and Class I–III rapids. Some flatwater paddling in lower sections. Portages at four dams. Frequent access sites. Trips of varied lengths and difficulties possible. Put-in at SR 93 bridge north of North Carolina border. Take-out at boat ramp at Claytor Lake State Park. 78 miles.

WEST NECK CREEK – Virginia Beach – 96 D3 Passes initially through an urban area before traversing scenic section through natural surroundings. Small tributaries extend into undisturbed swamps. Put-in at bridge on Princess Anne Road. Take-out 5 miles downstream at West Neck Road. West Neck Creek connects to North Landing River for longer trip.

SKIING

BRYCE RESORT – Mount Jackson – 22 F5 MOUNTAIN: 2 chairlifts and 3 surface lifts. 8 trails: 34% beginner, 33% intermediate and 33% advanced. VERTICAL DROP: 500 ft. FACILITIES: Restaurant, cafeteria, rentals, ski shop, night-skiing, snowtubing. Summer activities include golf, mountain biking, tubing, hiking and ziplines.

MASSANUTTEN – McGaheysville – 30 F5 MOUNTAIN: 4 chairlifts and 3 surface lifts. 14 trails: 30% beginner, 35% intermediate and 35% advanced. VERTICAL DROP: 1,110 ft. FACILITIES: Ski school, cafeteria, rentals, terrain parks, night-skiing, snowtubing. 4 season resort.

THE OMNI HOMESTEAD RESORT – George Washington National Forest – 36 E3 MOUNTAIN: 4 lifts including 1 chairlift. 9 trails: 33% beginner, 33% intermediate and 34% advanced. VERTICAL DROP: 700 ft. FACILITIES: Restaurant, rentals, ski shop, terrain park, snowtubing, Nordic skiing. 4 season resort.

WINTERGREEN RESORT – George Washington National Forest – 38 F3 MOUNTAIN: 5 chairlifts including 2 high-speed 6 packs. 26 trails: 23% beginner, 35% intermediate and 42% advanced. VERTICAL DROP: 1,003 ft. FACILITIES: Ski school, restaurants, rentals, ski shop, terrain parks, night-skiing, snowtubing. 4 season resort.

Unique Natural Features

BREAKS CANYON – Jefferson National Forest – 61 B8 Largest canyon east of the Mississippi River. Carved by Russell Fork Creek. 5 miles in length, with sheer vertical walls 1,600 feet high.

CALEDON NATURAL AREA – Caledon State Park – 34 F5 Hardwood forest along shores of the Potomac River includes 800 acres of 80–100-year-old trees. Site of rare floating primrose willow. 2,579 acres. Home to bald eagles among over 120 species of birds including uncommon Canadian warbler and gray-cheeked thrush. Mammals and 39 species of reptiles and amphibians. Closed to public during eagle mating season.

DARK HOLLOW FALLS – Shenandoah National Park – 31 D9 Series of small cascades falling 70 feet. Popular destination is the closest falls to Skyline Drive.

DIXIE CAVERNS – Salem – 66 C3 Underground caverns featuring rock formations including drapery formations, stalactites and towering chamber. Only caverns in southwest Virginia. Guided tours.

DOYLES RIVER FALLS – Shenandoah National Park – 39 B6 Two falls, 28 and 63 feet high. Hiking trail extends from the Appalachian National Scenic Trail to a vantage point with an excellent view of the falls.

ENDLESS CAVERNS – George Washington National Forest – 31 C6 Cavern rock formations include stalactites, stalagmites, giant columns, shields, flowstone and limestone pendants. Guided tours along lighted walkways.

FAIRY STONES – Fairy Stone State Park – 86 C4 Six-sided staurolite crystals found in Fairy Stone State Park. Commonly occur in pairs, intersecting at angles to form cross-like shapes. Combination of heat and pressure during formation of the Appalachian Mountains provided optimal conditions necessary for crystal formation.

GRAND CAVERNS – Grand Caverns Regional Park – 38 A4 Caverns featuring unique shield formations as well as draperies, flowstone, stalactites and stalagmites. Cathedral Hall, one of the largest cavern rooms in eastern US. 280 feet long, 70 feet high. Guided tours.

GREAT DISMAL SWAMP – Great Dismal Swamp National Wildlife Refuge – 95 E8 Remnant of larger swamp containing geological and ecological elements unique in US. Supports five forest types including pine, Atlantic white cedar, maple–blackgum, tupelo–bald cypress and sweetgum–oak–poplar. Unique plants include dwarf trillium, silky camellia and rare log fern. Remnant marsh, sphagnum bog and 3,100-acre Lake Drummond located in heart of swamp.

JONES RUN FALLS – Shenandoah National Park – 39 B6 Two small cascading streams fall 42 feet. Reachable by short 3.4 mile round-trip hike with gradual climbs from Skyline Drive.

LURAY CAVERNS – Luray – 31 B9 Caverns featuring cascades, columns, stalactites, stalagmites and underground pools. Unusual organ uses stalactites to play music. Guided tours. Car and carriage exhibits outline transportation history.

MONTPELIER FOREST – Somerset – 40 B2 200 acres of virgin oak, hickory and poplar forest. Many trees believed to be between 200 and 300 years old. Located on estate of fourth US President James Madison.

MT ROGERS – Jefferson National Forest – 83 E7 Highest point in Virginia at 5,729 feet is forested by the rare combination of red spruces and Fraser firs. Blazed trail departs the Appalachian National Scenic Trail and leads to summit.

NATURAL BRIDGE – Natural Bridge State Park – 50 D1 Limestone arch 215 feet high, 90 feet long and up to 150 feet wide. Joins two mountains, spans creek and supports highway.

NATURAL BRIDGE CAVERNS – Natural Bridge State Park – 50 D1 Cavern rock formations include stalactites, stalagmites, "hanging gardens", "totem poles." and the colossal Dome Room. Underground streams and waterfalls. Guided tours.

NATURAL CHIMNEYS – Natural Chimneys Park – 30 F2 Seven limestone towers rising 120 feet in astounding contrast to surrounding forested terrain. Various viewpoints.

NATURAL TUNNEL – Natural Tunnel State Park – 80 D3 Tunnel carved through limestone ridge by Stock Creek, beginning during the glacial recession. 850 feet long, 100–175 feet in width, with an average height of 100 feet. Deep, semicircular basin at south end of tunnel has vertical walls nearly 400 feet high.

OVERALL RUN FALLS – Shenandoah National Park – 32 A1 Lower falls is the highest waterfall in park at 93 feet high. Upper falls is 29 feet high. Both are accessible by a fairly difficult, 6-mile round-trip trail leaving from Skyline Drive.

SEASHORE NATURAL AREA – First Landing State Park – 96 A3 Coastal dune region covers 2,770 acres. Parallel sand dunes densely wooded with semitropical forest. Maritime forest of loblolly pines and live oaks. Lagoons rimmed with cypress trees.

SHENANDOAH CAVERNS – Quicksburg – 31 A6 Large, underground caverns. Unique rock formations include Capitol Dome, Oriental Garden and Bacon Formation. Caves accessible by elevator.

SKYLINE CAVERNS – Front Royal – 24 E2 Extensive caverns featuring delicate, flower-like calcite formations called anthodites. Three underground streams and 37-foot-high Rainbow Falls. Guided tours along lighted walkways. Miniature train ride. Mirror maze.

SOUTH RIVER FALLS – Shenandoah National Park – 31 F8 83 foot high waterfall drops in two immediate falls. Best viewed from an overlook that is easily reached by a short, 2.5 mile rountrip hike from the South River Picnic Area on the Skyline Drive.

WHITE OAK CANYON FALLS – Shenandoah National Park – 31 C10 Six waterfalls ranging from 35 to 86 feet high in steep, wooded gorge. Difficult hike traverses gorge, offering views of all falls.

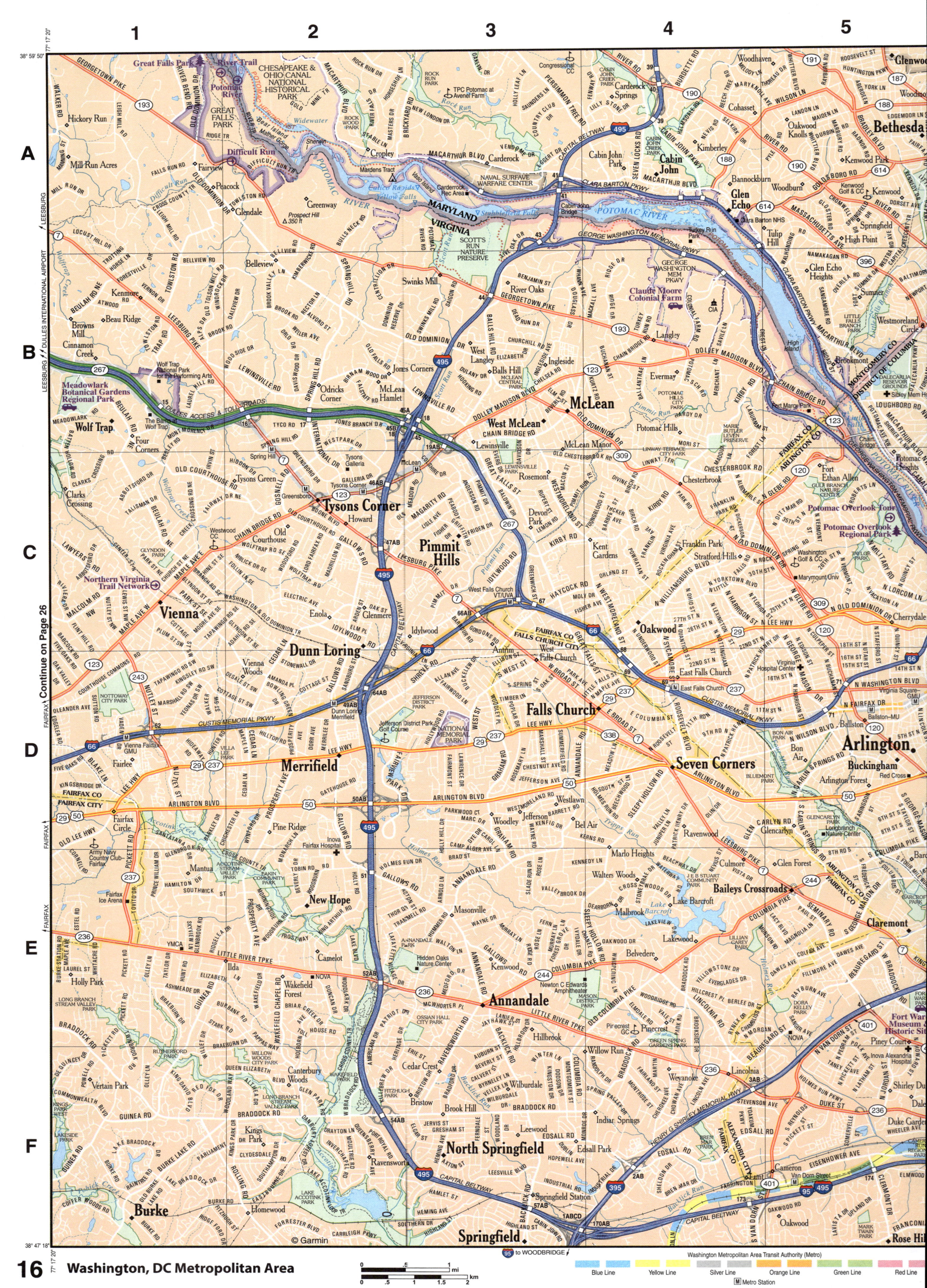

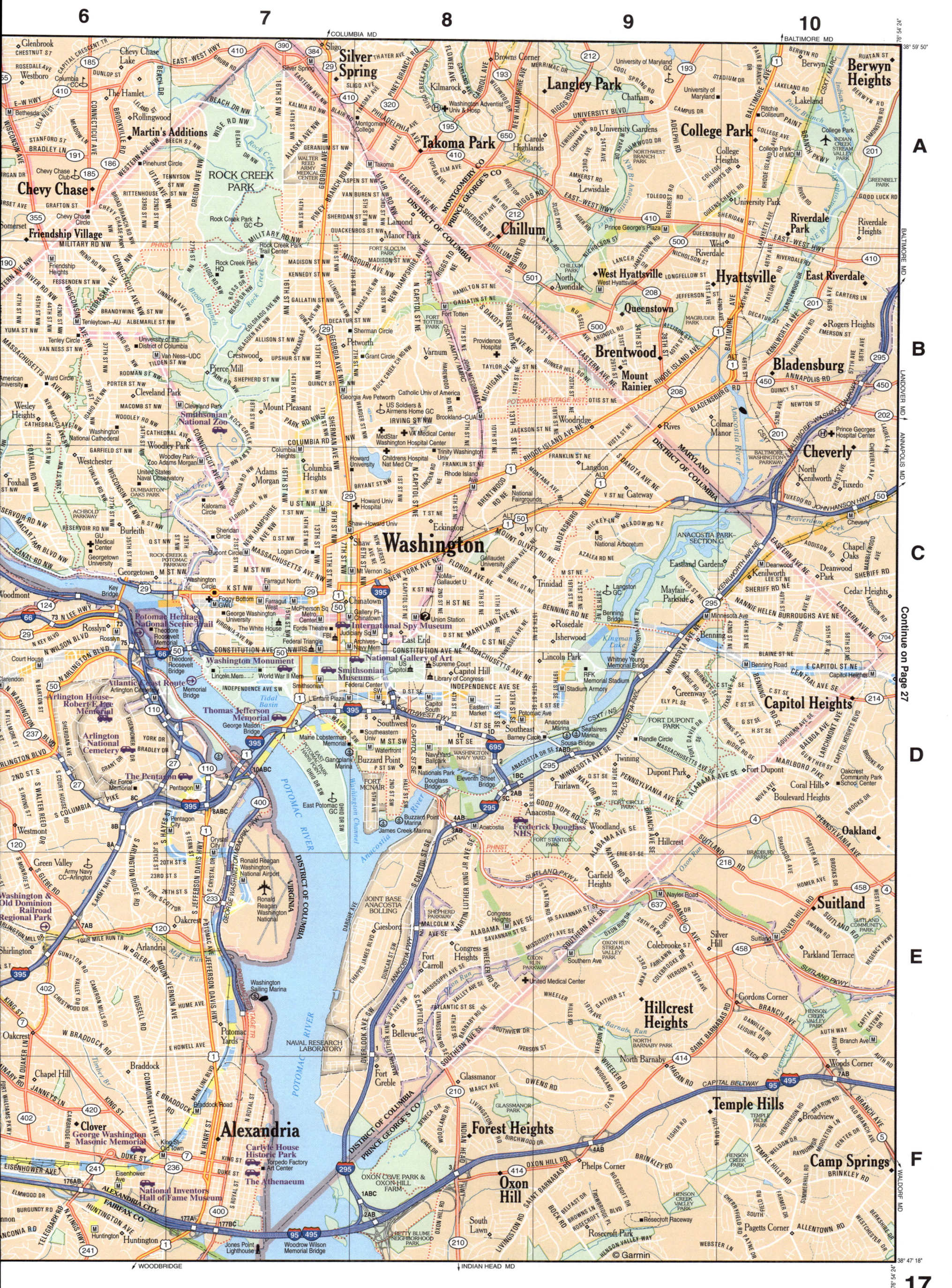

Washington, DC Metropolitan Area Map Road Name Indexes (see pages 16, 17)

MARYLAND

8th Ave 17 A8
19th Ave 17 E9
23rd Ave 17 A9
23rd Pkwy 17 E9
24th Ave 17 A9
28th Ave 17 E9
28th Pkwy 17 E9
29th St 17 B9
31st St 17 B9
34th St 17 B9
38th St 17 B9
40th St 17 B9
41st Ave 17 B9
42nd Ave 17 B10
46th Ave 17 B10
46th St 17 B10
48th Ave 17 B10
52nd Ave 17 B10
56th Ave 17 B10
57th Ave 17 B10
58th Ave 17 B10
Aberdeen Rd 16 A5
Addison Rd 17 C10
Adelphi Rd 17 A9
Ager Rd 17 A9
Allentown Rd 17 F10
Allison St 17 B9
Amherst Rd 17 A9
Annapolis Rd 17 B10
Arlington Rd 16 A5
Arundel Rd 17 B9
Auth Pl 17 E10
Auth Rd 17 E10
Auth Way 17 E10
Balboa Ave 17 D10
Baltimore Ave 16 B5; 17 A10,B10
Beach Dr 17 A6
Beech Rd 17 E10
Beech Tree Rd 16 A4
Belcrest Rd 17 A9
Belfast Dr 17 F9
Berkshire Dr 17 F10
Berwyn Rd 17 A10
Birchwood Dr 17 F8
Bladensburg Rd 17 B9
Blair Rd 17 A7
Bock Rd 17 F9
Bradley Blvd 16 A5
Bradley Ln 17 A6
Branch Ave 17 E10;F10
Branch Ave 17 E9
Brickyard Rd 16 A3
Brinkley Rd 17 F9,10
Broad St 16 B5
Brooke Rd 17 D10
Brooks Dr 17 D10;E10
Brookville Rd 17 A6
Browns Ln 17 F9
Burdette Rd 16 A4
Cabin John Pkwy 16 A4
Campus Dr 17 A9
Capital Gateway Dr 17 E10
Capitol Heights Blvd 17 D10
Carroll Ave 17 A8
Carters Ln 17 B10
Center Dr 17 F10
Chapman Rd 17 A9
Cherryfield Rd 17 F10
Chestnut St 17 A6
Cheverly Ave 17 B10
Chillum Rd 17 B8
Colebrooke Dr 17 E9
College Ave 17 A10
College Heights Dr 17 A9
Connecticut Ave 17 A6
Cool Spring Rd 17 A9
Country Club Dr 16 A3
Cree Dr 17 F8
Crest Ave 17 C10
Cromwell Dr 16 A5
Curtis Dr 17 E9
Danville Dr 17 E10
Decatur St 17 B10
Dorset Ave 16 A5
Dorset Ave 17 A6
Dunlop St 17 A6
Durbin Rd 16 A5
East–west Hwy 17 A6,7,9,10
Edgemoor Ln 16 A5
Edmonston Rd 17 A10;B10
Eggert Dr 16 A3
Elm Ave 17 A8
Emerson St 17 B10
Fairfax Rd 16 A5
Fairlawn St 17 E9
Farmer Dr 17 F10
Fenway Rd 16 A4
Fisher Rd 17 F9
Flower Ave 17 A8
Fort Sumner Dr 16 B5
Gaither St 17 E9
Garland Ave 17 A8
Gateway Dr 17 E10
Georgetown Pike 16 A1
Gloster Rd 16 A5
Goldsboro Rd 16 A5
Good Luck Rd 17 A10
Grafton St 17 A6
Grubb Rd 17 A7
Gumwood Dr 17 A9
Gunther St 17 D10
Hagan Rd 17 F9
Helmsdale Rd 16 A4
Henderson Rd 17 F10
Henson Valley Way 17 F9
Holly Leaf Ln 16 A3
Holton Ln 17 F9
Homer Ave 17 E10
Horseshoe Ln 16 A2
Huntington Pkwy 16 A5
Indian Head Hwy 17 F8
Iverson Pl 17 E9
Iverson St 17 E8,9
Jamestown Rd 17 B9
Jefferson St 17 B9
Kenilworth Ave 17 B10
Kennedy Dr 16 A5
Lafayette Ave 17 B10
Lakeland Rd 17 A10
Lancer Dr 17 B9
Landing Way 17 B10
Landon Ln 16 A5
Larchmont Ave 17 D10
Laurel Ave 17 B10
Leisure Dr 17 E10
Leland St 17 A6
Lewisdale Dr 17 A9
Lilly Stone Dr 16 A4
Little Falls Pkwy 16 A5
Livingston Rd 17 F8
Longfellow St 17 B9
Macarthur Blvd 16 A2-4;B5
Maiden Ln 16 A5
Maple Ave 17 A8
Marblewood Ave 17 C10
Marbury Rd 16 A5
Marcy Ave 17 F8
Marlboro Pike 17 D10
Maryknoll Ave 16 A4
Massachusetts Ave 16 A5
Masters Dr 16 A2
Meadow Ln 17 A6
Melody Ln 16 A4
Merrimac Dr 17 A8
Middleton Ln 17 F10
Morgan Dr 17 A6
Namakagan Rd 16 B5
Nevis Rd 16 A4
New Hampshire Ave 17 A8
New London Dr 16 A3
Newport Ave 16 B5
Newton St 17 B10
Nicholson St 17 B9
Nova Ave 17 D10
Oaklyn Dr 16 A3
Old Branch Ave 17 F10
Overlea Rd 16 B5
Owens Rd 17 F8
Oxon Hill Rd 17 F8
Oxon Run Dr 17 E9
Paint Branch Dr 17 A10
Paint Branch Pkwy 17 A10
Payne Dr 17 F10
Pennsylvania Ave 17 D10
Persimmon Tree Rd 16 A3
Philadelphia Ave 17 A8
Piney Branch Rd 17 A8
Poplar Ave 17 A8
Porter Ave 17 D10
Pyle Rd 16 A5
Queens Chapel Rd 17 A9
Queensbury Rd 17 A9
Quincy St 17 B10
Radnor Rd 16 A5
Ray Rd 17 A8,9
Rayburn Dr 17 F10
Rayburn Rd 16 A5
Red Top Rd 17 A8
Regency Pkwy 17 E10
Rhode Island Ave 17 A10;B9
Riggs Rd 17 A8,9
River Falls Dr 16 A2
River Rd 16 A4,5; 17 A10
Riverdale Rd 17 B10
Rock Run Dr 16 A2
Roosevelt St 16 A5
Rosecroft Blvd 17 F9
Rosecroft Dr 17 F9
Rosedale Ave 17 A6
Ruatan St 17 A10
Russell Ave 17 B9
Saint Barnabas Rd 17 E9;F8
Sangamore Rd 16 B5
Sargent Rd 17 B8
Saunders Ln 16 A3
Selkirk Dr 16 A4
Seneca Dr 17 F8
Seven Locks Rd 16 A4
Shadyside Ave 17 D10
Sharon Rd 17 F10
Sheridan St 17 A10
Sheridan St 17 A8
Silver Hill Rd 17 E10
Sligo Ave 17 A7
Sligo Creek Pkwy 17 A8
Sligo Pkwy 17 A9
Southfield Rd 17 F10
Southview Dr 17 E8
Springfield Dr 16 A5
Stable Ln 16 A2
Stadium Dr 17 A9
Stanford St 17 A6
Suitland Rd 17 E10;D9
Summerhill Rd 17 F10
Swann Rd 17 E10
Takoma Ave 17 A8
Tanglewood Dr 17 B10
Taylor Rd 17 B10
Temple Hills Rd 17 F10
Thayer Ave 17 A8
Thoreau Dr 16 A5
Toledo Rd 17 A9
Trowbridge Pl 17 F9
Tuxedo Rd 17 C10
University Blvd 17 A9
Vendome Dr 16 A3
W Park Dr 17 A9
Walhonding Rd 16 B5
Webster Ln 17 F9
Weldon Dr 17 F10
West Ave 17 E10
Westba Rd Ave 16 B5
Westchester Dr 17 F10
Wheeler Hills Rd 17 E9
Wheeler Rd 17 F9
Whittier Blvd 16 A5
Wildwood Dr 17 A8
Wilson Ln 16 A5
Wisconsin Ave 17 A6
Woodland Blvd 17 F9
Woodland Dr 17 F8
York Ln 16 A5

WASHINGTON, DC

1st St NE 17 B8
1st St NW 17 C8
3rd St NW 17 A8;B8
4th St NE 17 C8
4th St SE 17 D8;E8
5th Ave 17 D8
5th St NW 17 A8
6th St NW 17 C8
7th St NE 17 B8
7th St NW 17 B7;C7
8th St NE 17 C8
9th St NW 17 B7;C7
10th St NE 17 B8
11th St NE 17 C8
11th St NW 17 B7;C7
11th St SE 17 D8
12th St NE 17 B8
13th St NE 17 B8
13th St NW 17 B7;C7
13th St SE 17 D8
14th St NE 17 B8
14th St NW 17 A-C7
15th St NE 17 C8
15th St NW 17 C7
15th St SE 17 D8
16th St NW 17 A-C7
16th St SE 17 D8
18th St NE 17 B9
18th St NW 17 B7
19th St NE 17 C9
19th St SE 17 D9
20th St NE 17 B9
21st St NE 17 C9
21st St NW 17 C7
26th St NE 17 C9
27th St NW 17 B7
28th St NW 17 C7
2nd St NE 17 C8
2nd St SW 17 D8
30th St SE 17 D9
32nd St NW 17 A6
33rd St NW 17 A6
34th St NW 17 B6
35th St NW 17 C6
37th St NW 17 B6;C6
39th St NW 17 B6
42nd St NE 17 C10
42nd St NW 17 B6;C6
44th St NE 17 C10
44th St NW 17 B6
45th St NW 17 B6
47th St NW 17 B6
49th St NE 17 C10
49th St NW 17 B6;C6
55th St NE 17 C10
58th St NE 17 C10
Alabama Ave SE 17 D9;E8,9
Alaska Ave NW 17 A7
Albemarle St NW 17 B6
Allison St NW 17 B7
Anacostia Ave NE 17 D9
Anacostia Dr SE 17 D8
Arkansas Ave NW 17 B7
Aspen St NW 17 A7
Atlantic St SE 17 E8
Azalea Rd NE 17 C9
Barnaby Rd SE 17 E8
Beach Dr NW 17 A7;B7
Beech St NW 17 A6
Benning Rd NE 17 C9
Benning Rd SE 17 D10
Bladensburg Rd NE 17 C9
Blagden Ave NW 17 B7
Blaine St NE 17 D10
Blair Rd NW 17 A8
Branch Ave SE 17 D9
Brandywine St NW 17 B6
Brentwood Rd NE 17 C8
Broad Branch Rd NW 17 A6
Bryant St NW 17 C8
Bunker Hill Rd NE 17 B9
Burns St SE 17 D9,10
C St NE 17 C8
C St SE 17 D10
Canal Rd NW 16 C5; 17 C6
Cathedral Ave NW 17 B6
Central Ave SE 17 D10
Chappie James Blvd 17 E8
Chevy Chase Pkwy NW 17 A6
Colorado Ave NW 17 B7
Columbia Rd NW 17 B7;C7
Connecticut Ave NW 17 B6,7
Constitution Ave NE 17 D8
Constitution Ave NW 17 D7
D St NE 17 C8
D St SE 17 D8
Dalecarlia Pkwy 16 B5
Dargue Ave 17 E7
Decatur St NW 17 B7
Division Ave NE 17 C10
Duncan St SW 17 E8
E Capitol St NE 17 D10
E St SE 17 D9,10
Eastern Ave NE 17 A8;B8,9;C10
Eastern Ave NW 17 A7
Ely Pl SE 17 D9
Erie St SE 17 E9
Fessenden St NW 17 B6
Florida Ave NE 17 C8
Florida Ave NW 17 C7
Fordham Rd NW 16 B5
Fort Davis Dr SE 17 D9
Foxhall Rd NW 17 C6
Franklin St NE 17 C8,9
G St SE 17 D10
Gallatin St NE 17 B8
Gallatin St NW 17 B7
Garfield St NW 17 C6
Georgia Ave NW 17 A7
Georgia Ave NW 17 B7
Geranium St NW 17 A7
Good Hope Rd SE 17 D9
H St NE 17 C8
H St SE 17 D10
Half St SW 17 D8
Hamilton St NE 17 B8
Harewood Rd NE 17 B8
Hayes St NE 17 C9
Hickey Ln NE 17 C9
I St SE 17 D8
Idaho Ave NW 17 B6
Illinois Ave NW 17 B7
Independence Ave SE 17 D8
Independence Ave SW 17 D7
Iowa Ave NW 17 B7
Irving St NW 17 B8
Jackson St NE 17 B8
John McCormack Rd 17 B8
K St NE 17 C8
K St NW 17 C7
Kalmia Rd NW 17 A7
Kansas Ave NW 17 B8
Kennedy St NW 17 B7
Lee St NE 17 C10
Lincoln Rd NE 17 C8
Linnean Ave NW 17 B6
Livingston Rd SE 17 E8
Loughboro Rd NW 16 B5
M St NE 17 C9
M St NW 17 C6,7
M St SE 17 D8
M St SW 17 D8
Macarthur Blvd NW 16 B5
Macarthur Blvd NW 17 C6
Macomb St NW 17 B6
Madison St NW 17 B7,8
Malcolm X Ave SE 17 E8
Martin Luther King Jr Ave Se 17 E8
Martin Luther King Jr Ave SW 17 F8
Maryland Ave NE 17 C8
Massachusetts Ave NE 17 C8
Massachusetts Ave NW 17 B6;C7
Massachusetts Ave SE 17 D9
Meadow Rd NE 17 C9
Michigan Ave NE 17 B8
Military Rd NW 17 A7;B6
Minnesota Ave NE 17 D9
Minnesota Ave SE 17 D9
Mississippi Ave SE 17 E8
Missouri Ave NW 17 B7
Montana Ave NE 17 C8
Mount Olivet Rd NE 17 C8
N Capitol St NE 17 B8;C8
Nannie Helen Burroughs Ave NE 17 C10
Naylor Rd SE 17 D9
Neal St NE 17 C8
Nebraska Ave NW 17 B6
New Hampshire Ave NE 17 B8
New Hampshire Ave NW 17 C7
New Jersey Ave NW 17 C8
New Mexico Ave NW 17 B6
New York Ave NE 17 C8
Ohio Dr SW 17 D7
Oregon Ave NW 17 A7
Otis St NE 17 B9
Overlook Ave SW 17 F8
P St SW 17 D8
Park Rd NW 17 B7
Pennsylvania Ave SE 17 D9
Piney Branch Rd NW 17 A7
Porter St NW 17 B6
Potomac Ave NW 16 B5
Q St NW 17 C6,7
Q St SE 17 D9
Quackenbos St NW 17 A7
Quincy St NW 17 B7
R St NW 17 C6
Reno Rd NW 17 B6
Reno Rd NW 17 B6
Reservoir Rd NW 17 C6
Rhode Island Ave NE 17 C8
Ridge Rd NW 17 B7
Ridge Rd SE 17 D10
Ridge Rd SE 17 D9
Riggs Rd NE 17 B8
Rittenhouse St NW 17 A6
River Rd NW 17 B6
Rock Creek Church Rd NW 17 B8
Rock Creek Pkwy NW 17 B7
Rodman St NW 17 B6
Ross Dr NW 17 B7
S Capitol St SE 17 D8;E8
S Dakota Ave NE 17 B8;C9
Sargent Rd NE 17 B8
Savannah St SE 17 E8,9
Shepherd St NW 17 B7
Sheridan St NW 17 A7
Sherier Pl NW 16 B5
Sheriff Rd NE 17 C10
Sherman Ave NW 17 B7
Southern Ave SE 17 D10;E8,9
Southwest Fwy 17 D8
Spring St 17 A7
Stanton Rd SE 17 E9
T St NE 17 C8
T St NW 17 C7
Taylor St NE 17 B8
Tennessee Ave NE 17 D8
Tennyson St NW 17 A6
Texas Ave SE 17 D10
Tilden St NW 17 B6
Tunlaw Rd NW 17 C6
U St NW 17 C7
Upshur St NW 17 B7
Utah Ave NW 17 A6
V St NE 17 C9
Valley Ave SE 17 E8
Van Buren St NW 17 A7
Van Ness St NW 17 B6
Virginia Ave NW 17 C7
Vista St NE 17 B9
W St NW 17 C6,7
W Virginia Ave NE 17 C8
Warder St NW 17 B8
Water St SW 17 D7
Western Ave NW 17 A6;B6
Wheeler Rd SE 17 E8
Wisconsin Ave NW 17 B6;C6
Wise Rd NW 17 A7
Woodley Rd NW 17 B6
Yuma St NW 17 B6

VIRGINIA

11th Rd N 16 D4
11th St N 16 D4
14th St N 16 D5
15th St N 16 D5
16th St N 16 D5;E5
18th St N 16 C5
20th St S 17 E6
22nd St N 16 D4
22nd St S 17 E6
23rd St S 17 E6
25th St N 16 C5
26th St N 16 C4,5
26th St S 17 E6
27th St N 16 C4
2nd St S 17 D6
30th St N 16 C4
31st St S 17 E6
35th St N 16 C5
5th St N 16 D5
6th St S 16 D5
8th Rd S 16 E5
8th St S 16 D5
9th Rd N 16 D4
Abbotsford Dr 16 C1
Adahi Rd SE 16 C2
Allan Ave 16 D3
Alps Dr 16 B1
Althea Dr 16 F2
Alvord St 16 B2
Amanda Pl 16 D2
Americana Dr 16 F2
Anderson Rd 16 C3
Annandale Rd 16 D3;E3
Arden St 16 C2
Arlington Blvd 16 D1,3,4
Arnold Ln 16 E3
Ashmeade Dr 16 E1
Aston St 16 E2
Atwood Rd 16 B1
Auburn St 16 F3
Axton St 16 F3
Babcock Rd 16 C1
Backlick Rd 16 E3;F3
Baldwin Dr 16 C3
Ballantrae Ln 16 B4
Balls Hill Rd 16 B3
Barbee St 16 C4
Barbour Rd 16 C3
Barkley Dr 16 D1
Barrett Rd 16 D3
Batten Hollow Rd 16 B1
Beachway Dr 16 E4
Beauregard St 16 E5;F4
Beechwood Ln 16 D4
Bellview Rd 16 B1,2
Benjamin St 16 B3
Berlee Dr 16 E4
Besley Rd 16 C1
Beulah Rd NE 16 B1;C1
Beverly Dr 16 E2
Beverly Rd 16 B3
Beverly St 16 F3
Birch Rd 16 C4
Birnam Wood Dr 16 B2
Blake Ln 16 D1
Boone Blvd 16 C2
Bowling Green Dr 16 D2
Brad St 16 E3
Braddock Rd 16 E1,4;F2-4
Bradford Dr 16 F3
Bradley Dr 17 D6
Braeburn Dr 16 E1;F1
Branch Rd SE 16 C1
Bren Mar Dr 16 F4
Briar Creek Dr 16 E2
Bristow Dr 16 F3
Brook Rd 16 B1,2
Brook Valley Ln 16 B2
Brookside Dr 16 E4
Buchanan St 16 B4
Buckelew Dr 16 D3
Bulls Neck Rd 16 A2
Burbank Rd 16 E1
Burgundy Rd 17 F6
Burke Lake Rd 16 F1
Burke Rd 16 F1
Burke Station Rd 16 E1
Byrneley Ln 16 F3
Cabin John Rd 16 F3
Calvert St 16 F3
Cambridge Rd 17 F6
Cameron Mills Rd 17 E6
Camp Alger Ave 16 D3
Carol Ln 16 D3
Carrleigh Pkwy 16 F2
Cedar Ln 16 D2
Center St N 16 C1
Centrillion Dr 16 B2
Chain Bridge Rd 16 B3-5;C2
Chanel Rd 16 E3
Chelsea Rd 16 B3
Cherokee Ave 16 F4
Chesterbrook Rd 16 C4
Chestnut Ave 16 D3
Chichester Ln 16 D1
Chowan Ave 16 F4
Church St NE 16 C1
Churchill Rd 16 B3
Clarks Crossing Rd 16 C1
Clermont Dr 16 F5
Clydesdale Rd 16 F2
Coffer Woods Rd 16 F1
Colfax Ave 16 E5
Colonial Farm Rd 16 B4
Colshire Dr 16 C3
Columbia Pike 16 E3,4
Columbia Rd 16 F3
Commonwealth Ave 17 F6
Commonwealth Blvd 16 F1
Cornell Rd 16 E1
Cottage St SW 16 C1; D1
Cottage St 16 D2
Courthouse Commons Rd 16 D1
Creek Crossing Rd NE 16 C1
Crest Ln 16 B5
Crestwood Dr 17 E6
Crosswoods Dr 16 E4
Daleview Dr 16 B2
Danbury Forest Dr 16 F2
Davidson Rd 16 C3
Daviswood Dr 16 B2
Dawes Ave 16 E5
De Quincey Dr 16 F1
Dead Run Dr 16 B3
Dearborn Dr 16 E4
Desale St SW 16 D1
Divine St 16 C4
Dodson Dr 16 F3
Dolley Madison Blvd 16 B3,4
Dominion Reserve Dr 16 B2
Dorr Ave 16 D2
Douglass Dr 16 B3
Drayton Ln 16 F2
Dublin Ave 16 F3
Duke St 16 F5
Duke St 17 F6,7
Dulany Dr 16 B3
Duncan Dr 16 E2
Dye Dr 16 D3
E Braddock Rd 17 F6
E Broad St 16 D4
E Columbia St 16 D4
E Howell Ave 17 E7
Eastbourne Dr 16 F2
Edgelea Rd 16 D1
Edsall Rd 16 F3,4
Eisenhower Ave 16 F5; 17 F6
Eisenhower Dr 17 D6
Electric Ave 16 C2
Elgar St 16 F3
Elizabeth Dr 16 B3
Elizabeth Ln 16 E1
Ellison St 16 D3
Elm Pl 16 C2
Elm St 16 B3
Elmdale Rd 16 E4
Elmwood Dr 16 F5; 17 F6
Erie St 16 F3
Estel Rd 16 E1
Everglades Dr 16 E4
Evers Dr 16 C3
Fairland St 16 F4
Fairmont St 16 D3
Fairview Park Dr 16 D2
Fairway Dr NE 16 C1
Fairwood Ln 16 D3
Falls Run Rd 16 A1
Falstaff Rd 16 B2
Farrington Ave 16 F4
Fern Ln 16 E3
Ferndale St 16 F3
Fillmore Ave 16 E5
Fisher Ave 16 C3
Fisher Dr 16 C3
Fitzhugh St 16 F1
Five Oaks Rd 16 C1;D1
Flint Hill Rd 16 C1
Follin Ln SE 16 C2
Forest Grove Dr 16 E3
Forest Ln 16 C4
Forestville Dr 16 B1
Forrester Blvd 16 F2
Fort Williams Pkwy 17 F6
Franconia Rd 16 F5
Franconia Rd 17 F6
Franklin Ave 16 C4
Franklin Park Rd 16 C4
Friden Dr 16 C3
Frost Way 16 E2
Galleria Dr 16 C2
Gallows Rd 16 C-E2,3
Gatehouse Rd 16 D2
Georgetown Pike 16 B3
Glen Carlyn Rd 16 D4
Glen Park Rd 16 F2
Glenbrook Rd 16 E1
Glyndon St SE 16 C1,2
Gordons Rd 16 C3
Gosnell Rd 16 C2
Graham Rd 16 D3
Grant Dr 17 D6
Great Falls St 16 C3
Greensboro Dr 16 C2
Greenwich St 16 C3
Gresham St 16 F3
Griffith Rd 16 C3
Guinea Rd 16 E1;F1
Gunston Rd 17 E6
Hamilton Dr 16 E1
Hamlet St 16 F3
Hardy Dr 16 B4
Haycock Rd 16 C3
Heming Ave 16 F3
Heritage Dr 16 F2
Hideaway Rd 16 D1
Higdon Dr 16 C2
Highland St 16 F3
Hillbrook Dr 16 F3
Hillcrest Pl 16 E4
Hilltop Rd 16 D2
Hine St SE 16 C1
Holborn Ave 16 F2
Holly Hill Dr 16 E3
Holly Rd 16 E2
Hollywood Rd 16 D3
Holmes Run Dr 16 E2
Holmes Run Pkwy 16 F5
Holmes Run Rd 16 D4
Hooking Rd 16 B3
Hopewell Ave 16 F3
Hume Ave 17 E7
Hummer Rd 16 E3
Hunt Rd 16 E1
Hunter Rd 16 D1
Huntington Ave 17 F6
Idylwood Rd 16 C2,3
Industrial Dr 16 F4
Industrial Rd 16 F3
Ingleside Ave 16 B3
International Dr 16 B2
Inverchapel Rd 16 F2
Irvin St 16 C1
Ivydale Dr 16 E3
Janneys Ln 17 F6
Jayhawk St 16 E3
Jefferson Ave 16 D3
Jefferson Davis Hwy 17 E7
Jervis St 16 F3
Jones Branch Dr 16 B2
Juniper Ln 16 D4
Kenfig Dr 16 D3
Kennedy Ln 16 E3
Kerns Rd 16 D3
Killebrew Dr 16 F2
Kimberwicke Rd 16 B2
King Arthur Rd 16 E2
King David Blvd 16 F1
King St 16 E5; 17 E6;F6,7
Kings Park Dr 16 F2
Kingsbridge Dr 16 D1
Kingsley Rd SW 16 D1
Kingston Dr 16 F3
Kirby Rd 16 B4;C3,4
Kurtz Rd 16 B4
Laburnum St 16 B4
Lacy Blvd 16 E5
Lafayette Village Dr 16 E2
Lake Blvd 16 E2
Lake Braddock Dr 16 F1
Lakeview Dr 16 E4
Lanier St 16 E3
Laurel Hill Rd 16 B1
Laurel St 16 E1
Lavista Dr 16 F5
Lawrence Dr 16 D3
Lawyers Rd 16 C1
Lee Hwy 16 D1-3
Leesburg Pike 16 B1;C2;D4
Leesville Blvd 16 F3
Leigh Mill Rd 16 A1
Lemon Rd 16 C3
Lewinsville Rd 16 B2,3
Lewis St NW 16 C1
Lincoln Ave 16 F4
Lincolnia Rd 16 E4
Linway Ter 16 C4
Lisle Ave 16 C3
Little Falls St 16 D4
Little River Tpke 16 E1,3
Live Oak Dr 16 B3
Locust Hill Dr 16 A1
Lord Fairfax Rd 16 C2
Mackall Ave 16 B4
Macon St 16 C3
Maddux Ln 16 C4
Madrillon Rd 16 C2
Magarity Rd 16 C3
Magnolia Ln 16 E3
Main Line Blvd 17 F7
Malcolm Rd NW 16 C1
Manning St 16 A1
Maple Ave E 16 C1
Maple Ave W 16 C1
Maple Ave 16 E1
Maple Ln 16 D2
Marc Dr 16 D3
Marshall Rd SW 16 D1
Marshall St 16 D3
Martin St 16 F4
McWhorter Pl 16 E3
Meadow Ln 16 D4
Meadowlark Rd 16 B1
Medford Dr 16 E3
Merchant Ln 16 B4
Merrilee Dr 16 D2
Mill Run Dr 16 A1
Moly Dr 16 C3
Monarch Ln 16 E2
Monroe Dr 16 F4
Montgomery St 16 F3
Montmorency Dr 16 B1
Montrose St 16 F4
Moore Ave SE 16 C1
Mori St 16 B4
Morningside Dr 16 E2
Moultrie Rd 16 F2
Mount Vernon Ave 17 E6
Munson Rd 16 E4
Murray Ln 16 E3
N Albemarle St 16 C4
N Arlington Blvd 17 D6
N Barton St 17 D6
N Buchanan St 16 D5
N Carlin Springs Rd 16 D5
N Chambliss St 16 E4
N Culpeper St 16 C5
N Dickerson St 16 C4
N Dittmar Rd 16 C5
N Edison St 16 C5
N Fairfax Dr 16 D5
N Fillmore St 17 D6
N Florida St 16 C4
N George Mason Dr 16 C5
N Glebe Rd 16 C5
N Harrison St 16 C4;D5
N Henry St 17 F7
N Highland St 17 D6
N Howard St 16 E5
N Jackson St 16 D5
N Jordan St 16 F5
N Key Blvd 17 C6
N Kings Hwy 17 F6
N Kirkwood Rd 16 C5
N Latham St 16 F5
N Lee Hwy 16 C5
N Lee Hwy 17 C6
N Lexington St 16 C4
N Lincoln St 16 D5
N Little Falls Rd 16 C4
N Lorcom Ln 16 C5
N Maple Ave 16 D4
N Military Rd 16 C5
N Morgan St 16 E4
N Nottingham St 16 C4
N Ohio St 16 C4
N Old Dominion Dr 16 C4,5
N Patrick Henry Dr 16 D4
N Pegram St 16 F5
N Pickett St 16 F5
N Quaker Ln 17 F6
N Quantico St 16 C4
N Quincy St 16 C5
N Roberts Ln 16 C5
N Rock Spring Rd 16 C4
N Roosevelt St 16 D4
N Royal St 17 F7
N Stafford St 16 C5
N Sycamore St 16 C4
N Underwood St 16 C4
N Utah St 16 C5
N Vacation Ln 16 C5
N Van Dorn St 16 F5
N Vermont St 16 C5
N Washington Blvd 16 D5; 17 D6
N Westmoreland St 16 C4
N Williamsburg Blvd 16 C4
N Wilson Blvd 16 D5; 17 D6
N Yorktown Blvd 16 C4
Nevius St 16 E4
Niblick Dr SE 16 C2
Nutley St NW 16 C1
Nutley St 16 D1
Oak St 16 C2
Oak Valley Dr 16 D1
Oakwood Dr 16 E4
Oakwood Rd 16 F5
Old Burke Lake Rd 16 F1
Old Chesterbrook Rd 16 C3
Old Columbia Pike 16 E4
Old Courthouse Rd 16 C1,2
Old Dominion Dr 16 A1;B3
Old Dominion Dr 16 B3
Old Falls Rd 16 B2
Old Lee Hwy 16 D1
Old Meadow Rd 16 C2
Old Tolson Mill Rd 16 B1
Oleander Ave 16 D1
Olin Dr 16 D4
Olley Ln 16 E1;F1
Orland St 16 C4
Orlo Dr 16 B2
Pappas Way 16 E2
Park Ave 16 D3
Park Rd 16 C4;E4
Park St NE 16 C1
Park St SE 16 C1
Parkwood Ct 16 D3
Parliament Dr 16 F1
Patrick Henry Dr 16 D4
Patriot Dr 16 E2
Paul St 16 E5
Peabody Dr 16 C3
Pickett Rd 16 E1;F1
Pimmit Dr 16 C3
Plum St SW 16 C1
Polk Ave 16 E5
Poplar Dr 16 D3
Port Royal Rd 16 F2
Potomac Ave 17 E7
Potomac River Rd 16 A3
Potomac School Rd 16 B4
Powell Rd 16 F1
Powhatan St 16 C4
Prince William Dr 16 E1
Prosperity Ave 16 D2;E2
Queen Elizabeth Blvd 16 F1
Queensberry Ave 16 F2
Raintree Rd 16 F1
Randolph Dr 16 F4
Ravensworth Rd 16 F3
Rayburn Ave 16 E5
Rector Ln 16 B2
Red Fox Dr 16 F1
Ridge Dr 16 B4
Ridge Ford Dr 16 F1
Ridge Rd 16 E3
Ridgelea Dr 16 E1
River Bend Rd 16 A1
Riviera Dr 16 C1
Rockingham St 16 C4
Rolling Rd 16 F2
Roosevelt Blvd 16 D4
Rose Ln 16 E3
Rosemary Ln 16 D3
Rupert St 16 C3
Russell Rd 17 E6
Rynex Dr 16 E4
S Abingdon St 16 D5
S Arlington Mill Dr 17 E6
S Arlington Ridge Rd 17 D6
S Army Navy Dr 17 E6
S Carlin Springs Rd 16 D5
S Columbia Pike 16 E5; 17 D6
S Columbus St 16 E5
S Court House Rd 17 D6
S Crystal Dr 17 E7
S Fern St 17 D7
S Fort Scott Dr 17 E6
S Four Mile Run Dr 16 E5; 17 E6
S Frederick St 16 E5
S George Mason Dr 16 D5;E5
S Glebe Rd 17 E6
S Hayes St 17 D6
S Irving St 17 D6
S Jefferson Davis Hwy 17 E7
S Joyce St 17 D6
S Monroe St 17 E6
S Oak St 16 D3
S Pickett St 16 F5
S Quincy St 16 D5; 17 E6
S Reynolds St 16 F5
S Royal St 17 F7
S Spring St 16 D3
S Taylor St 16 D5
S Van Dorn St 16 F4
S Walter Reed Dr 17 D6
S West St 16 D3
Saigon Rd 16 B3
Sandburg St 16 D2
Sanger Ave 16 E5
Santayana Dr 16 D1
Savile Ln 16 B4
Seminary Rd 16 E5; 17 F6
Sheldon Dr 16 F4
Sheridan Ave 17 D6
Shreve Rd 16 D3
Skyview Ln 16 E1
Slade Run Dr 16 E3
Sleepy Hollow Rd 16 D4;E4
Somerville St 16 F5
South St 16 D4
Southampton Dr 16 F2
Southern Dr 16 F2
Southwick St 16 E1
Spring Hill Rd 16 B2
Spring Valley Dr 16 F4
Stark Rd 16 E1
Stevenson Ave 16 F4
Stonewall Dr 16 D2
Stoneybrae Dr 16 E4
Summerfield Rd 16 D3
Sutton Rd 16 D1
Swinks Mill Rd 16 B3
Talisman Dr 16 C1
Taney Ave 16 F5
Tapawingo Rd SE 16 C1; D1
Taylor Dr 16 E1
Telegraph Rd 17 F6
Thor Dr 16 E2
Timber Ln 16 D3
Tobin Rd 16 E2
Toll House Rd 16 E2
Tovito Dr 16 E1
Towlston Rd 16 A2;B1
Trammell Rd 16 E2
Trap Rd 16 B1
Trotting Horse Ln 16 B1
Tucker Ave 16 C4
Turkey Run Rd 16 B4
Twinbrook Rd 16 E1
Tyco Rd 16 B2
Upland Dr 16 F5
Vaden Dr 16 D1
Vale St 16 E4
Valley Brook Dr 16 E3
Valley Dr 17 E6
Valley Ln 16 D4
Vellex Ln 16 F3
Vernon Dr 16 B1
Virginia Ave 16 C4
Virginia Ln 16 C2
Vista Dr 16 E4
W Braddock Rd 16 E5;F2; 17 E6
W Broad St 16 D3
W Glebe Rd 17 E6
Wakefield Chapel Rd 16 E2
Wakefield Dr 16 E2
Walker Rd 16 A1
Walker St SW 16 D1
Walton Ln 16 E3
Waterway Dr 16 E4
Wayne Dr 16 E3
Wayne Rd 16 D3
Weller Ave 16 B2
West St 16 D3
Westmoreland Rd 16 D3
Westmoreland St 16 C3
Westpark Dr 16 B2
Whann Ave 16 B3
Wheeler Ave 16 F5
Whispering Ln 16 E4
Whitacre Rd 16 E1
Wilburdale Dr 16 F3
Willet Dr 16 F1
Windrock Dr 16 B1
Winter Ln 16 F3
Wolftrap Rd SE 16 C2
Wolftrap Rd 16 C2
Woodburn Rd 16 E2
Woodford Rd 16 C2
Woodland Dr 16 F3
Woodland Way 16 F1
Woodlark Dr 16 E2
Woodley Pl 16 D3
Woodridge Rd 16 E4
Woodside Dr 16 B2
Wynford Dr 16 D2
Yellowstone Dr 16 E4
Yeonas Dr SW 16 D1
Yoakum Pkwy 16 F4
York Dr 17 D6
Youngblood St 16 C4

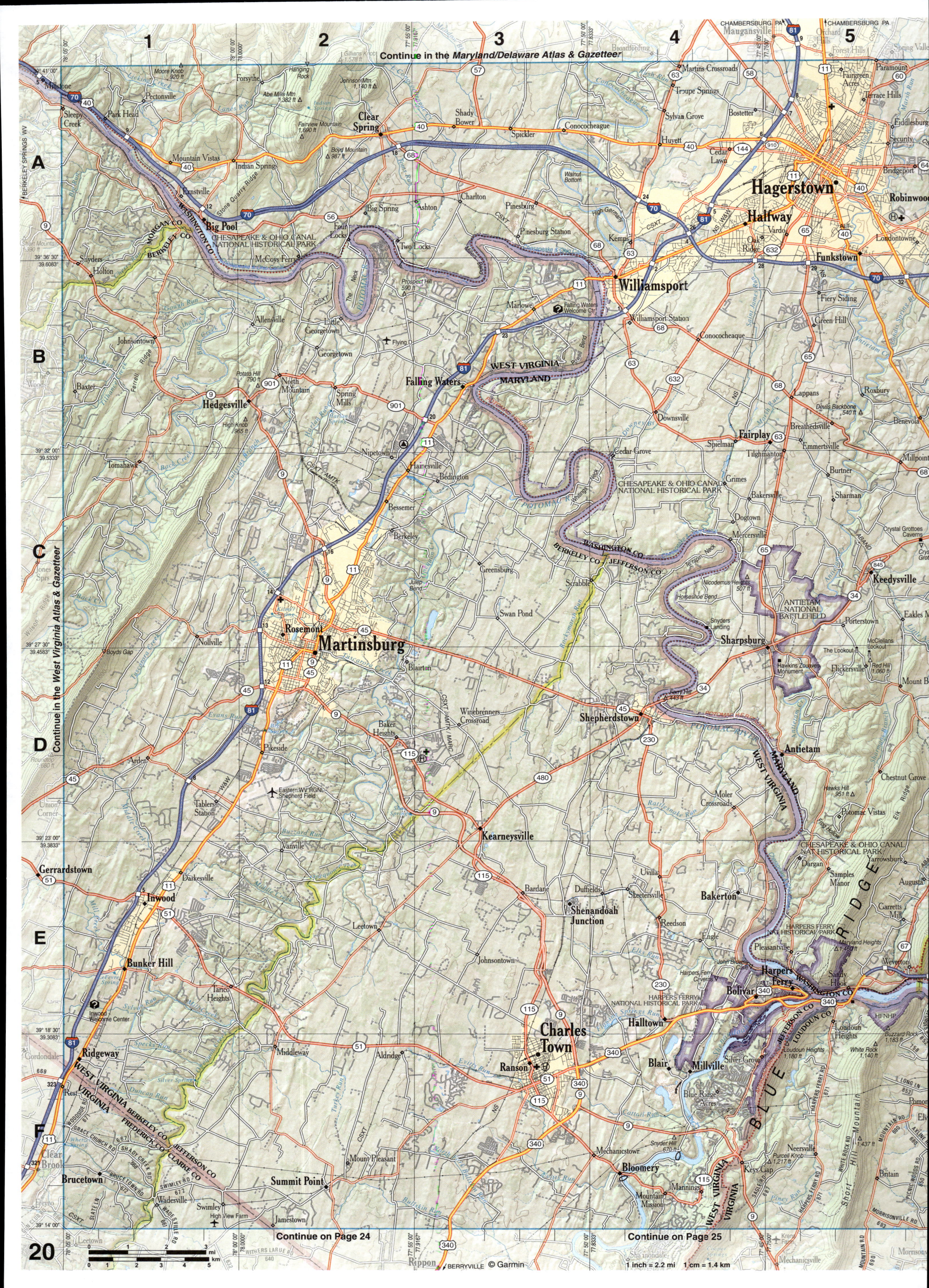

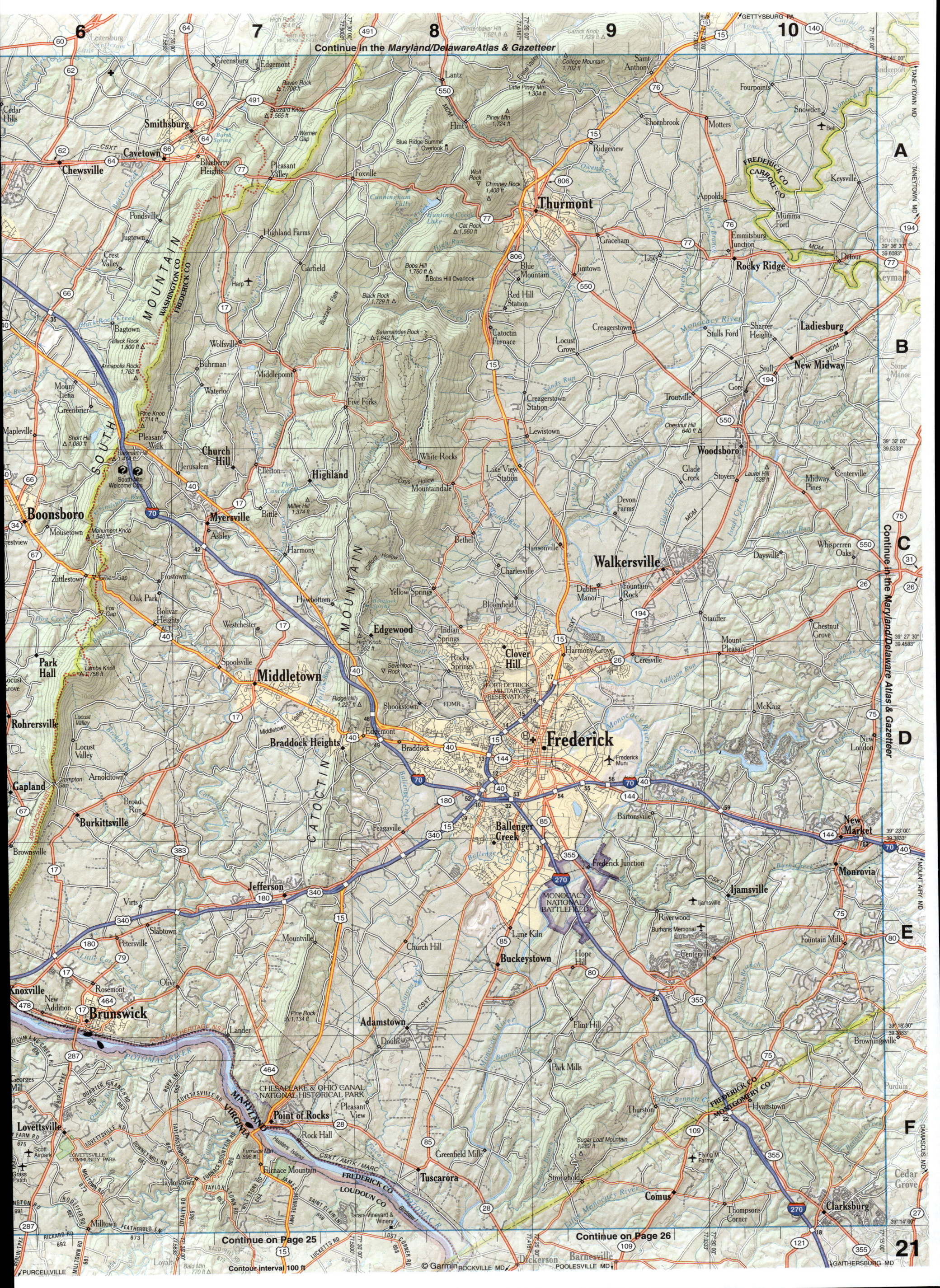

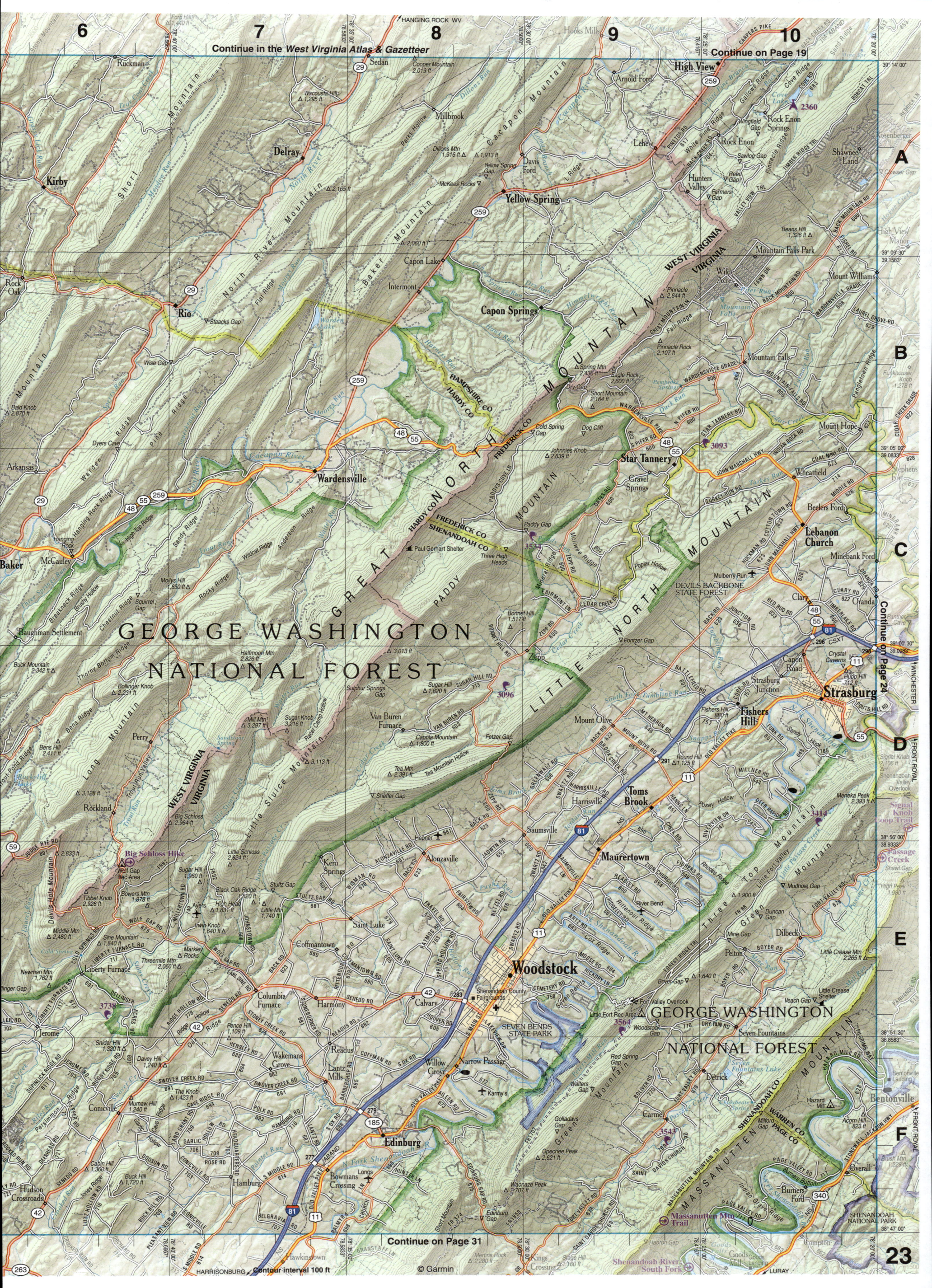

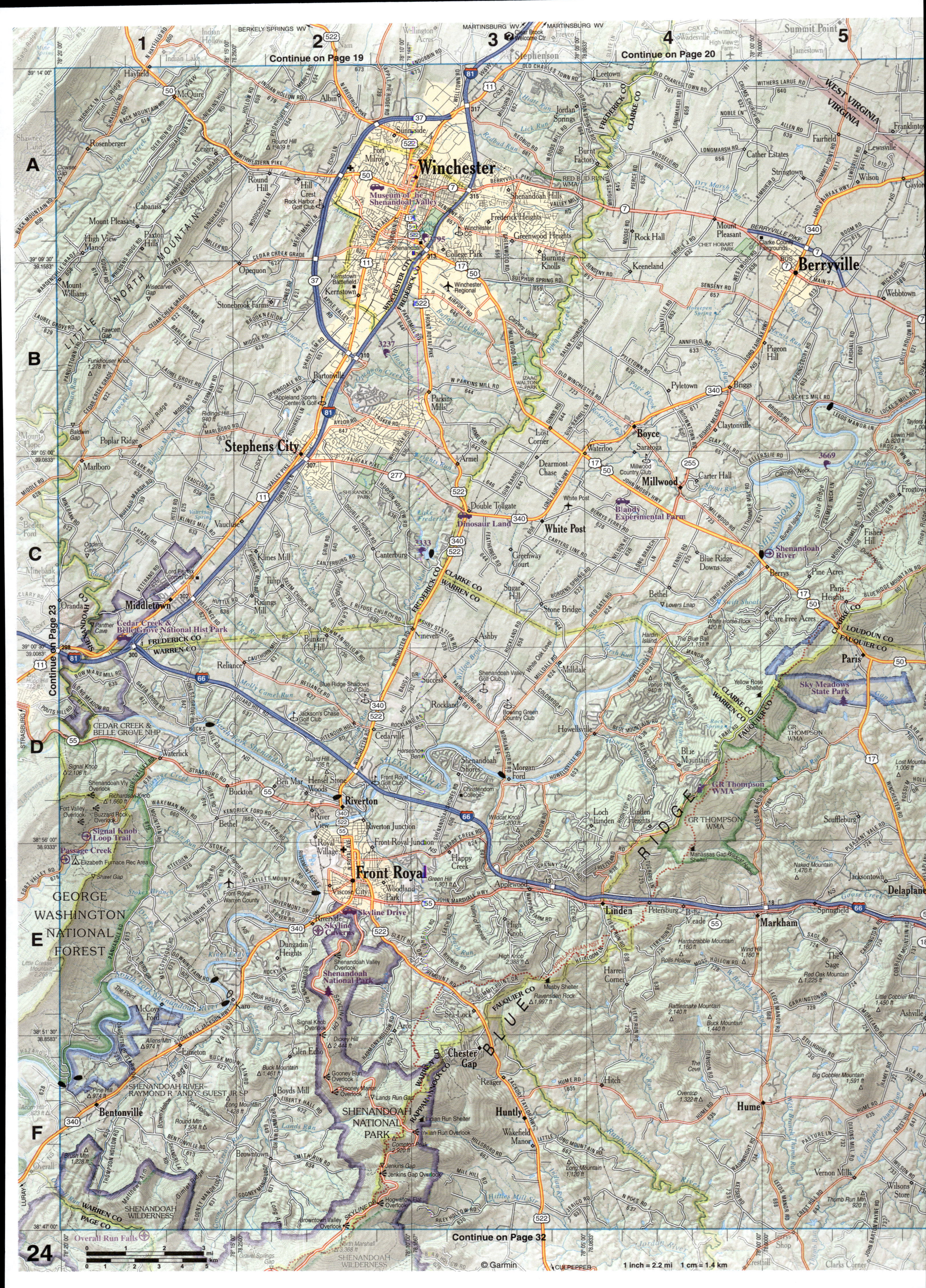

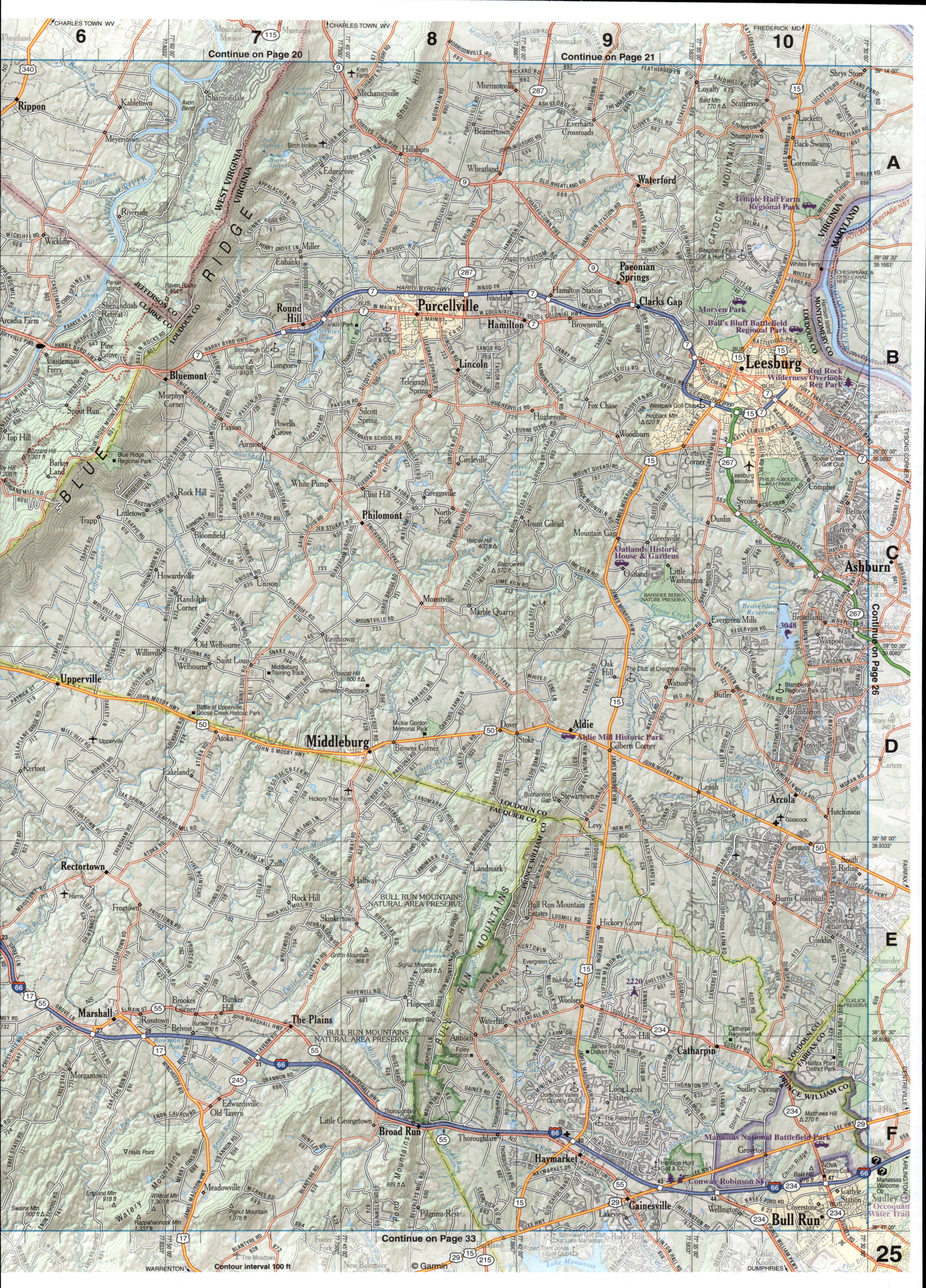

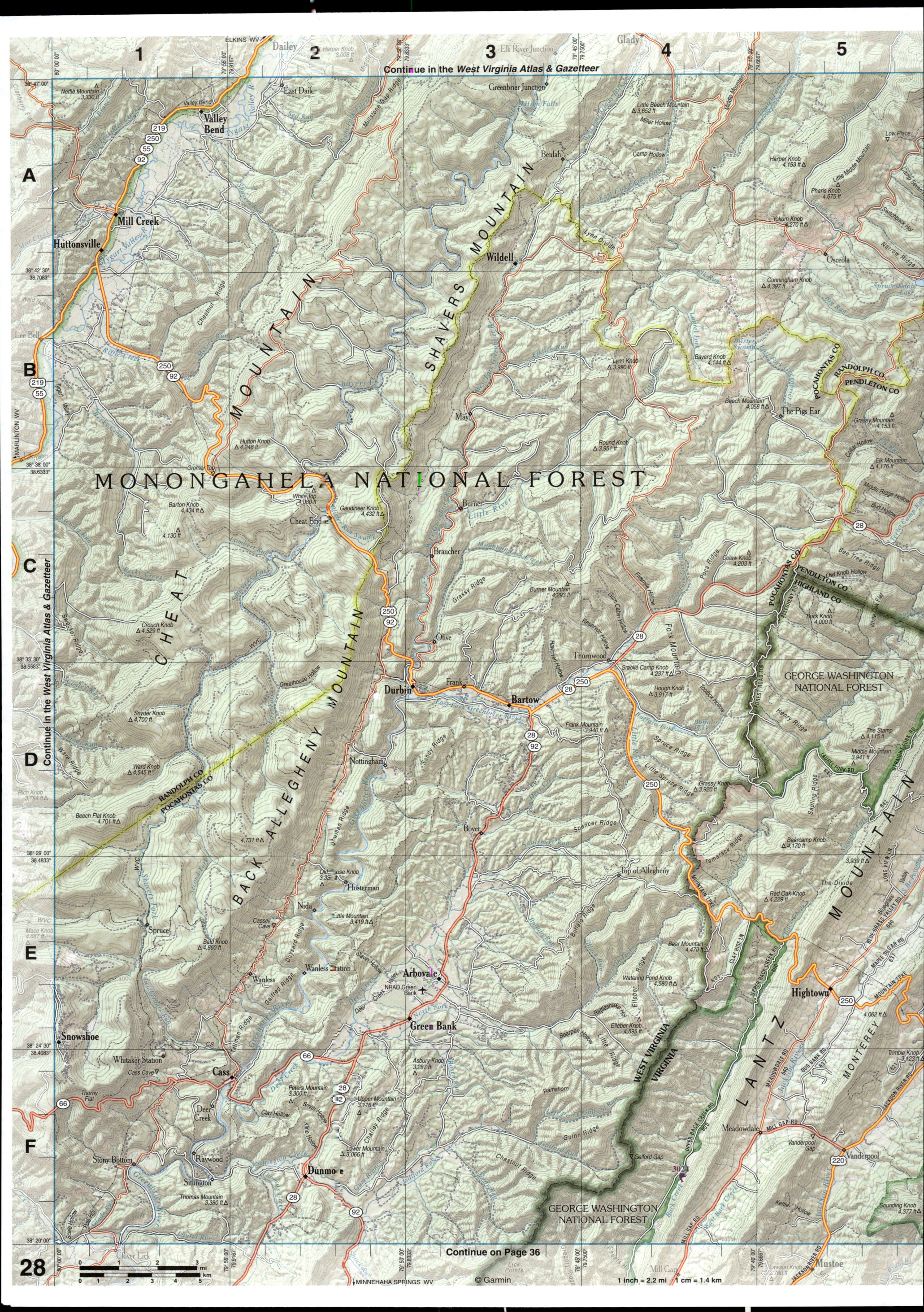

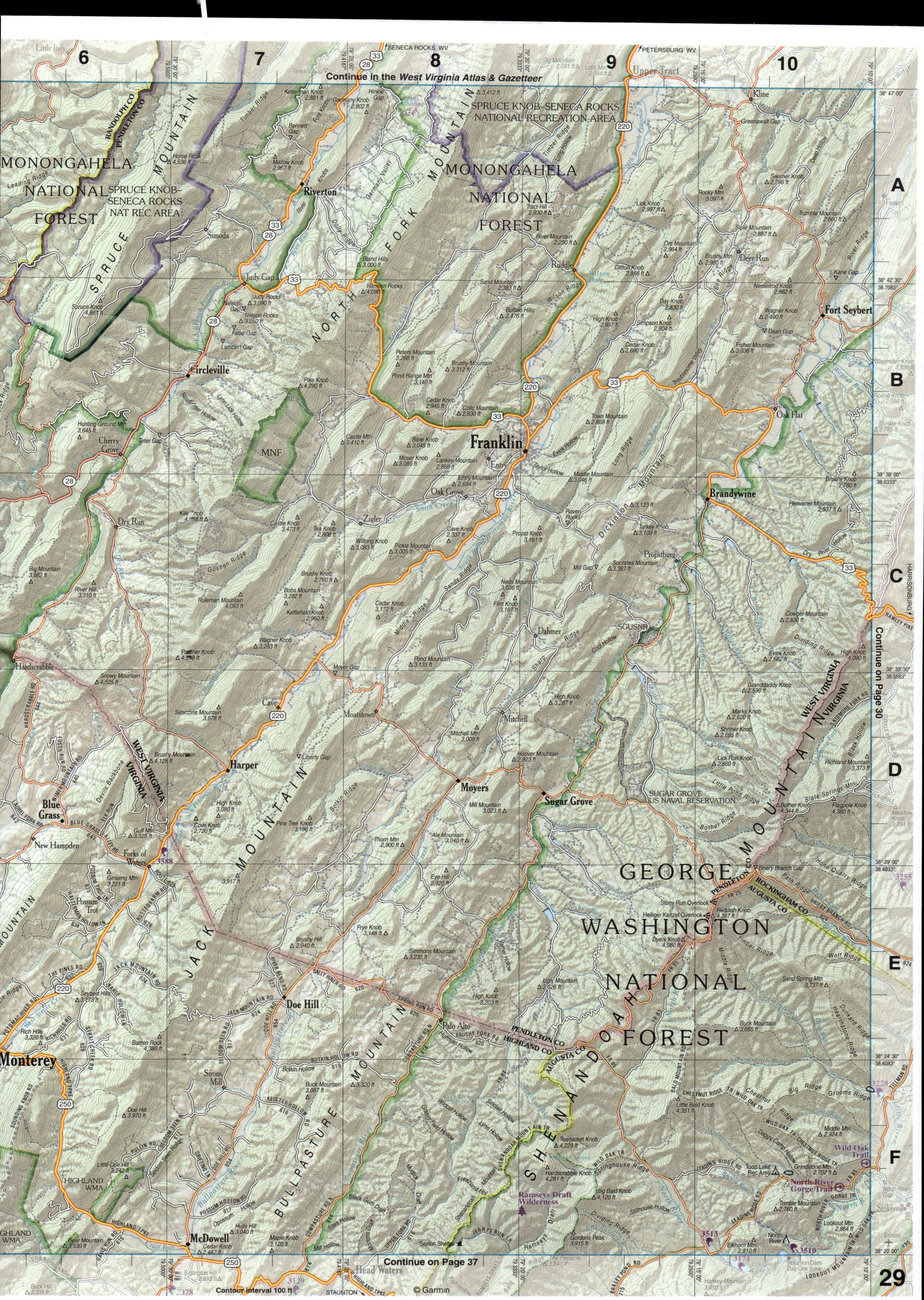

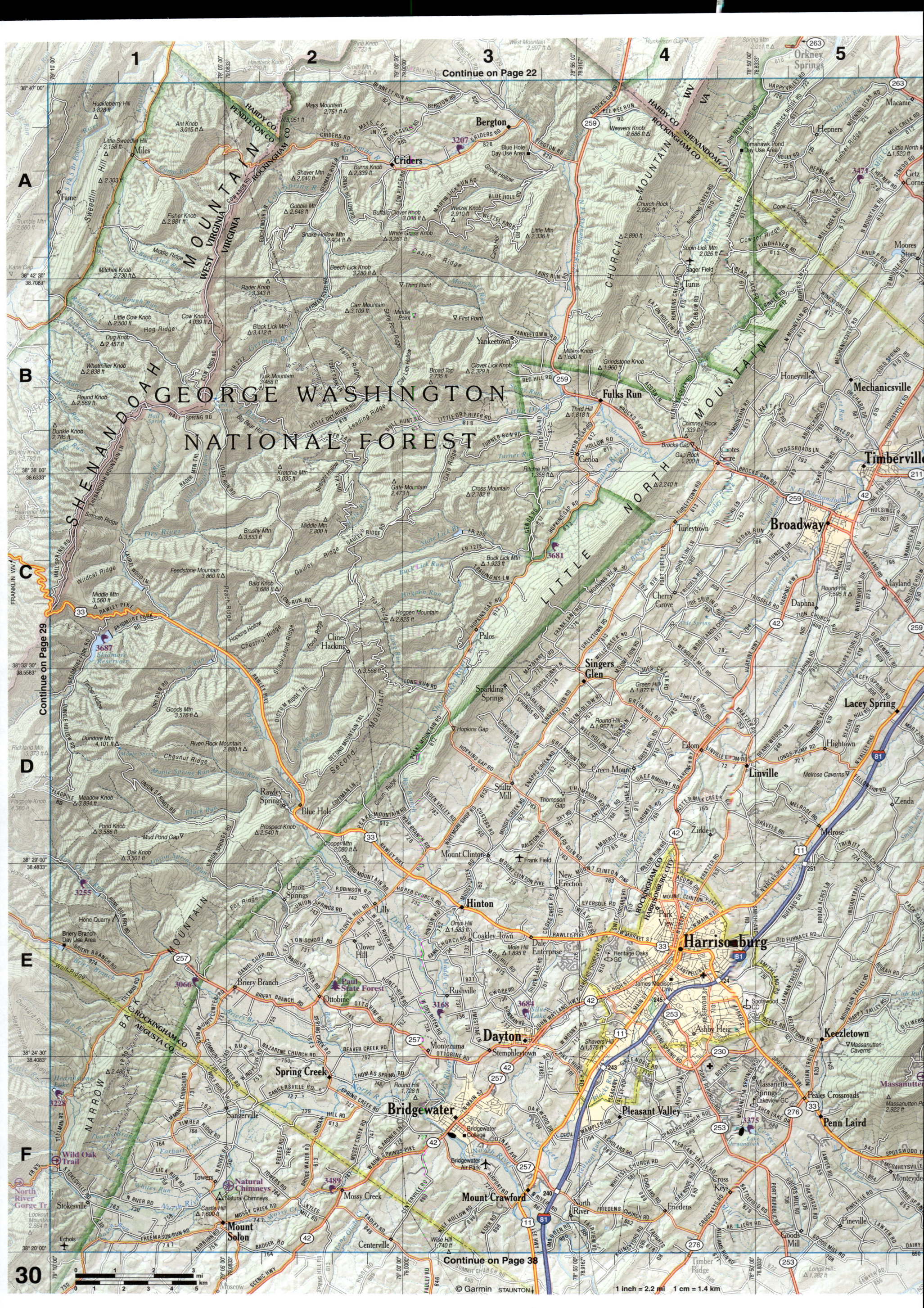

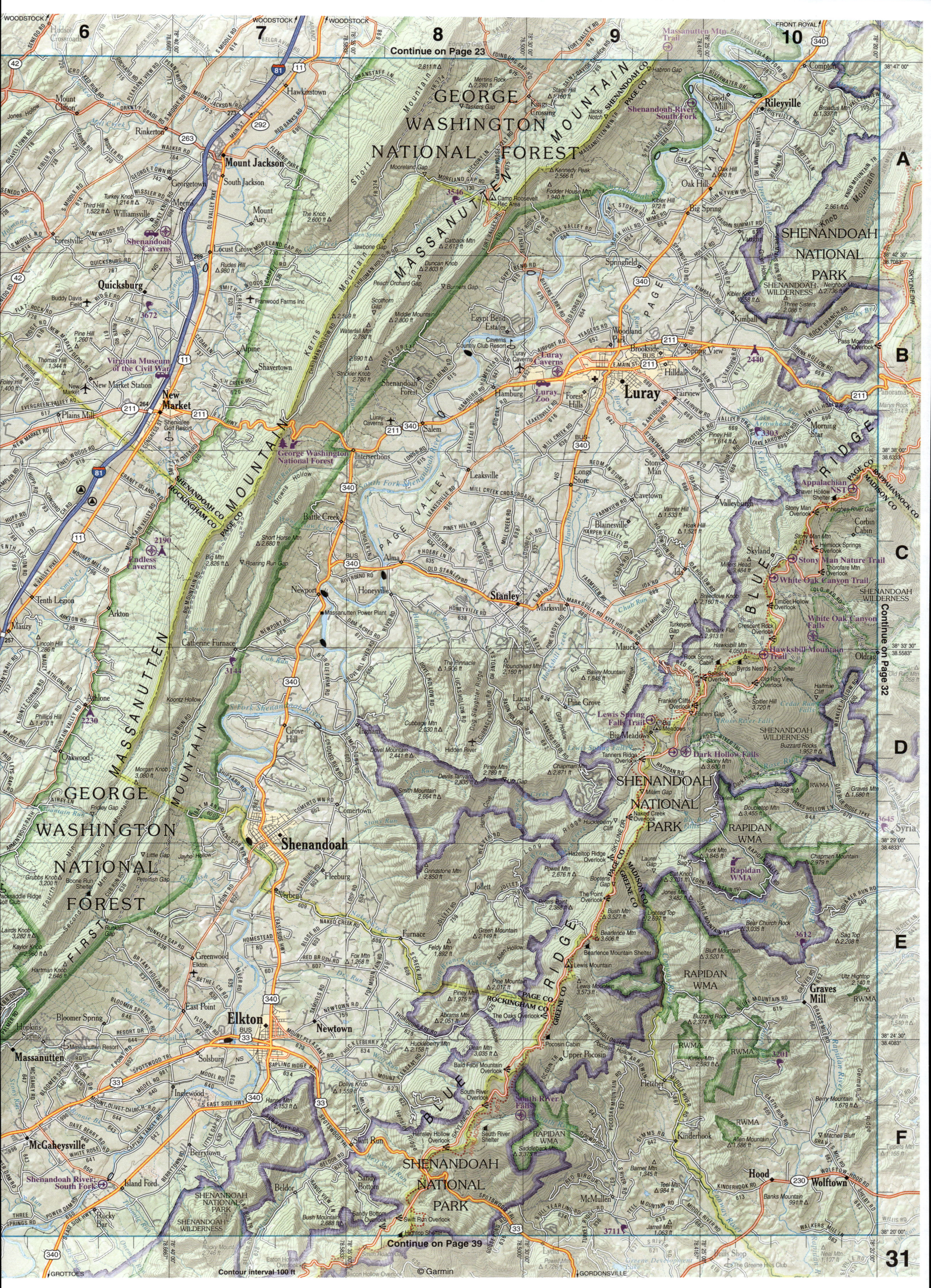

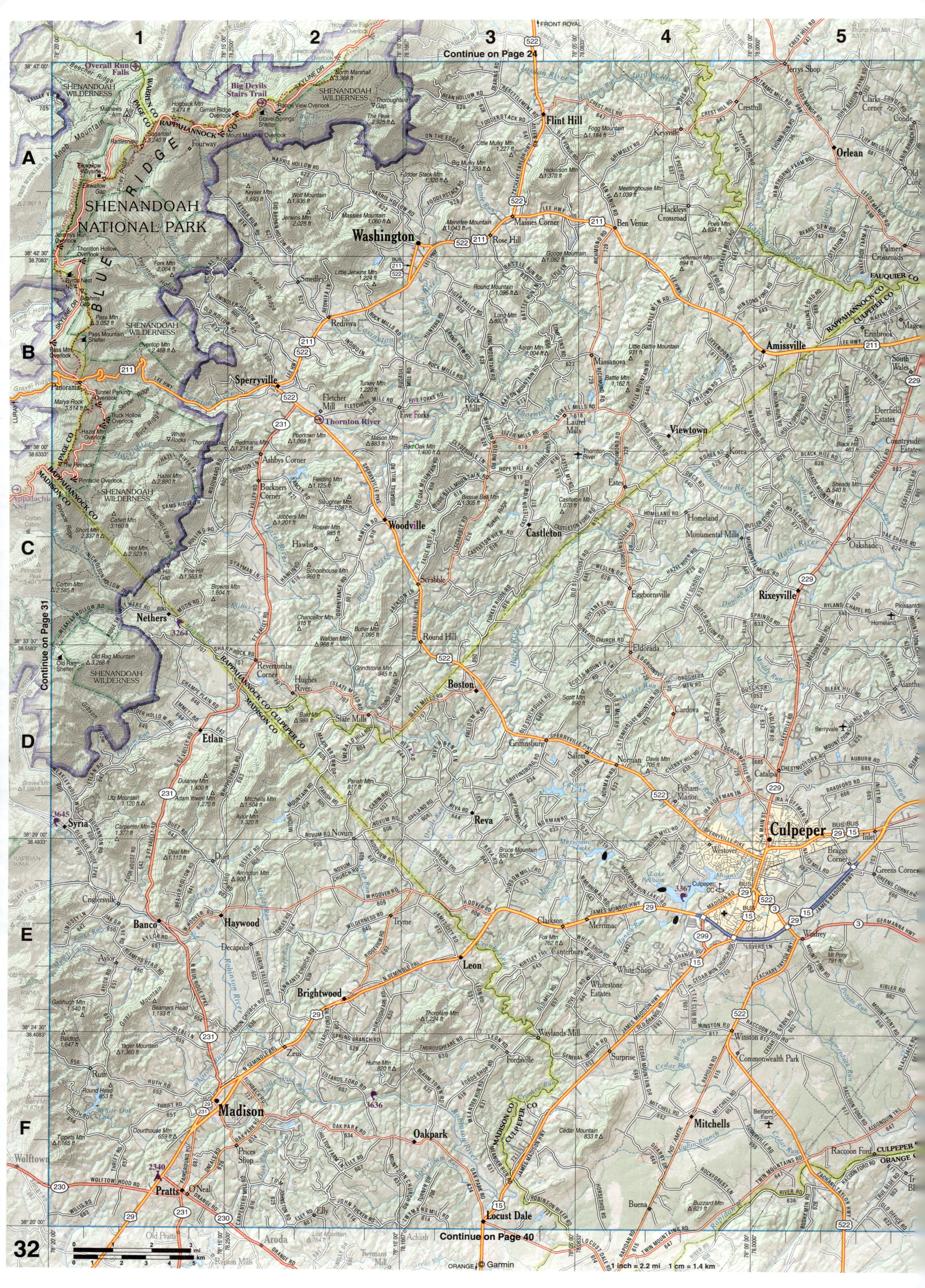

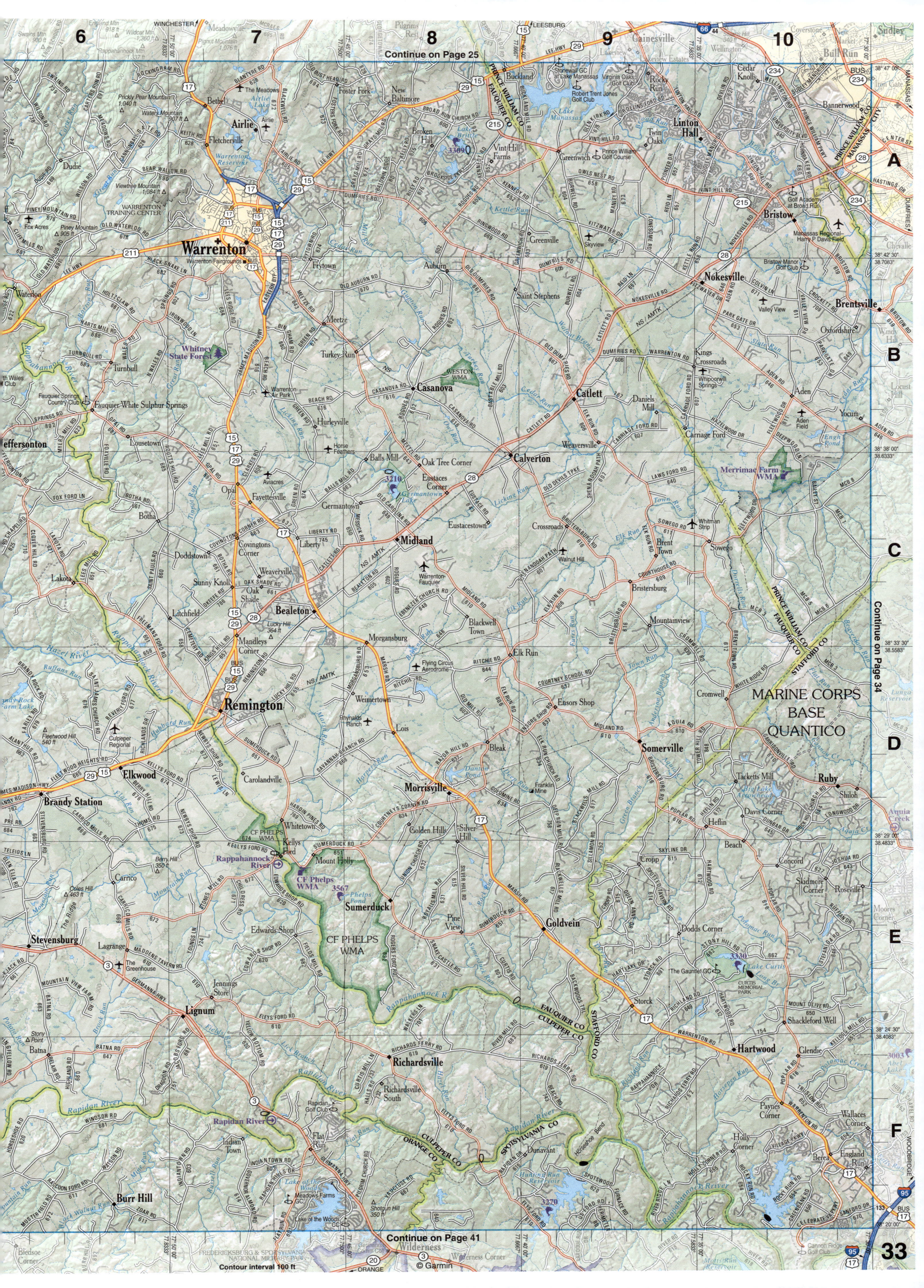

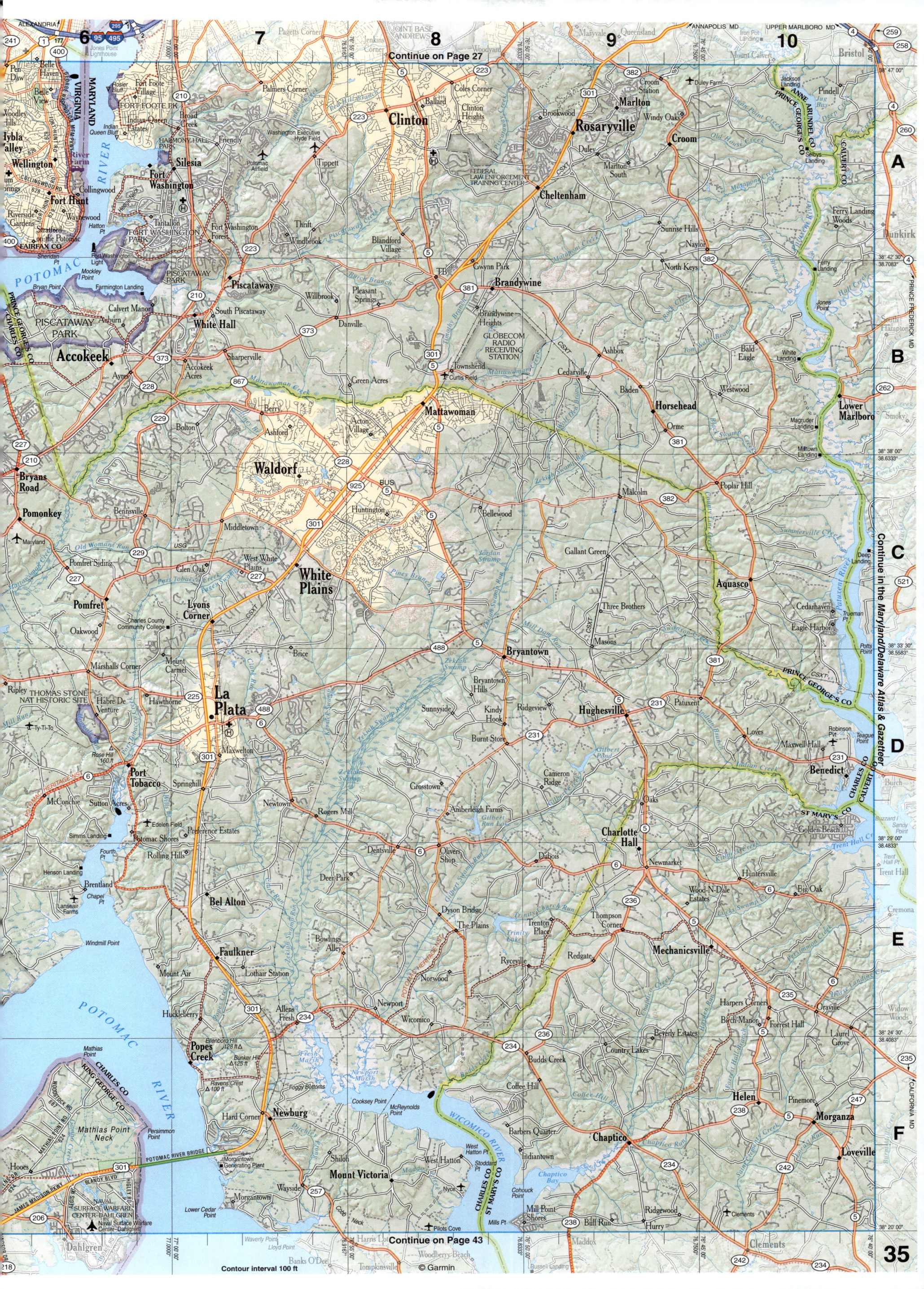

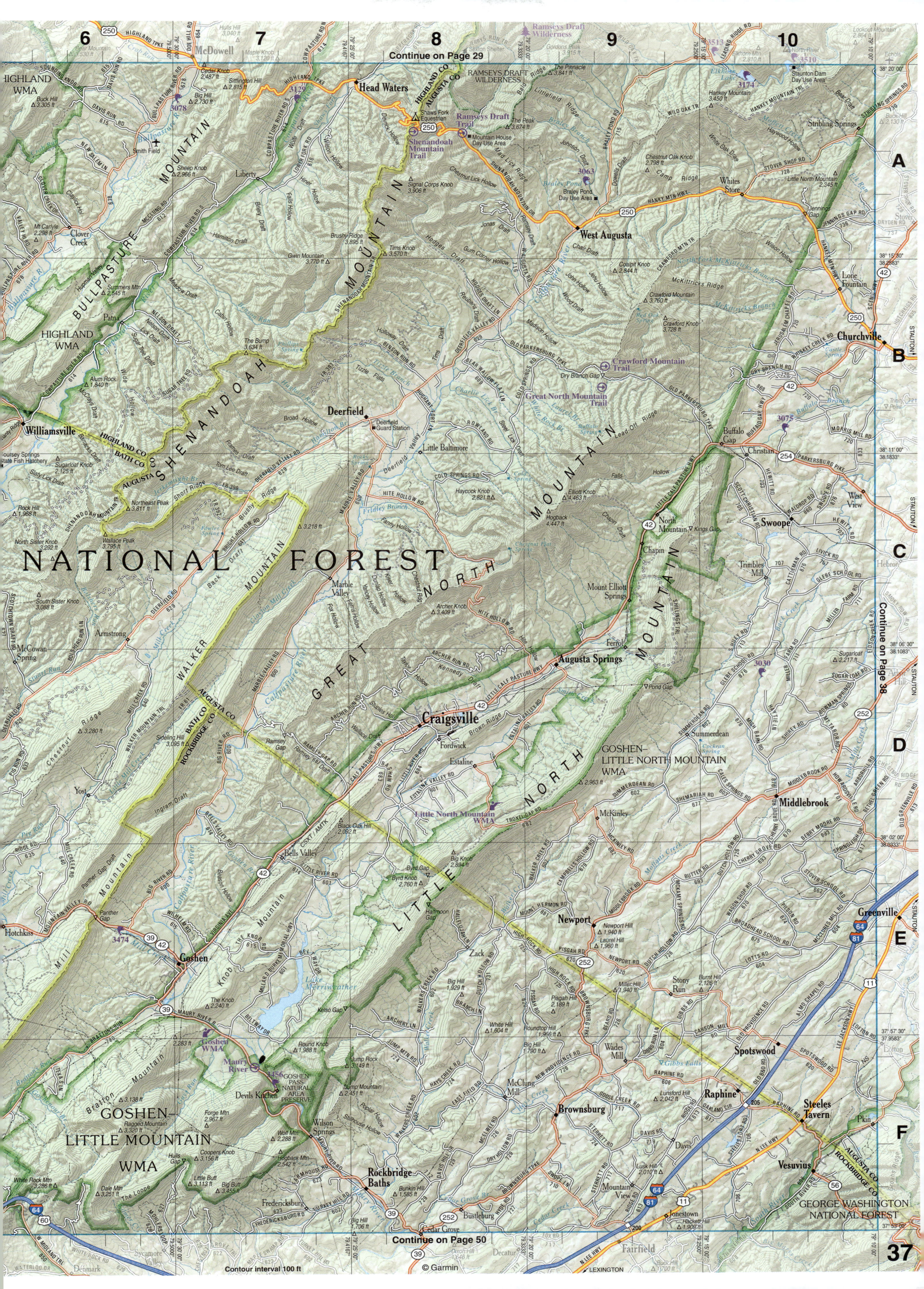

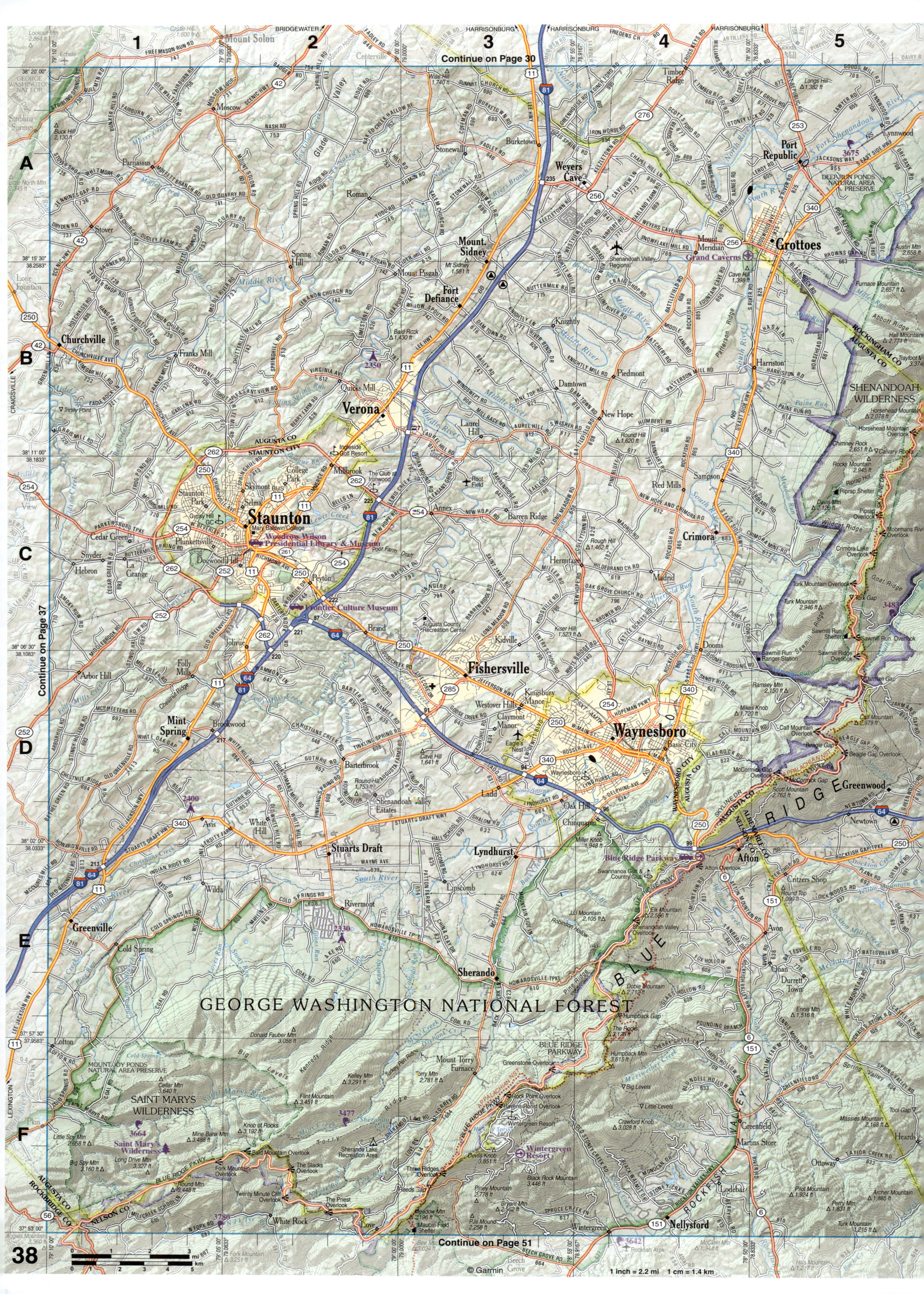

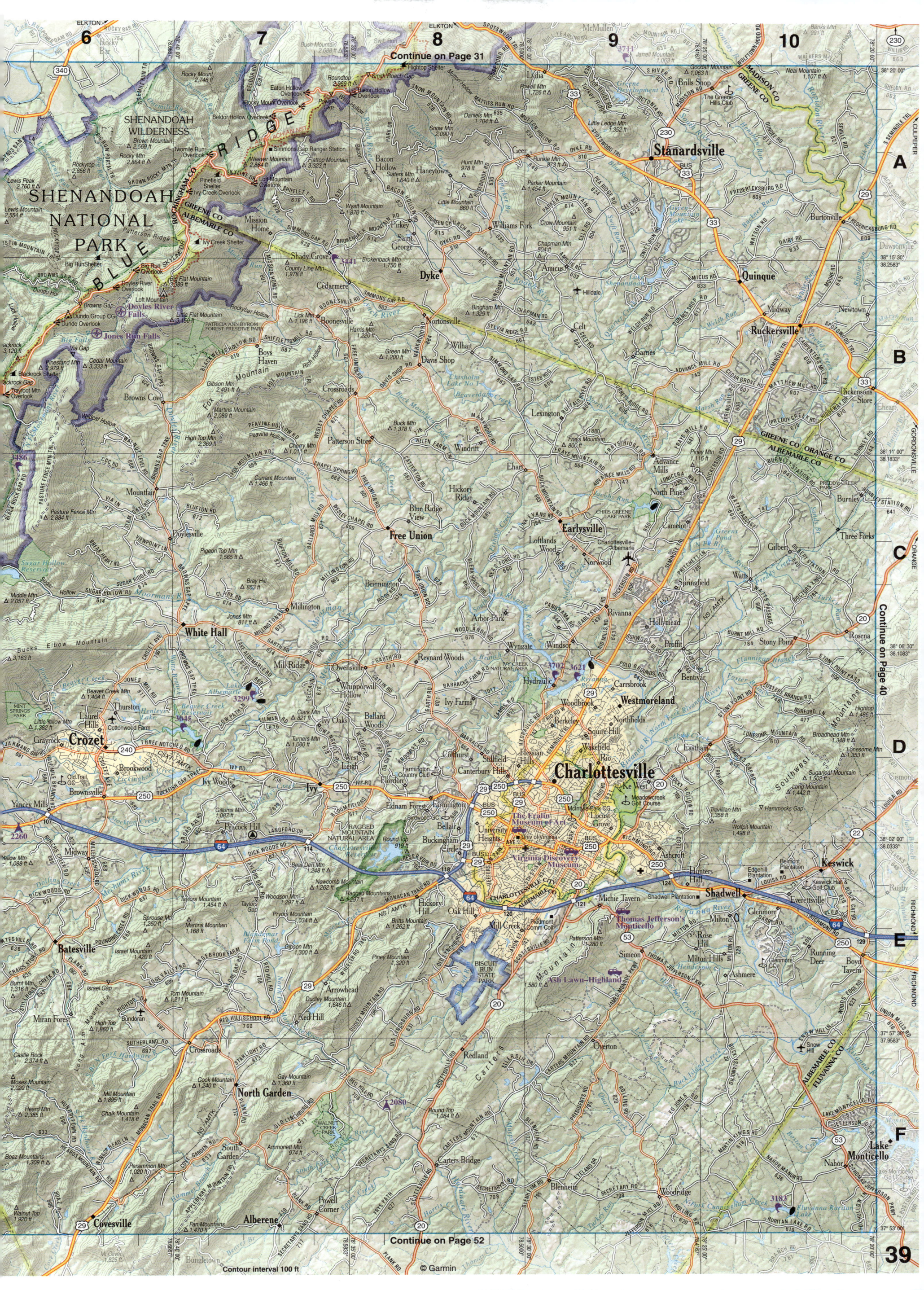

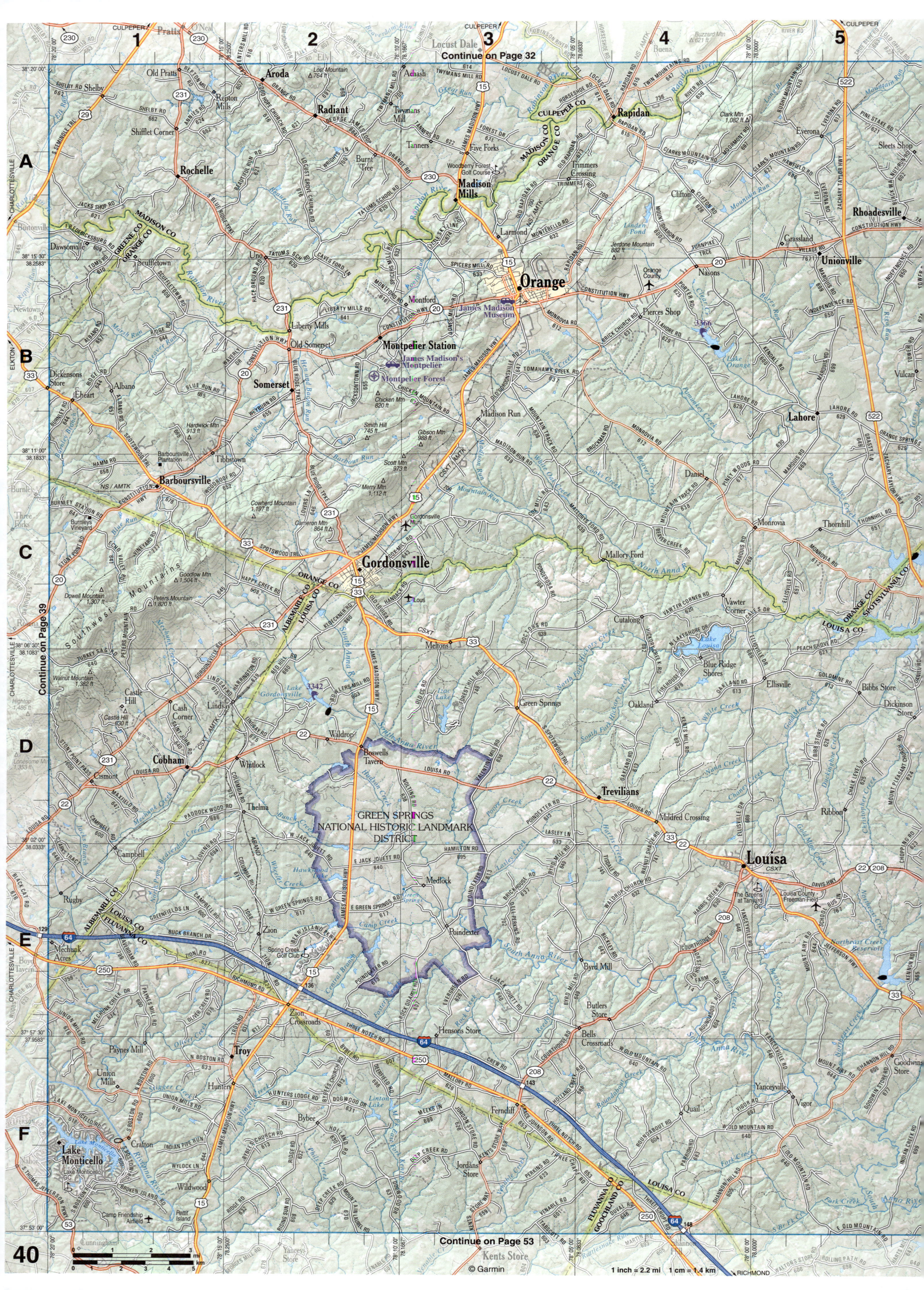

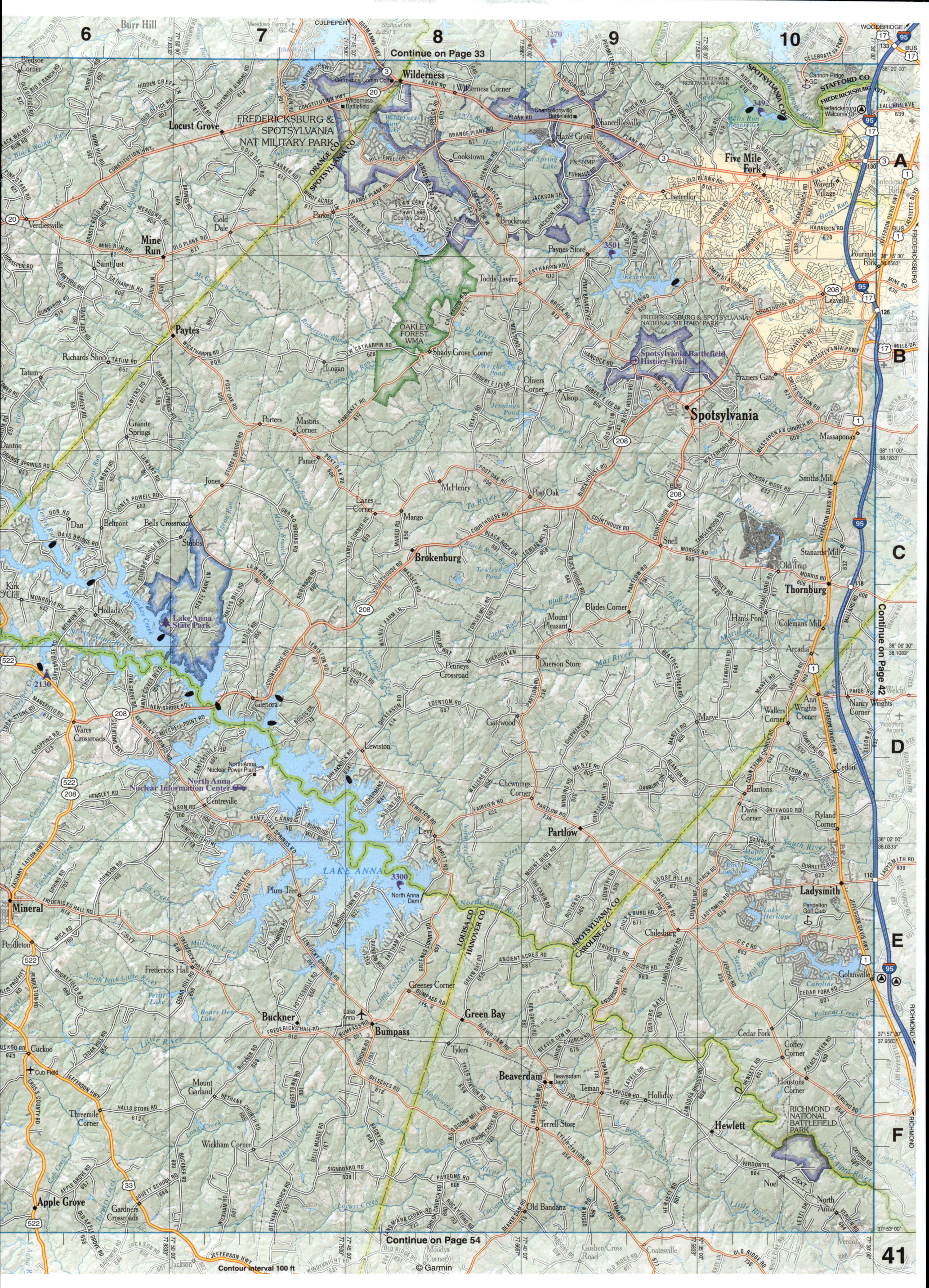

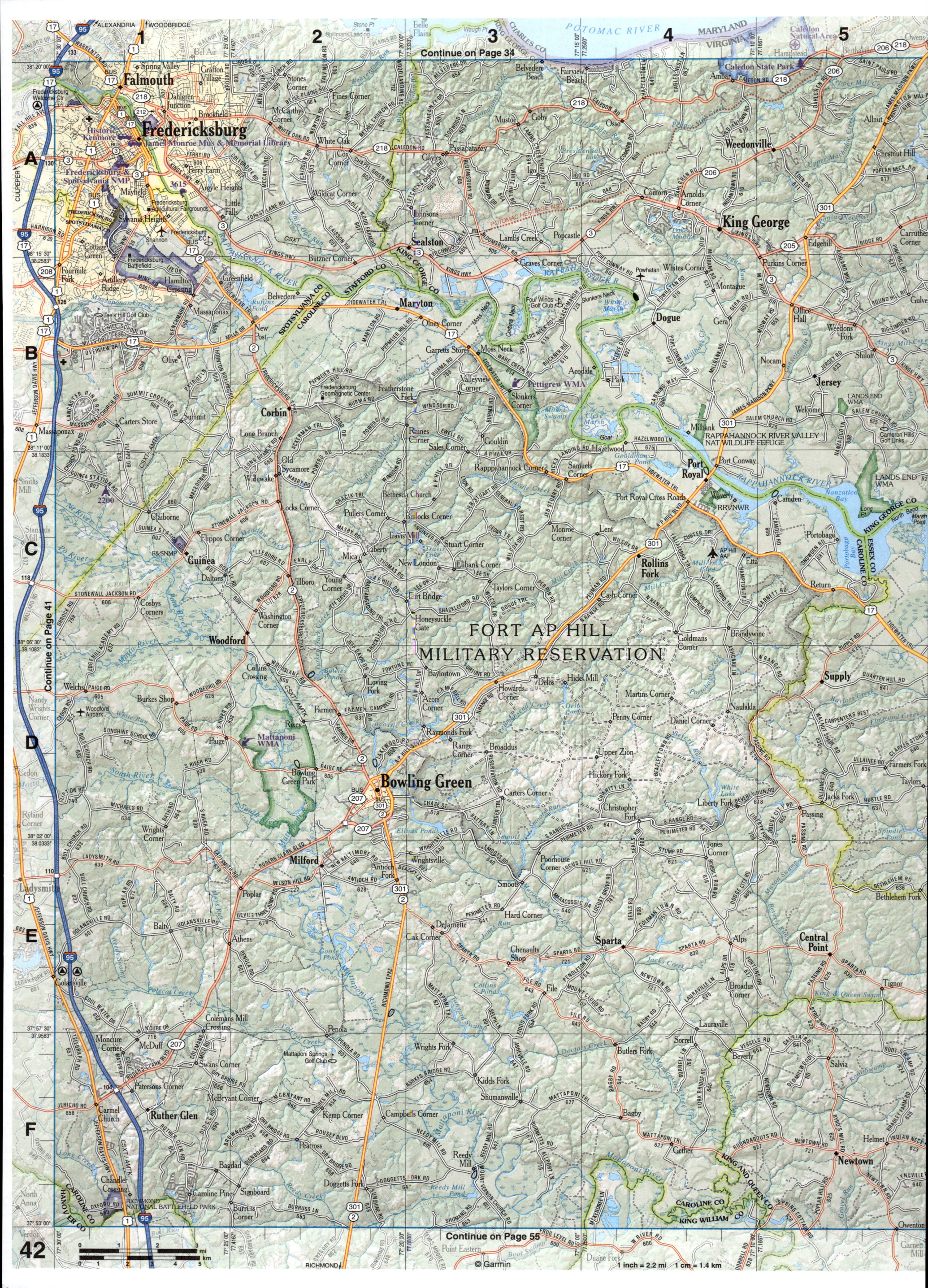

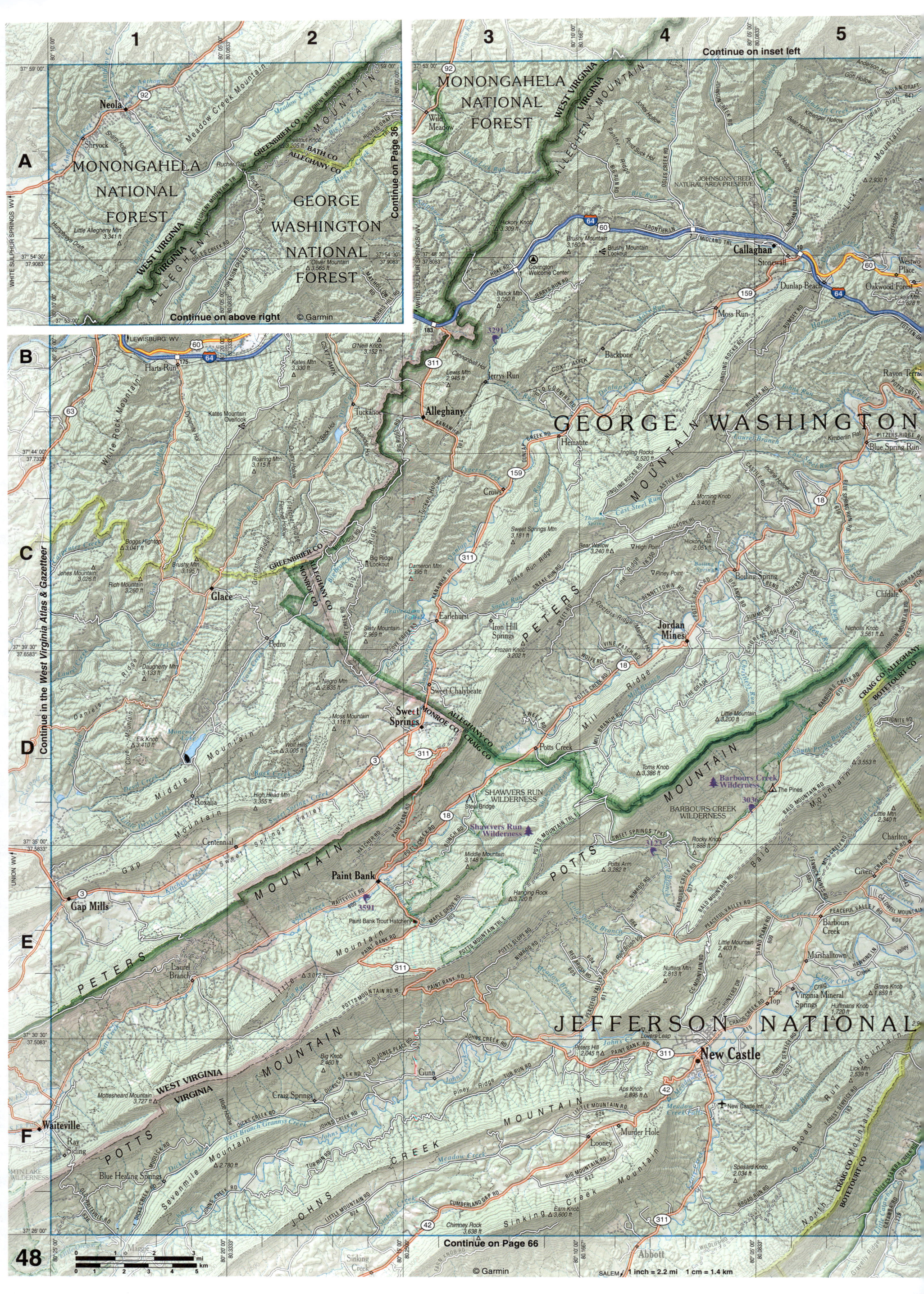

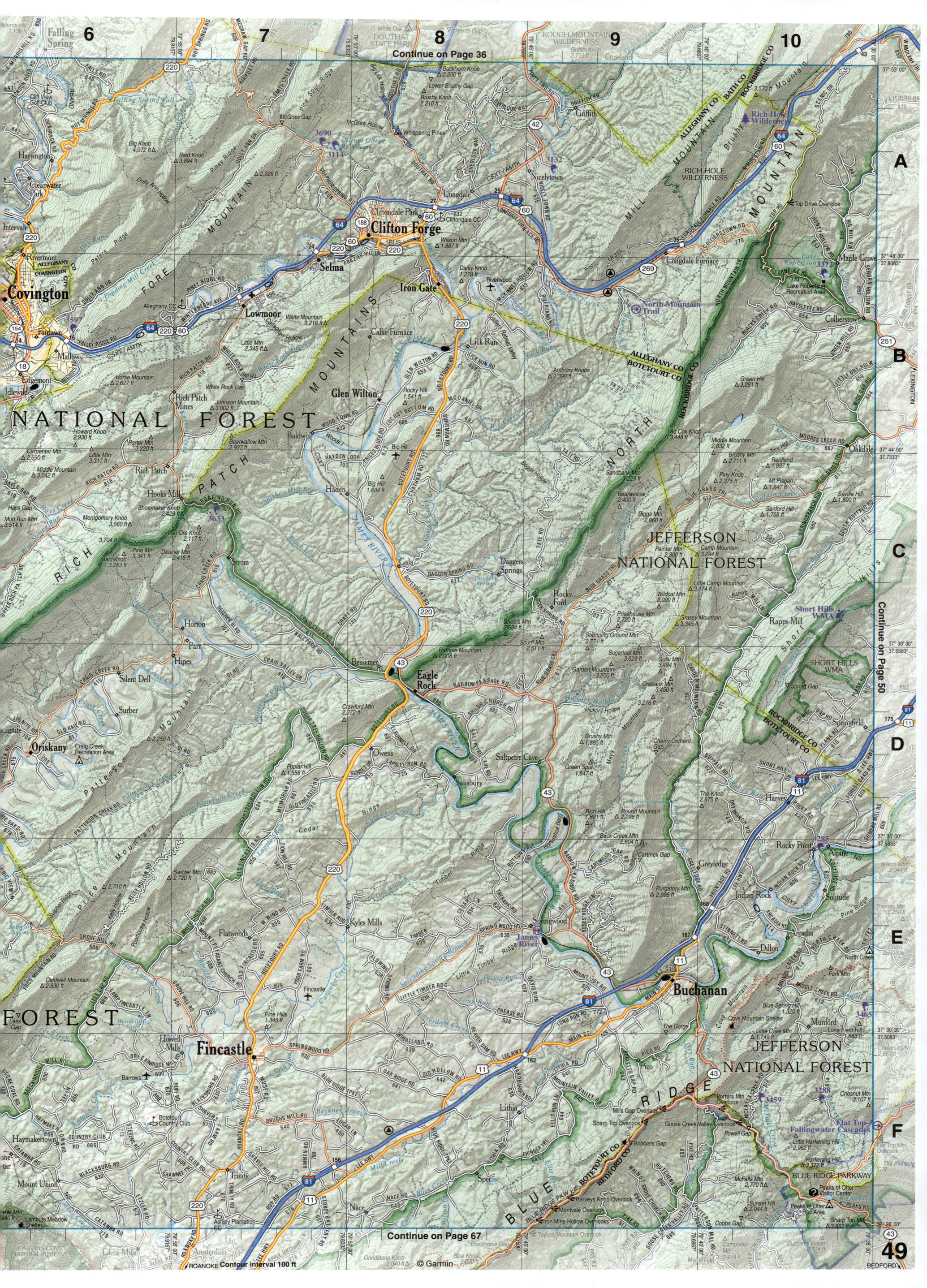

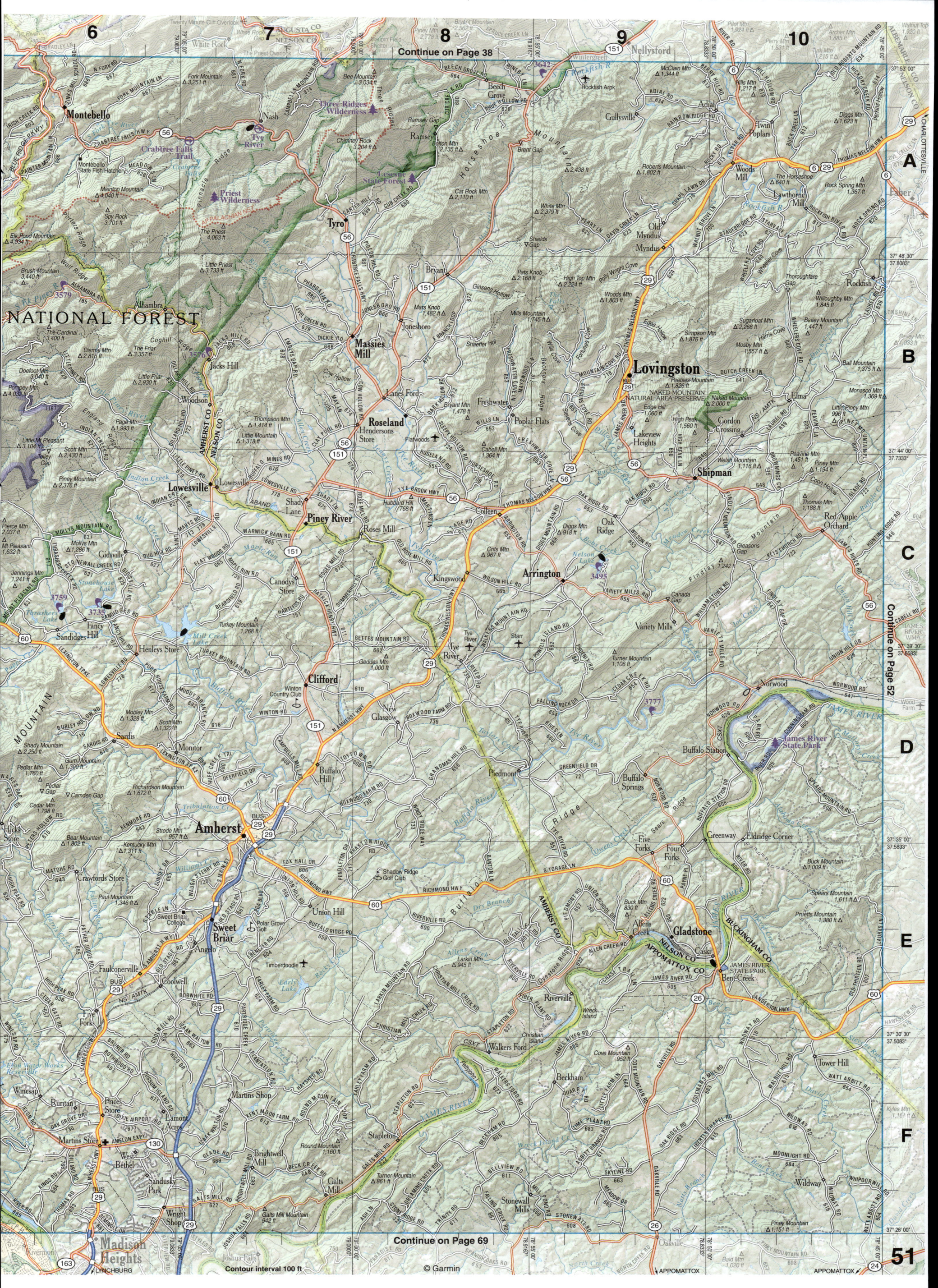

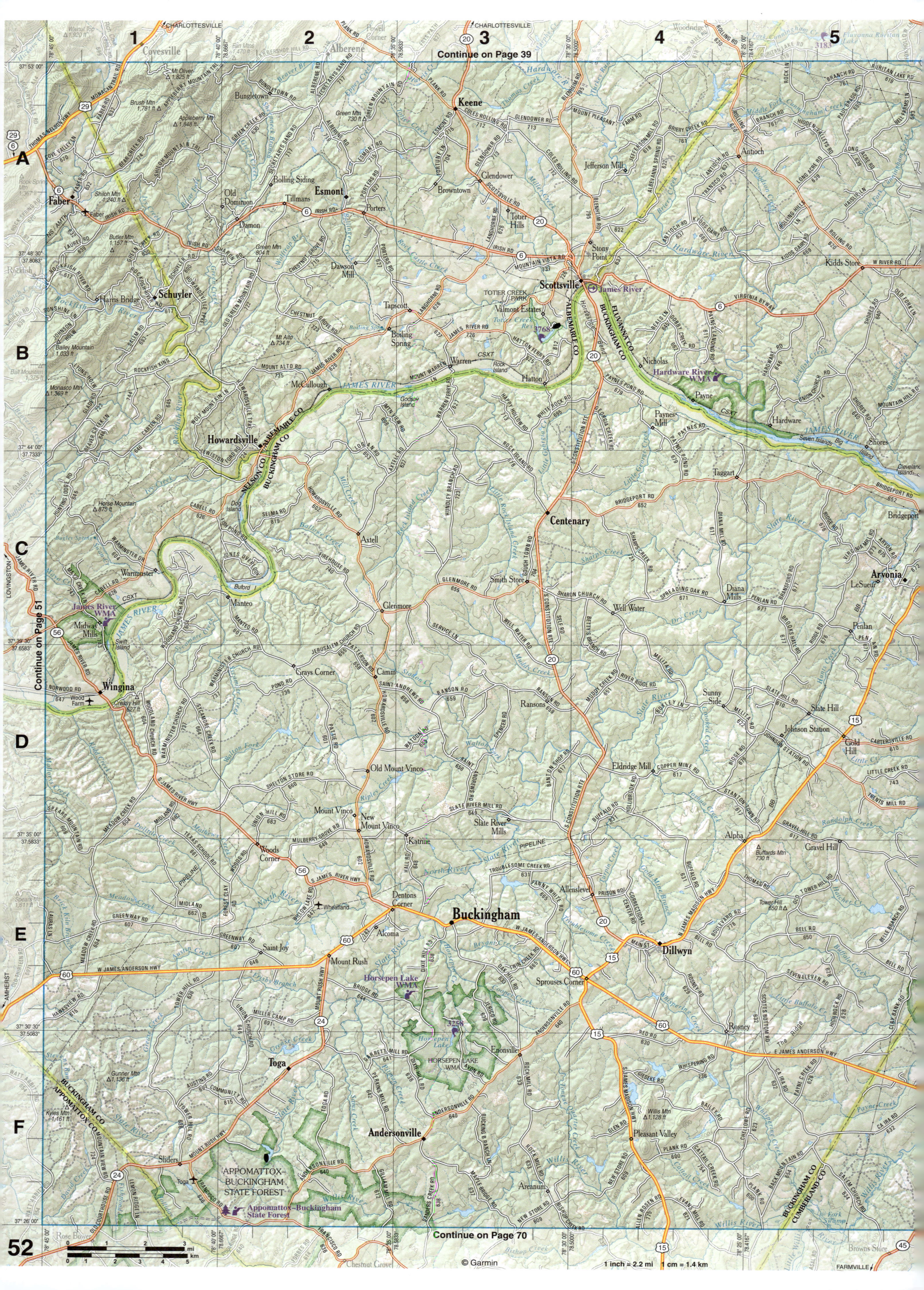

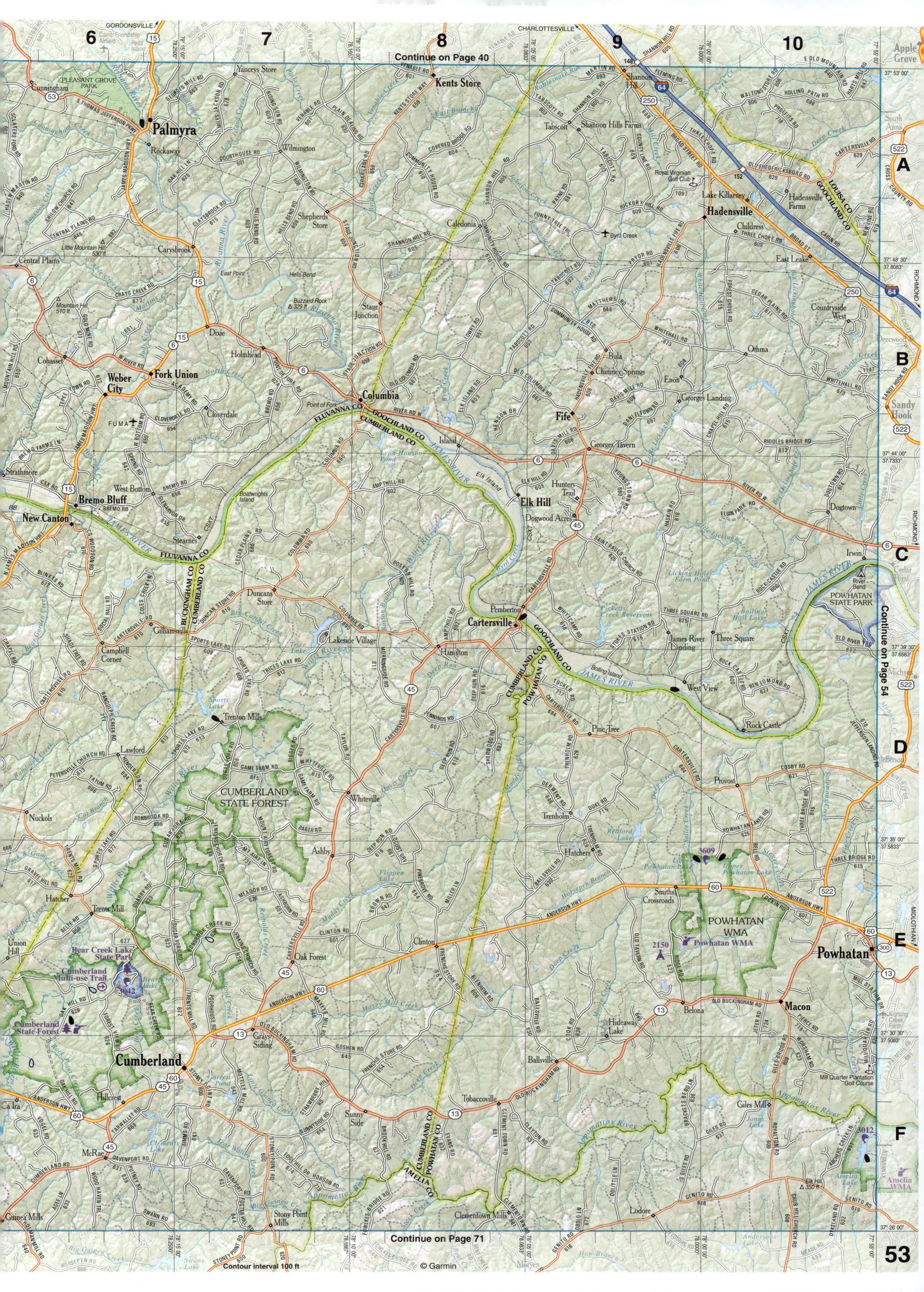

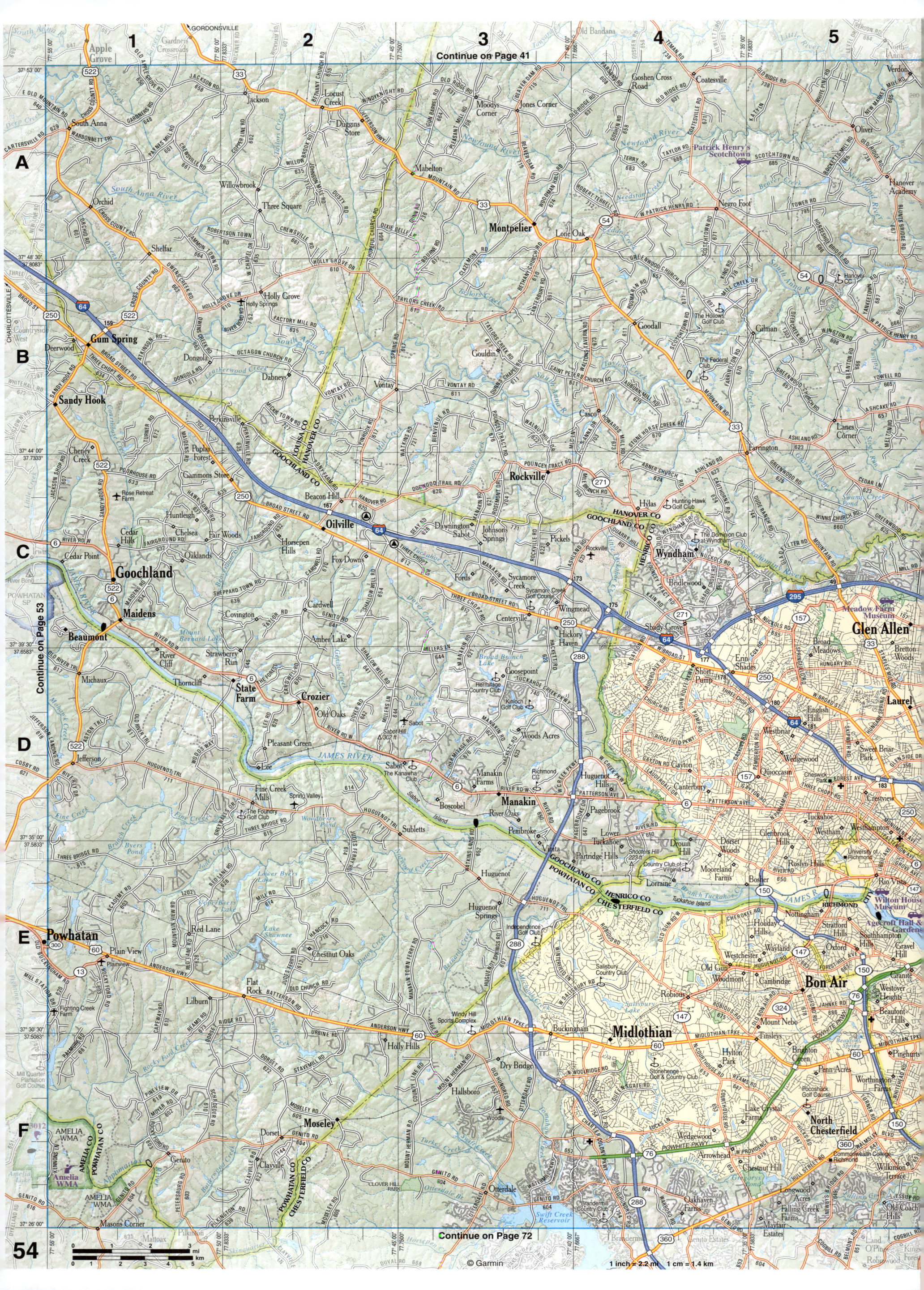

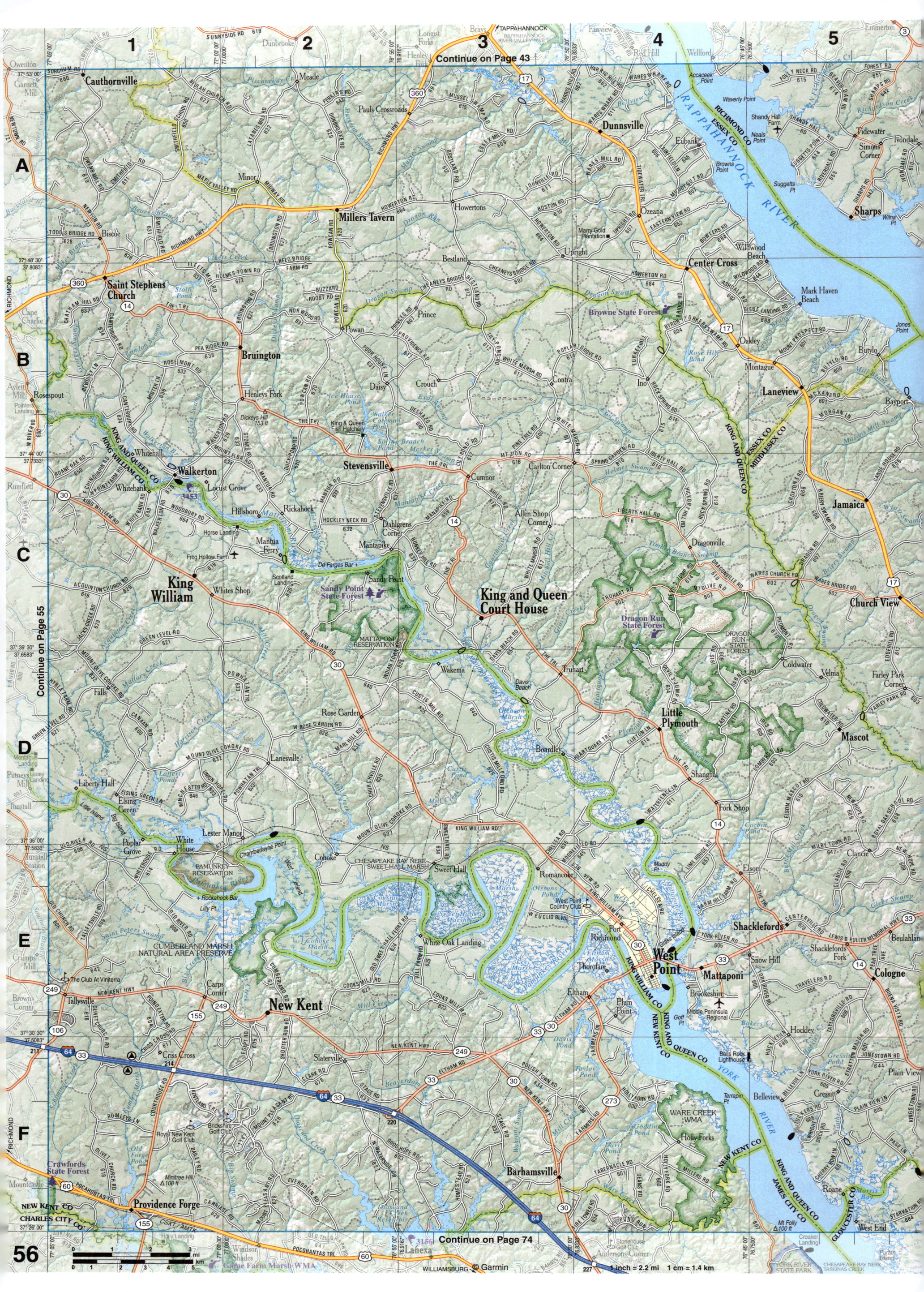

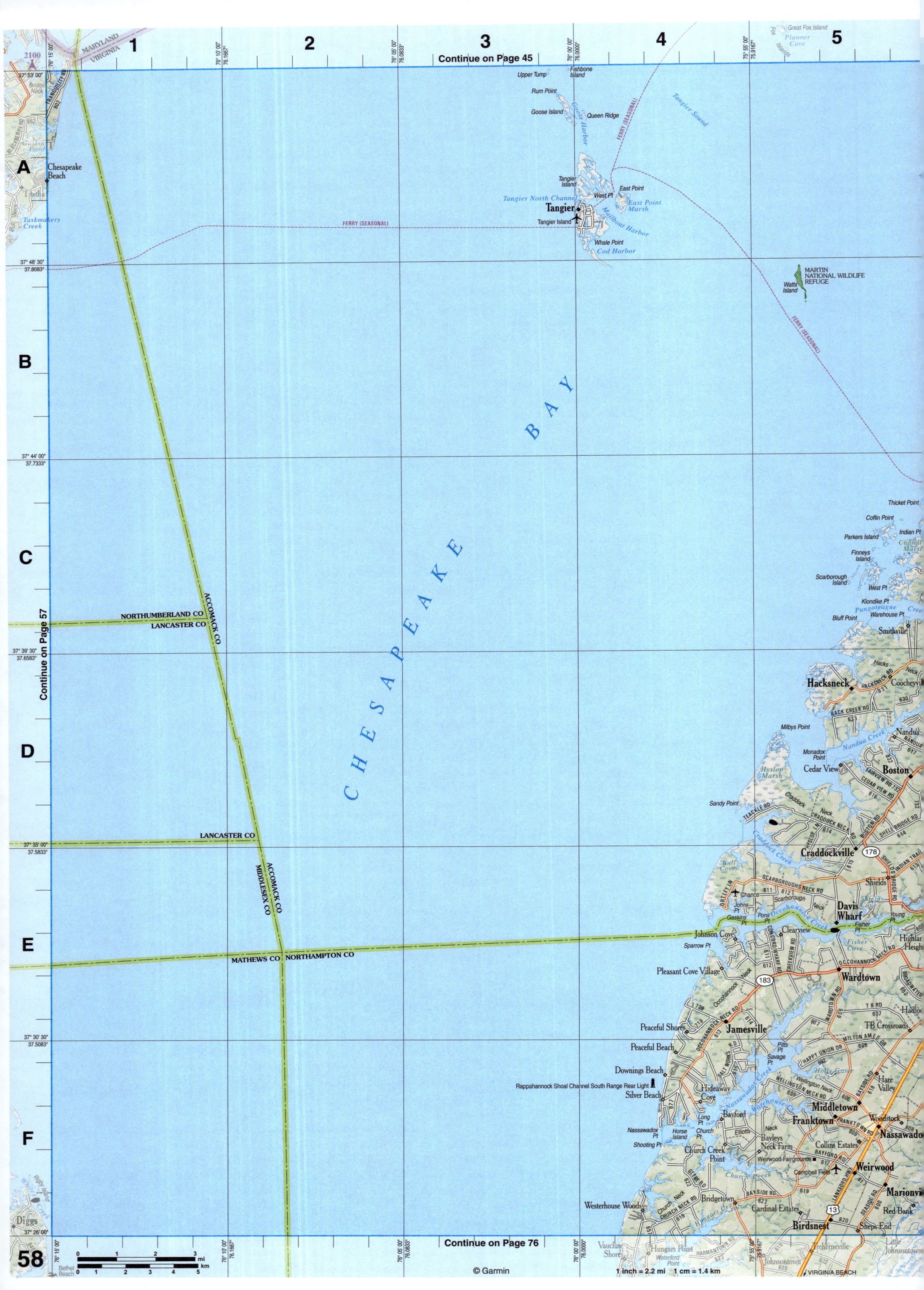

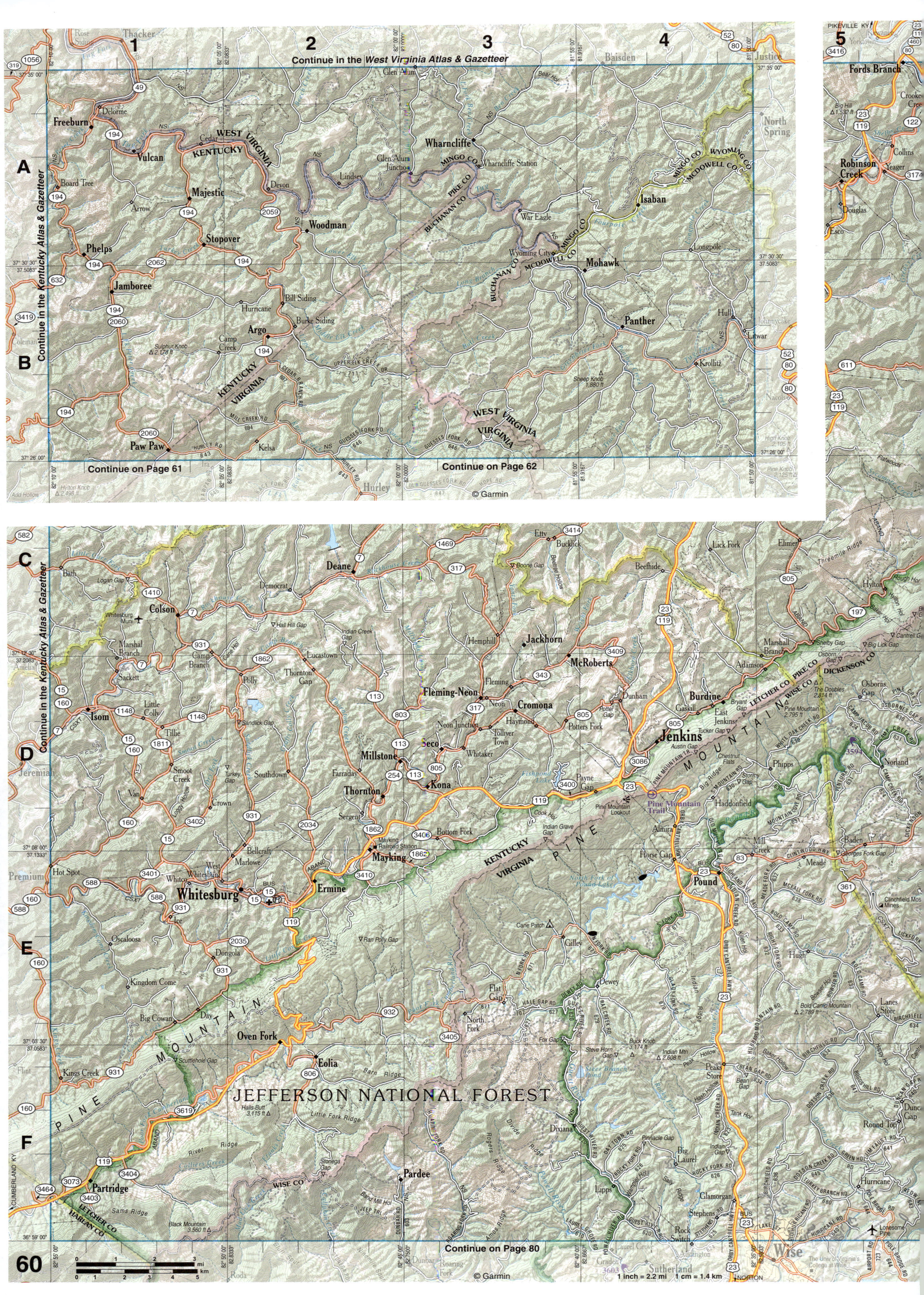

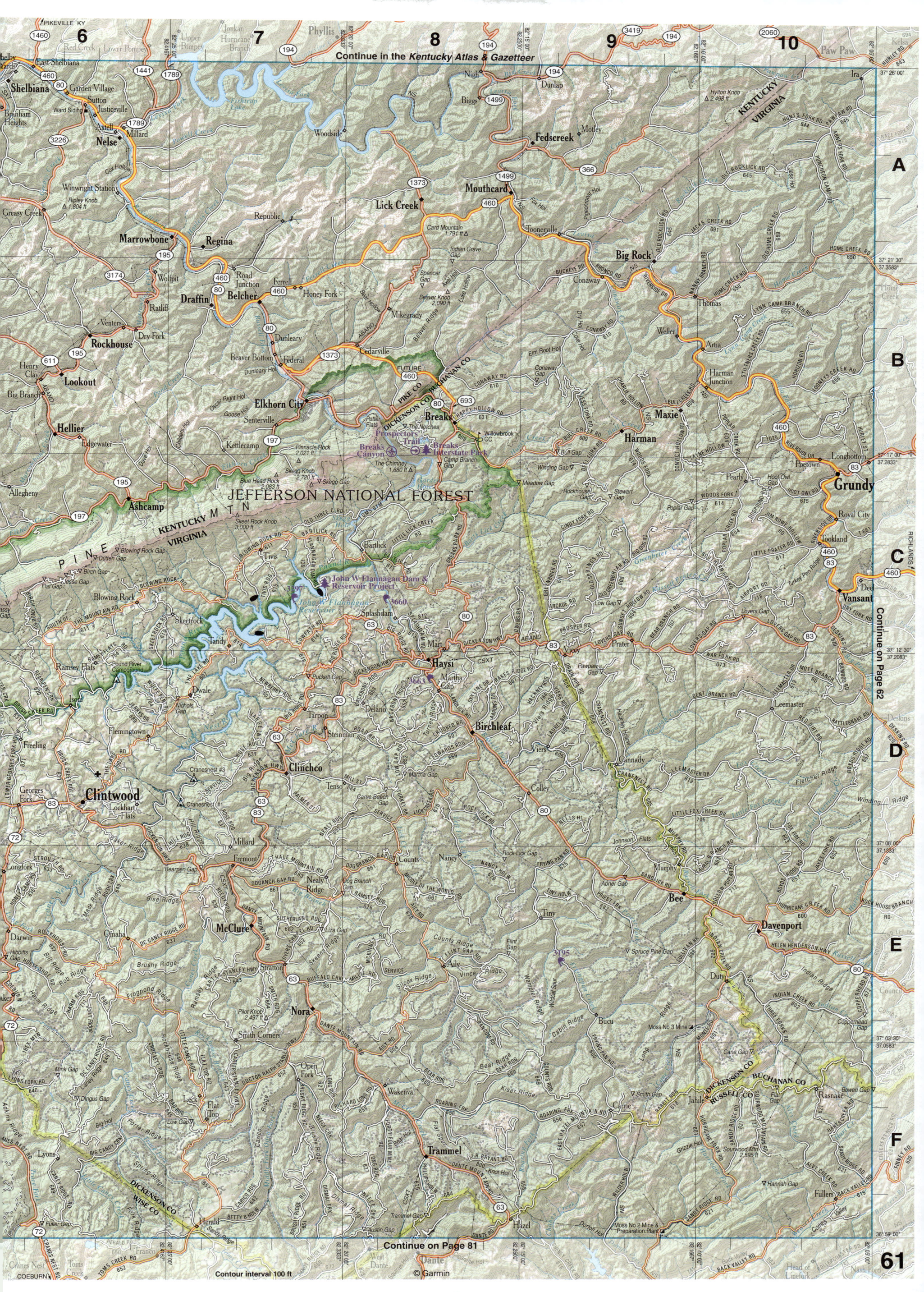

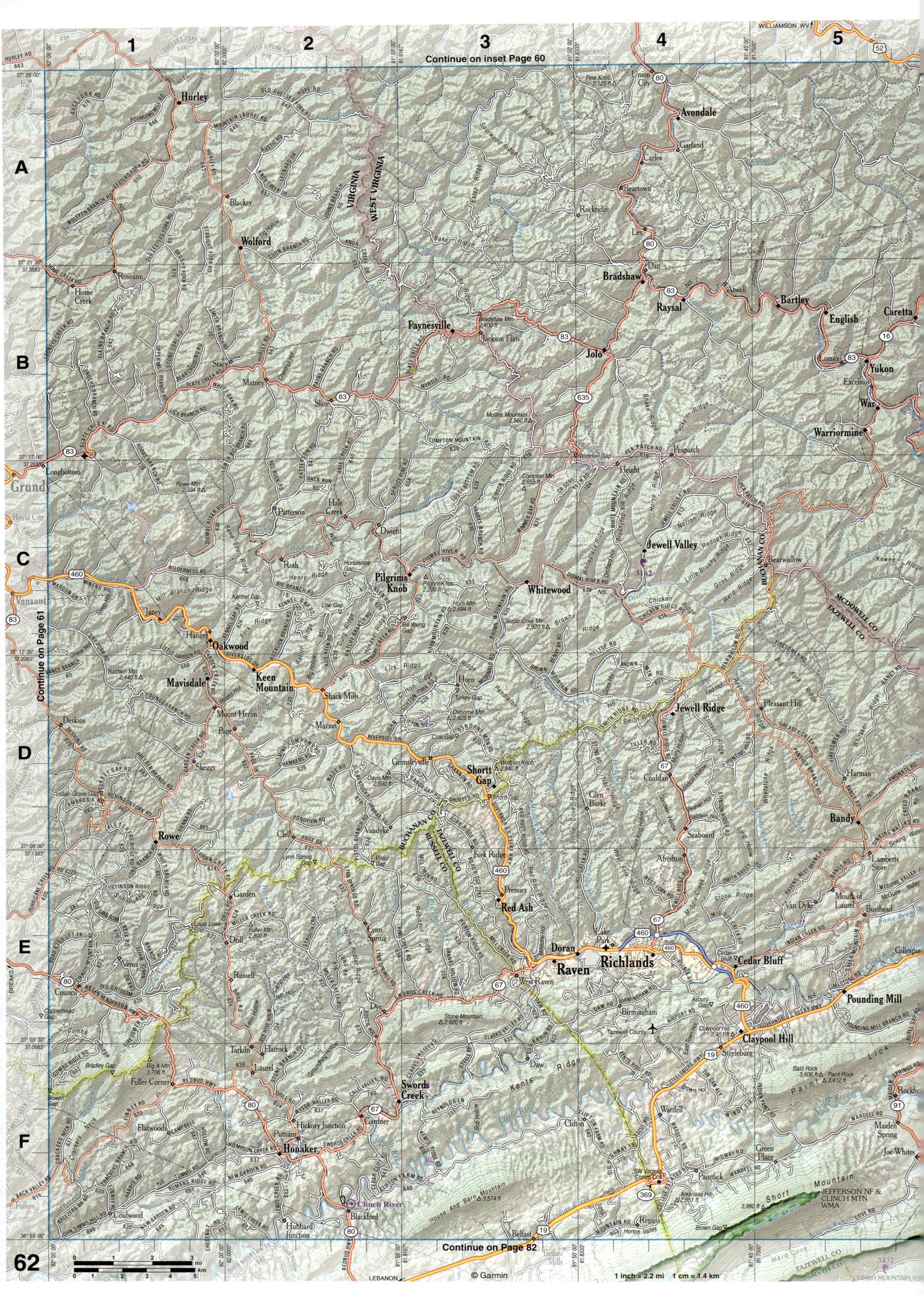

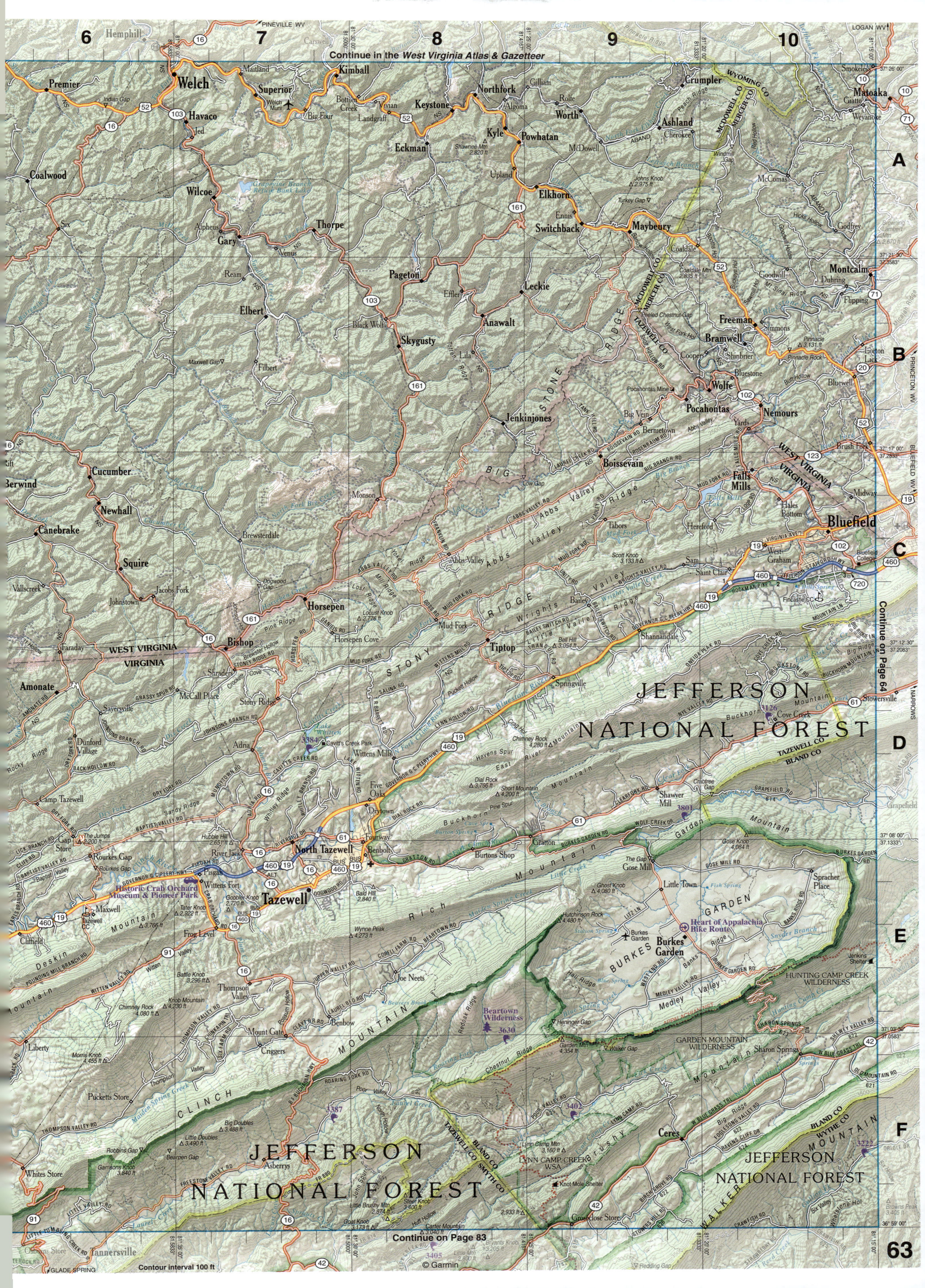

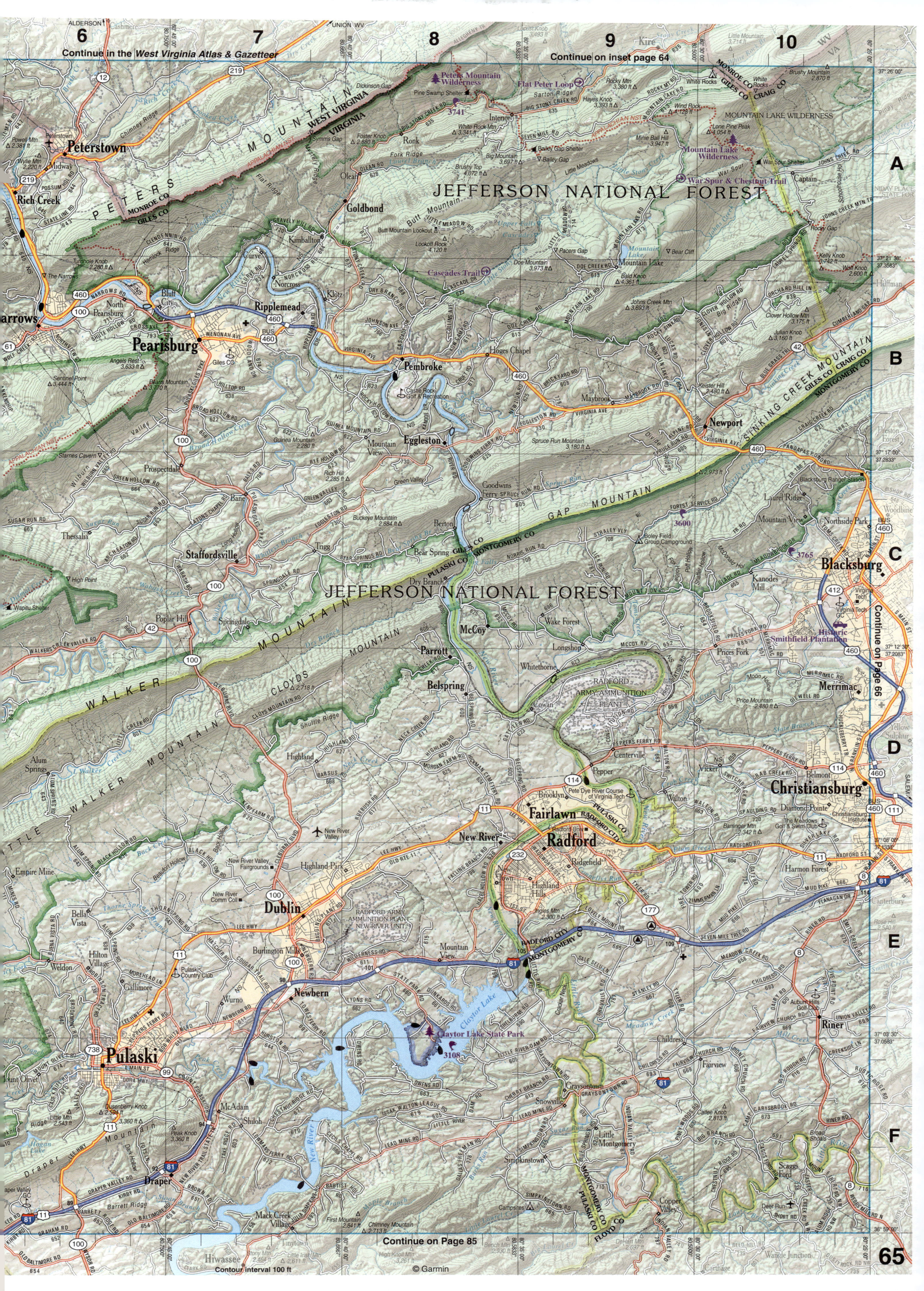

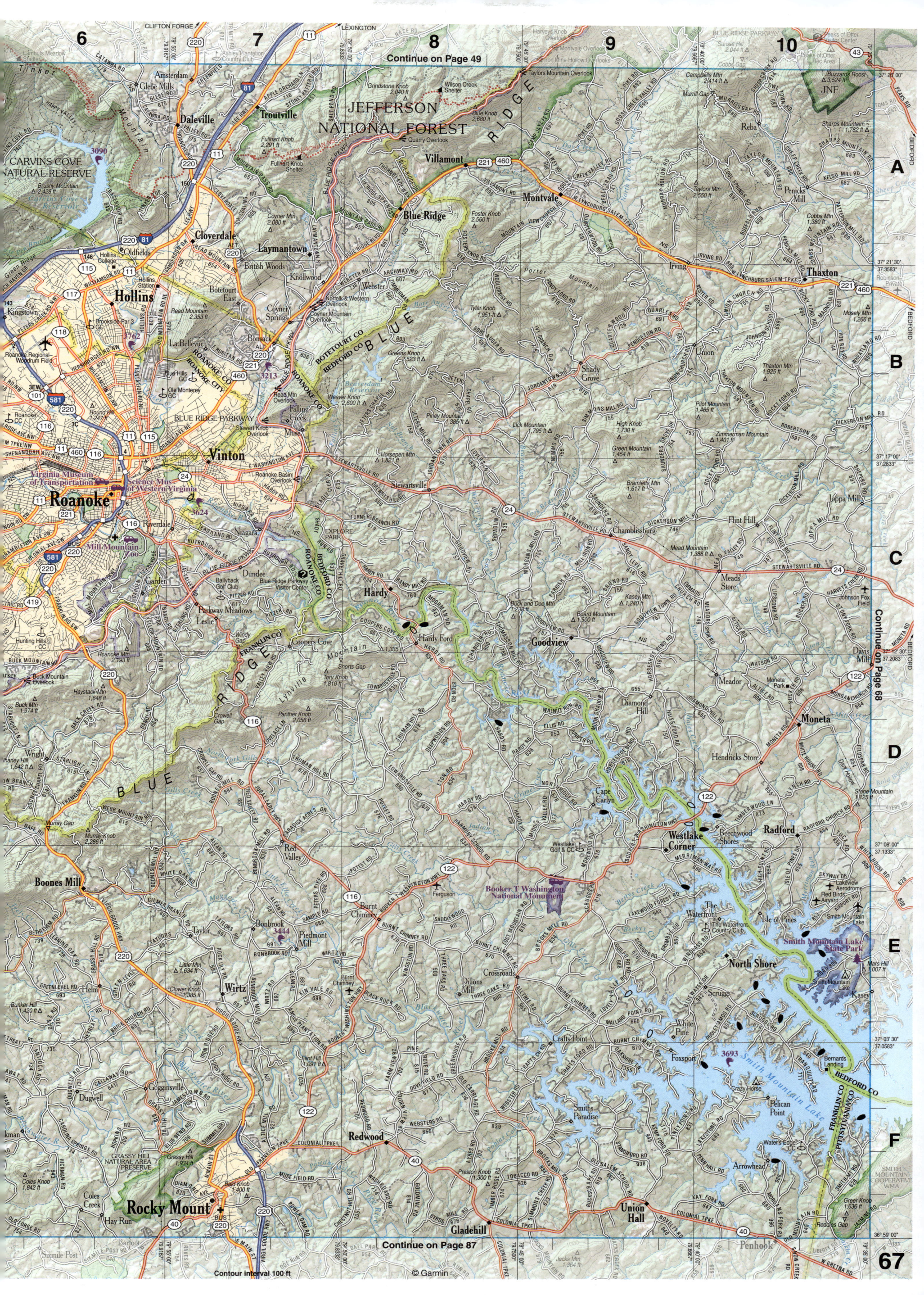

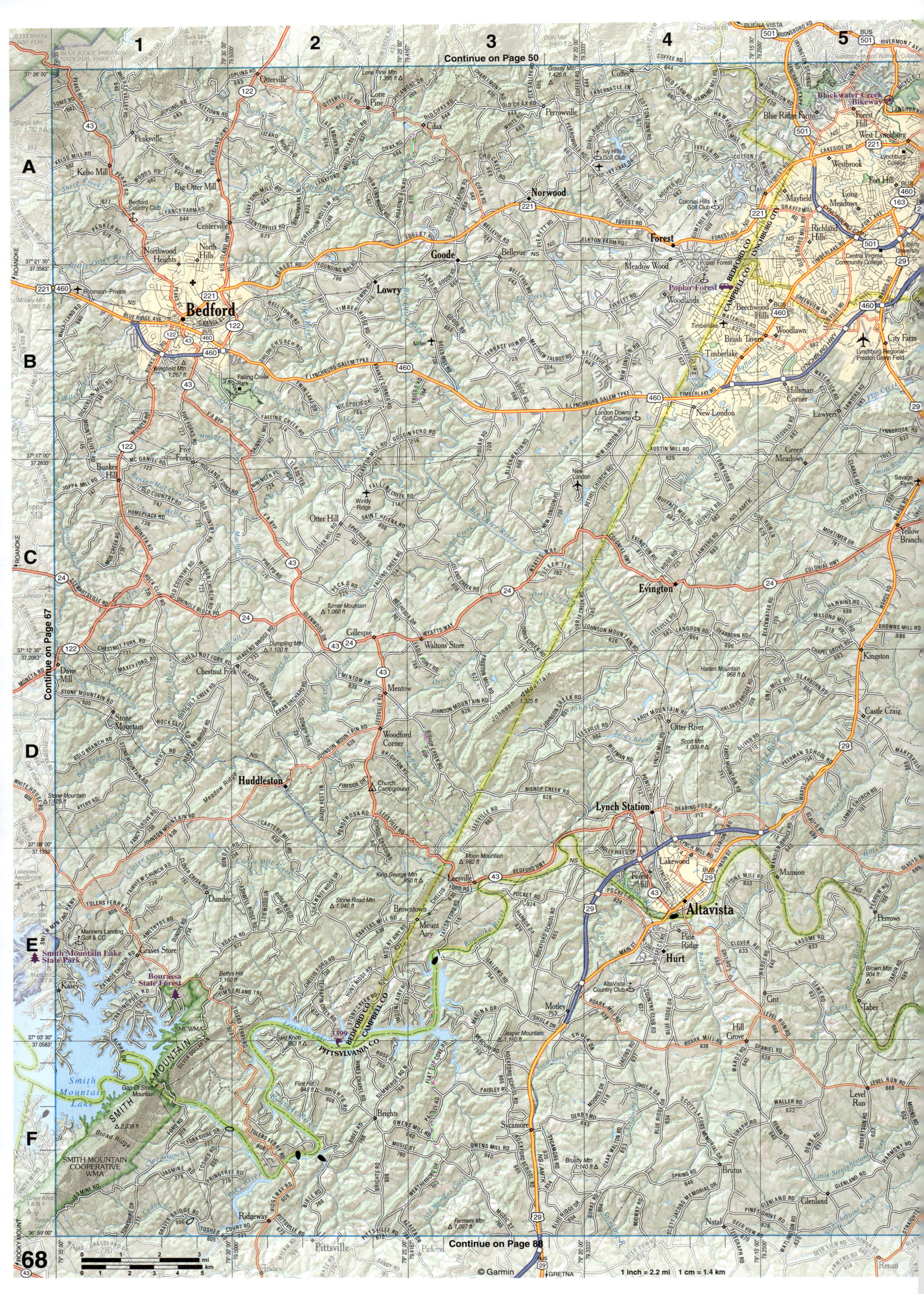

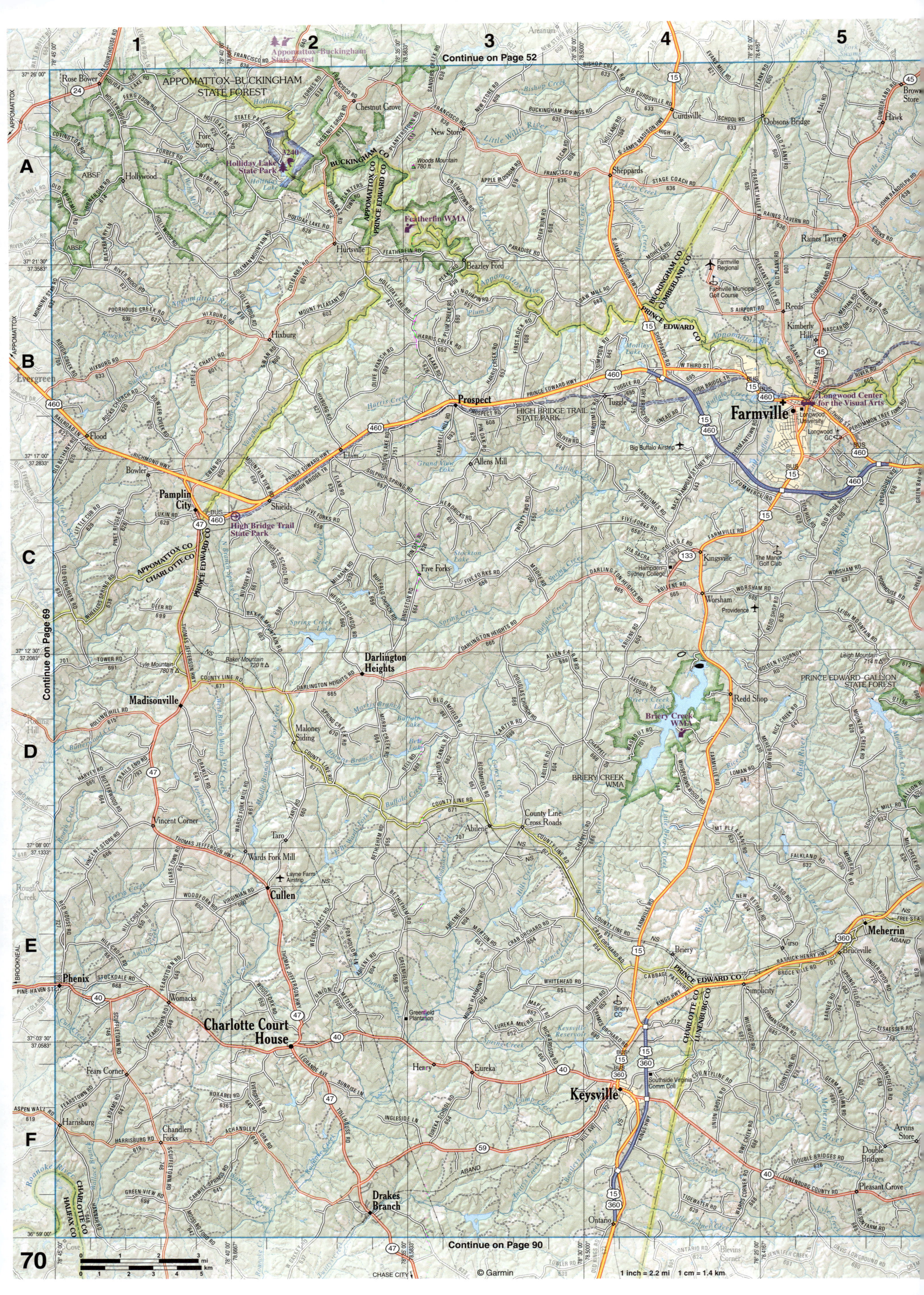

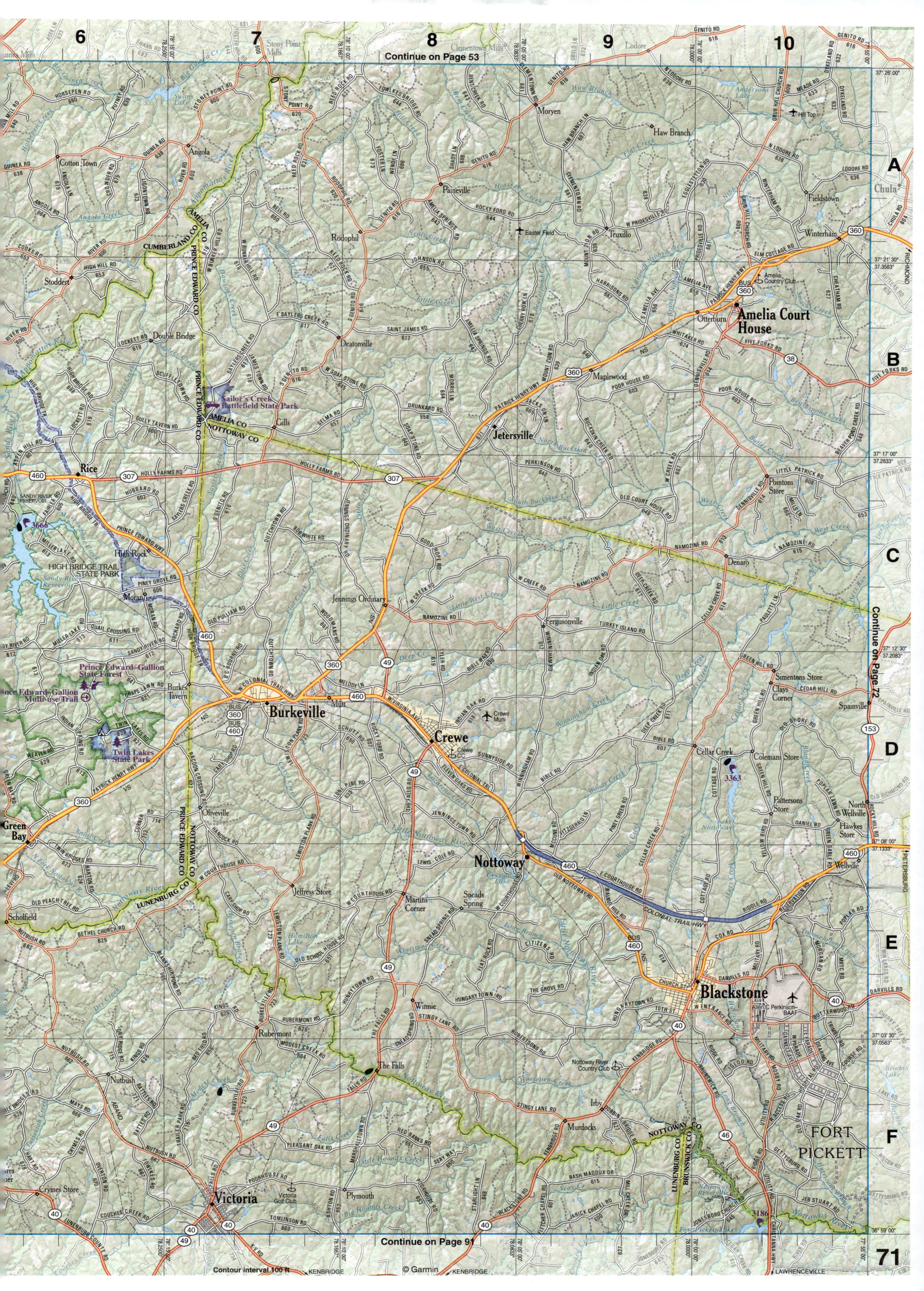

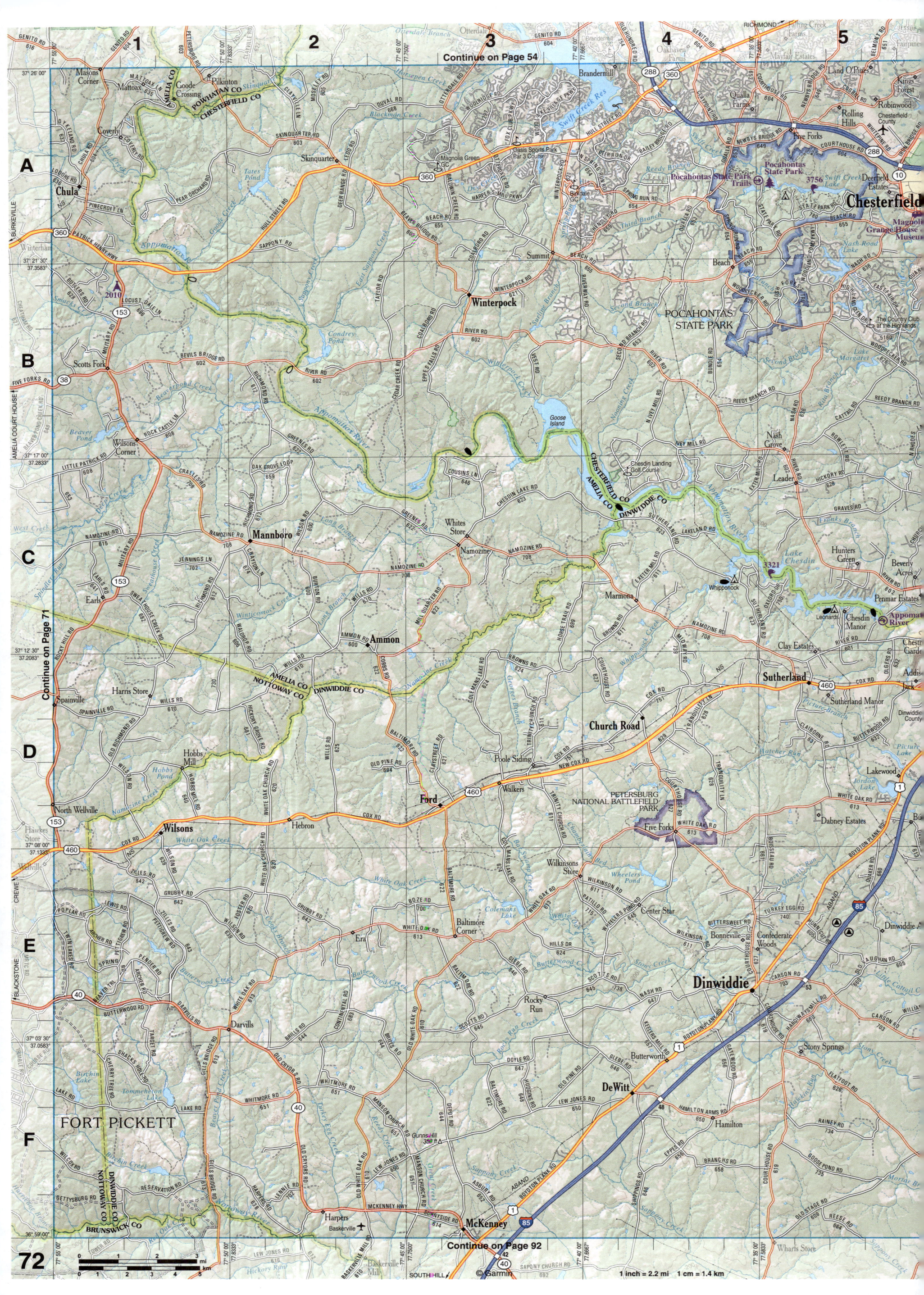

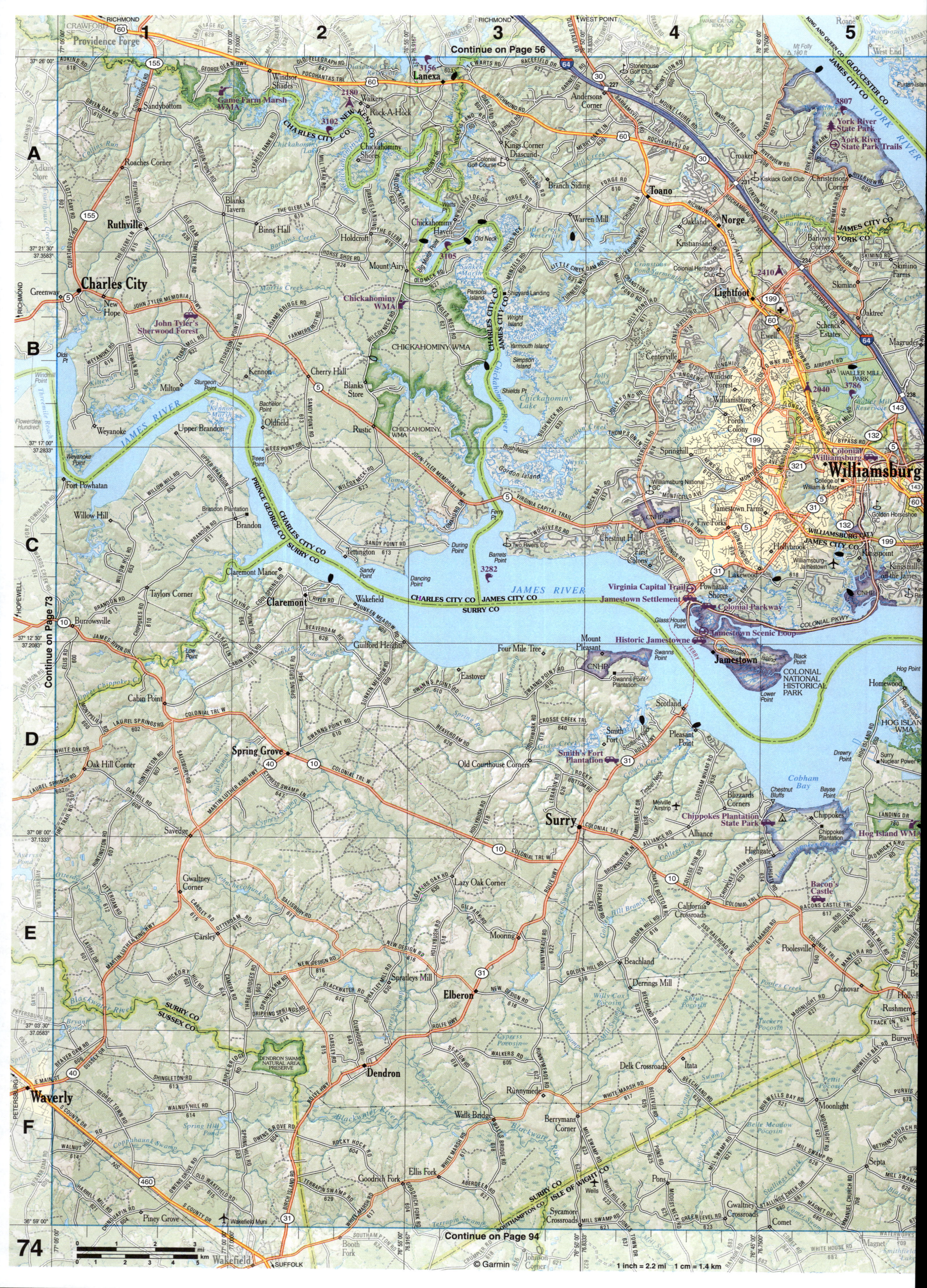

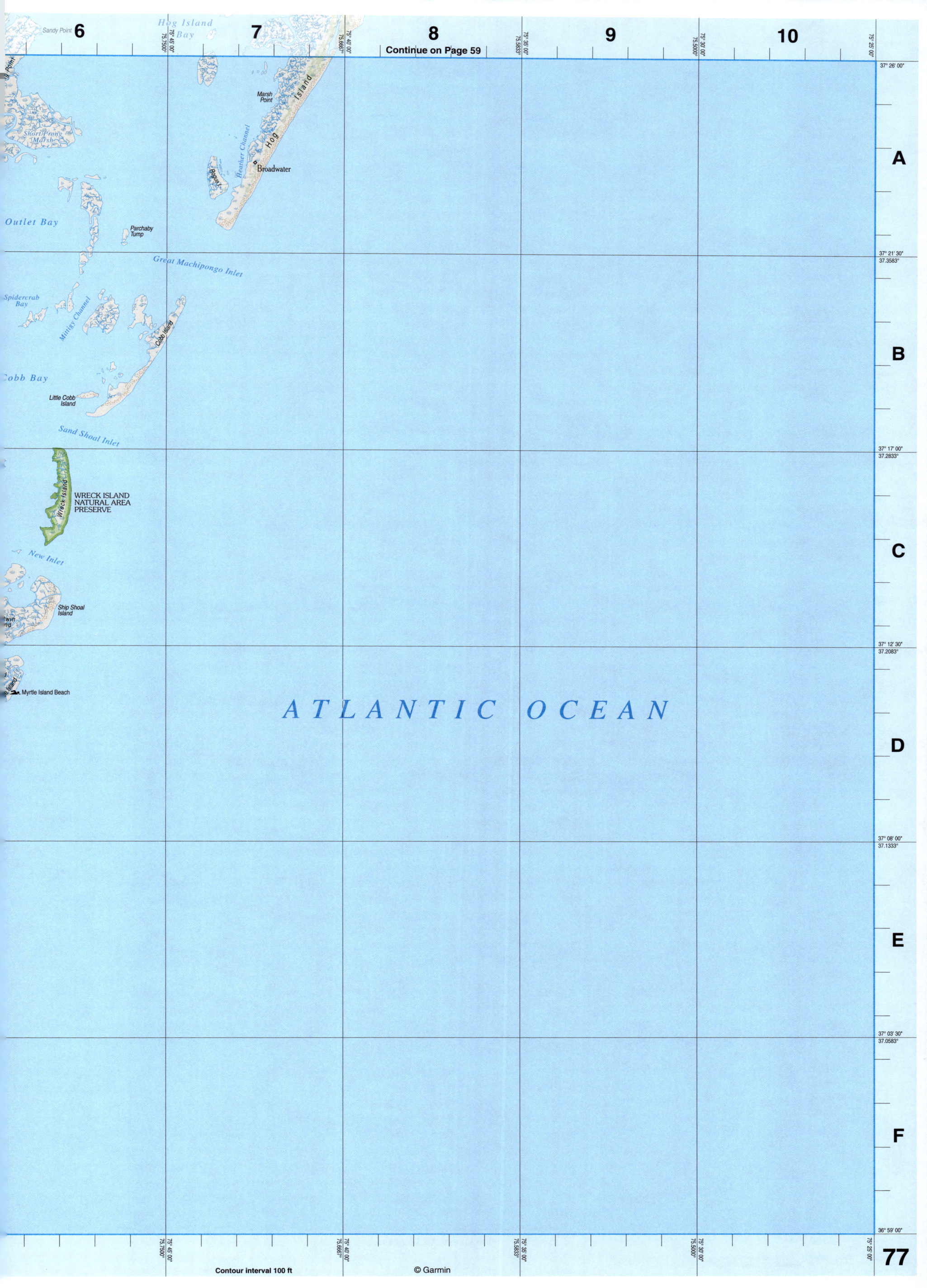

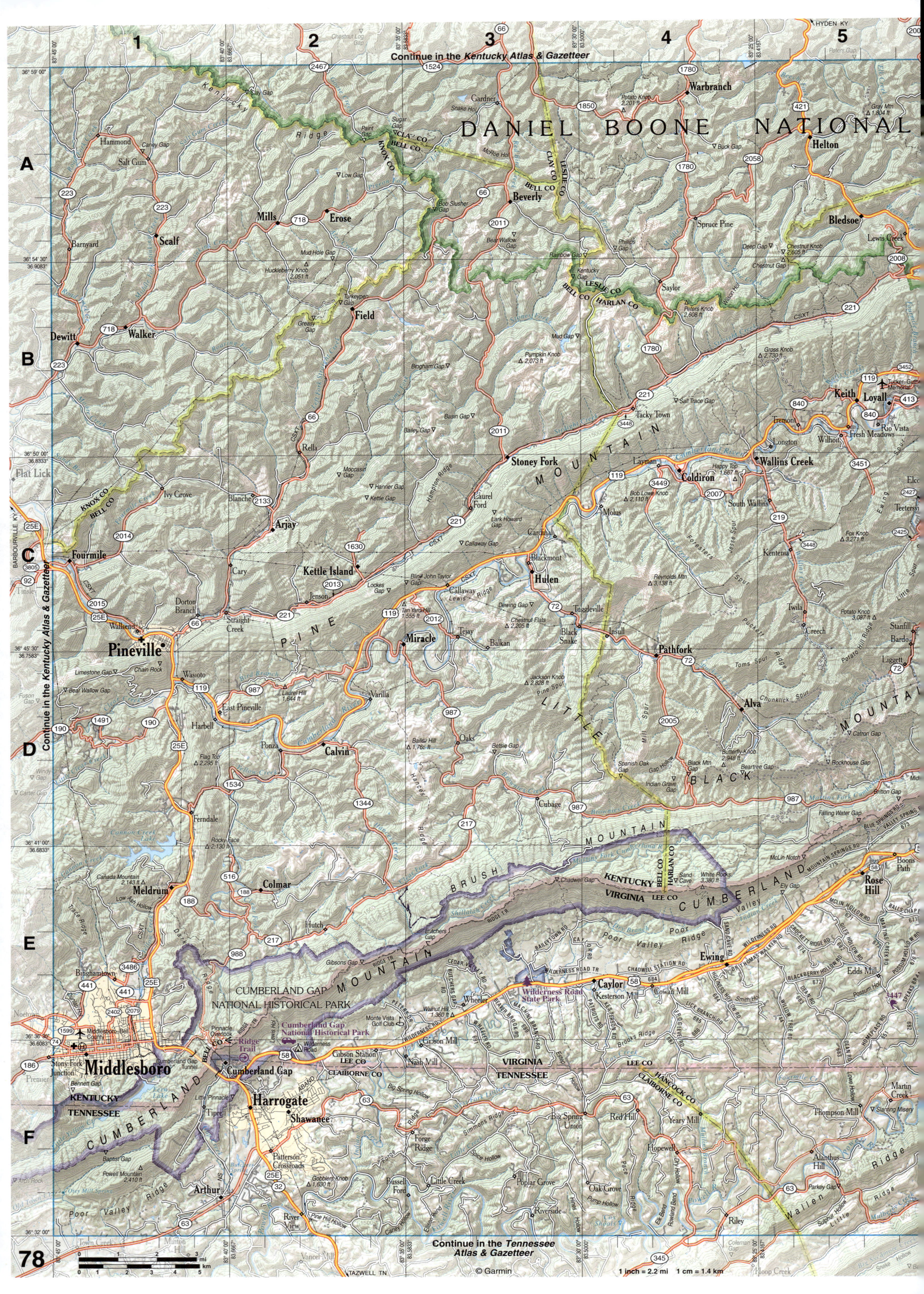

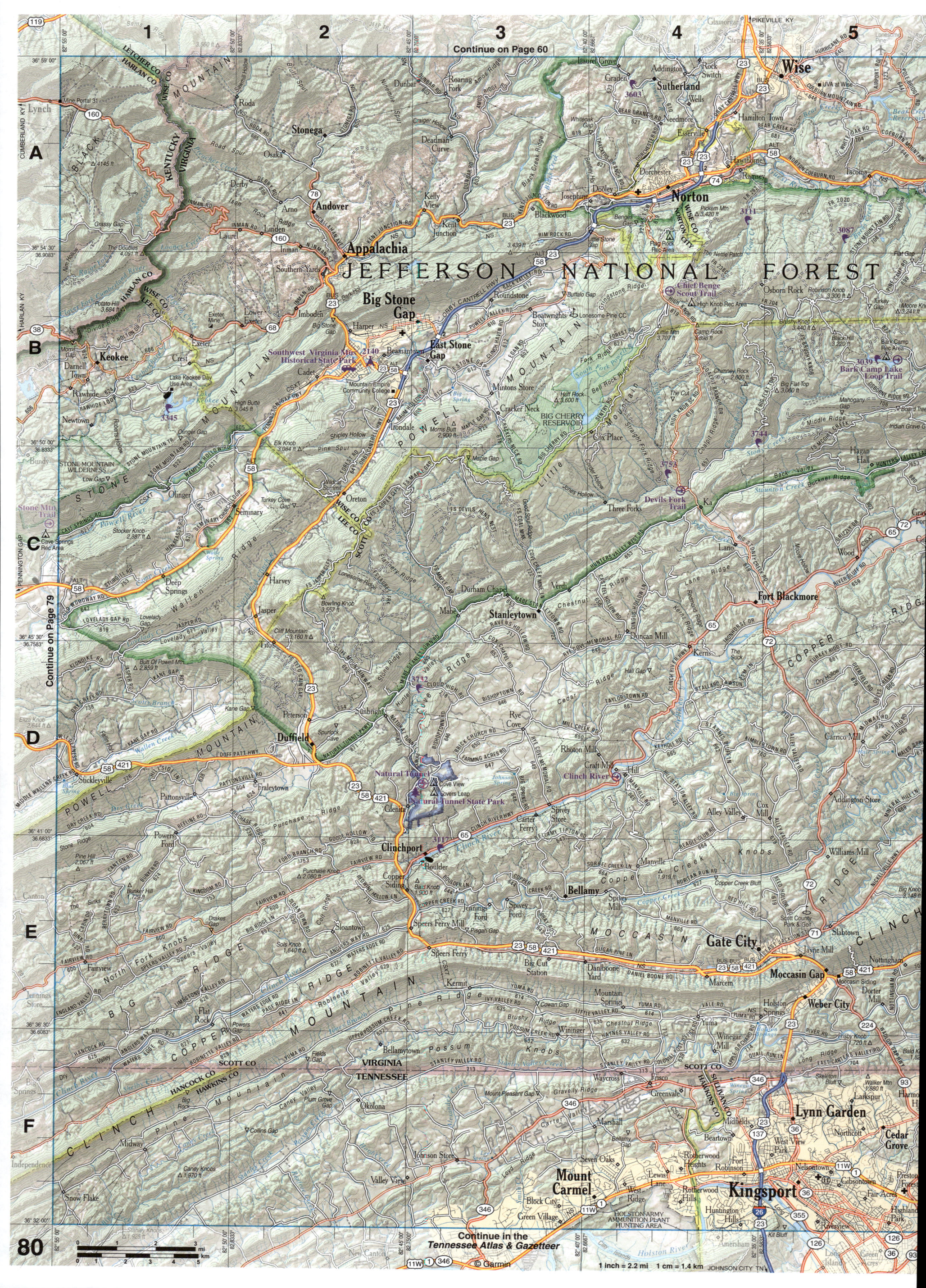

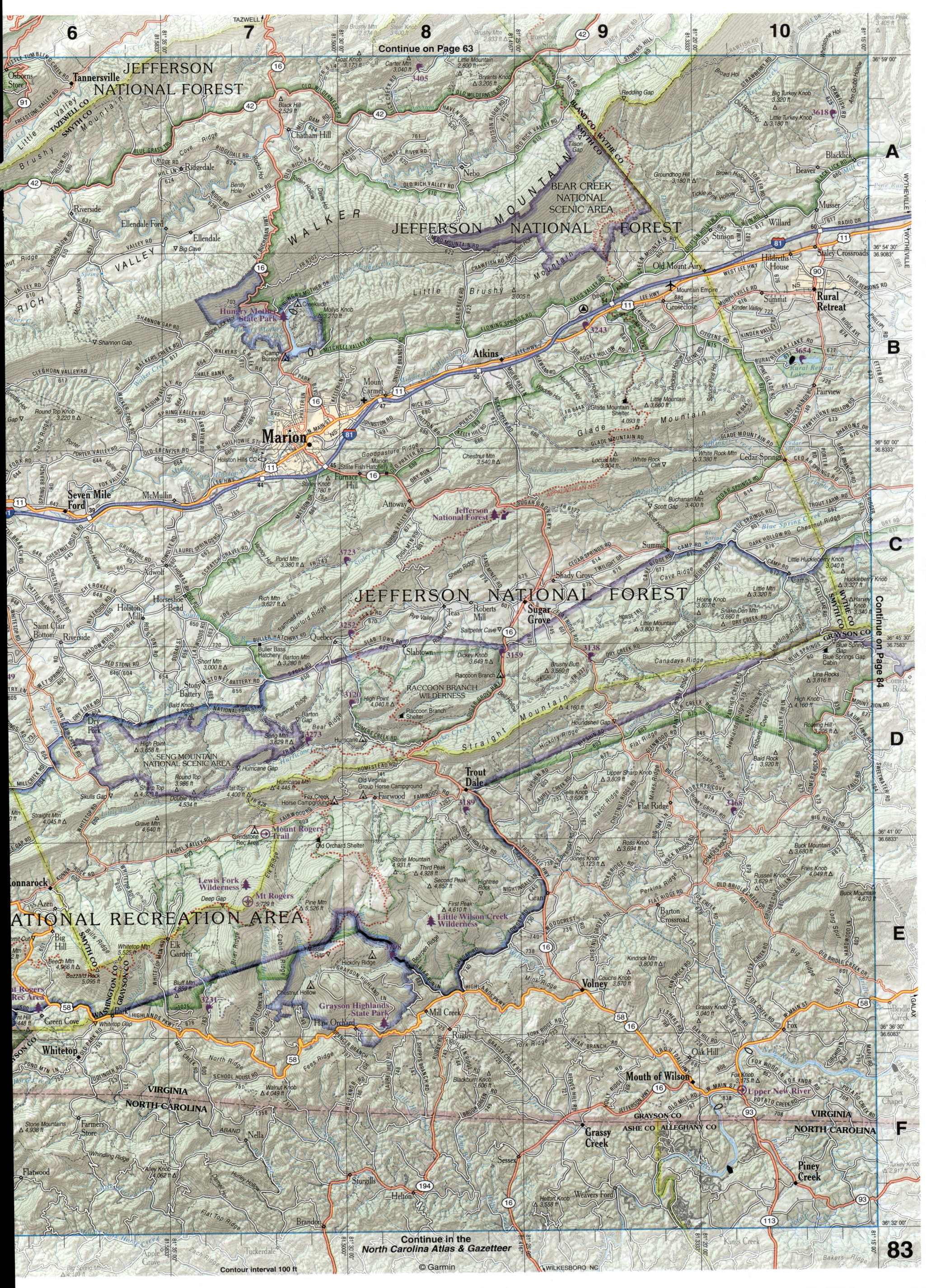

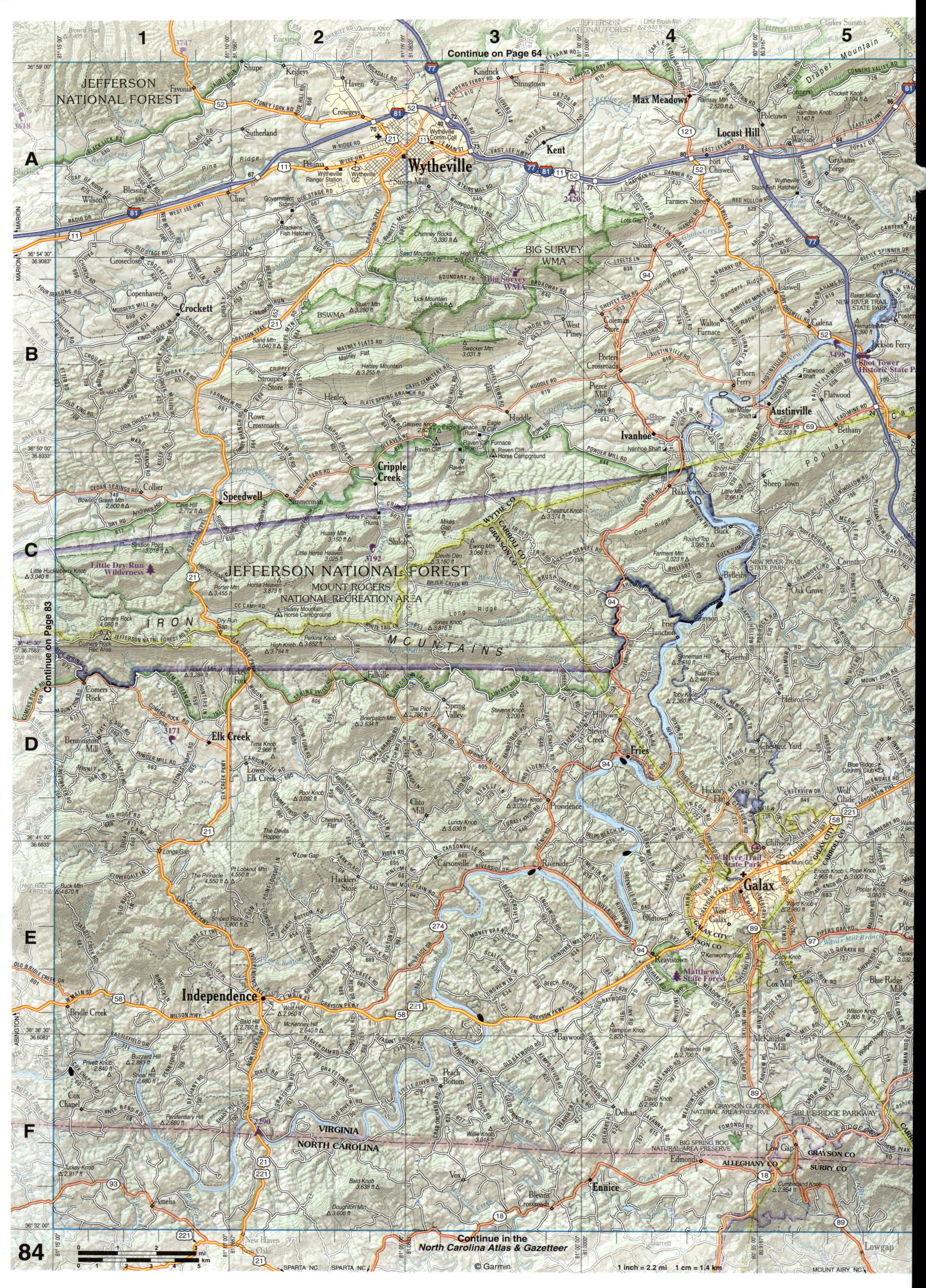

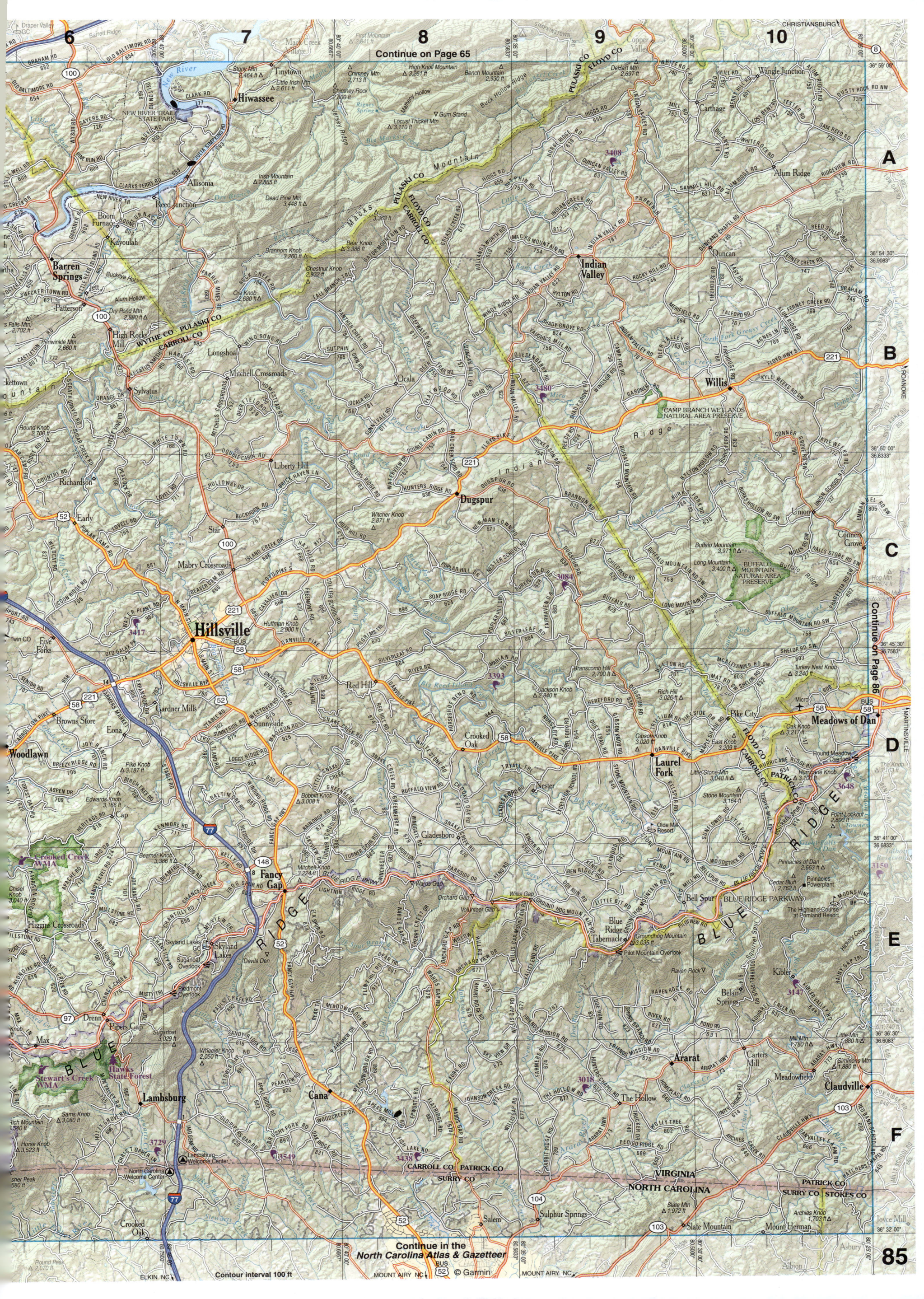

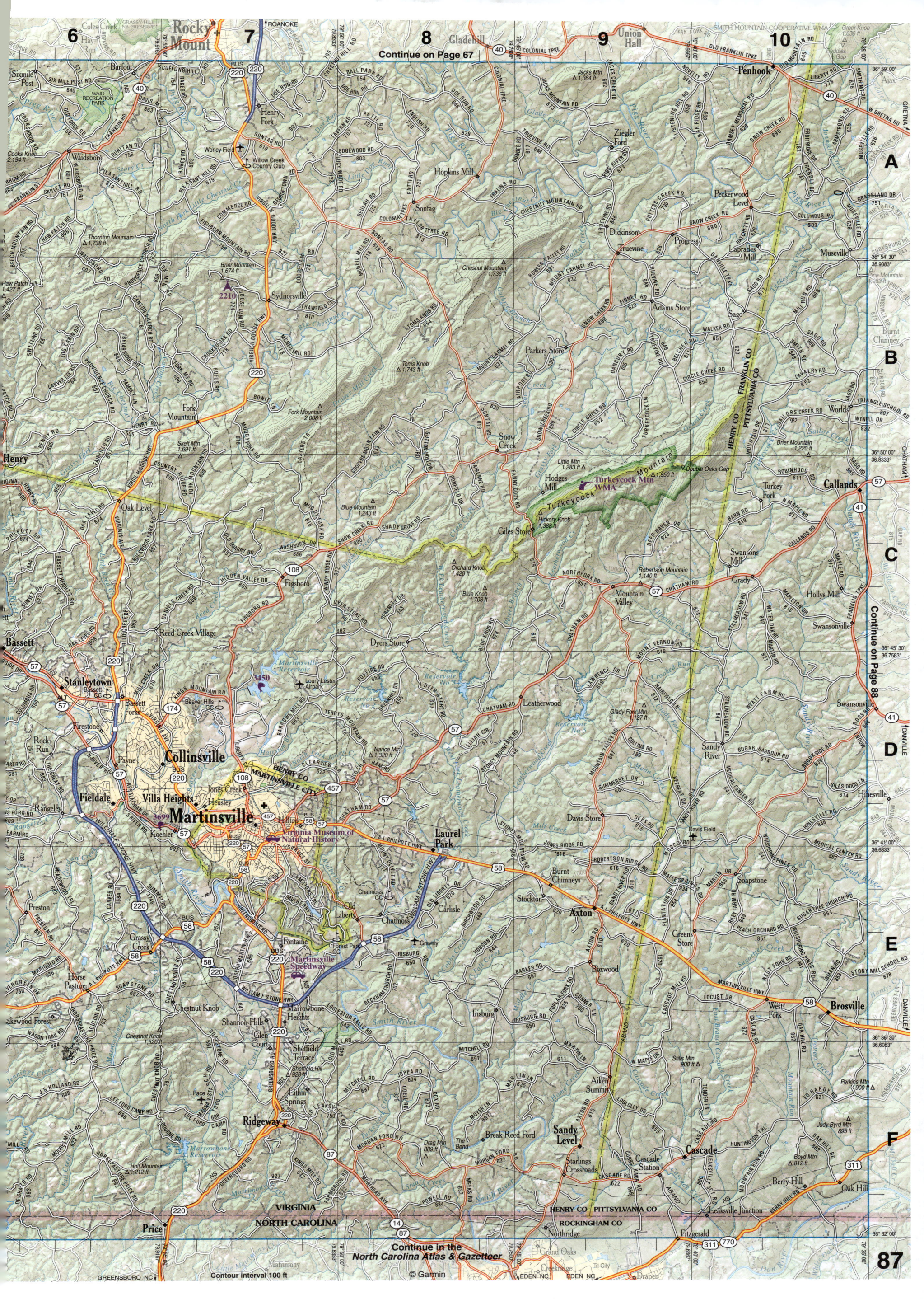

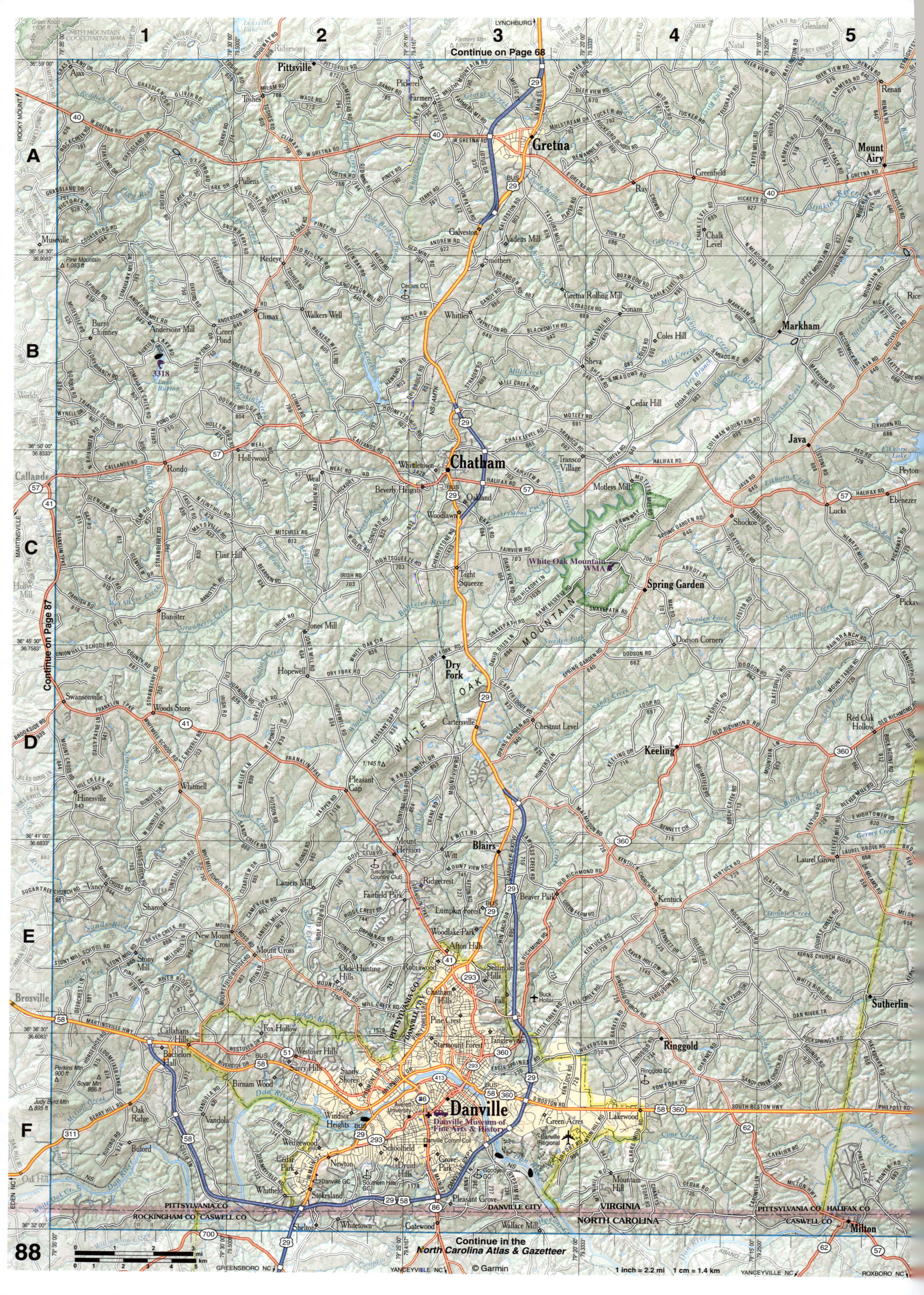

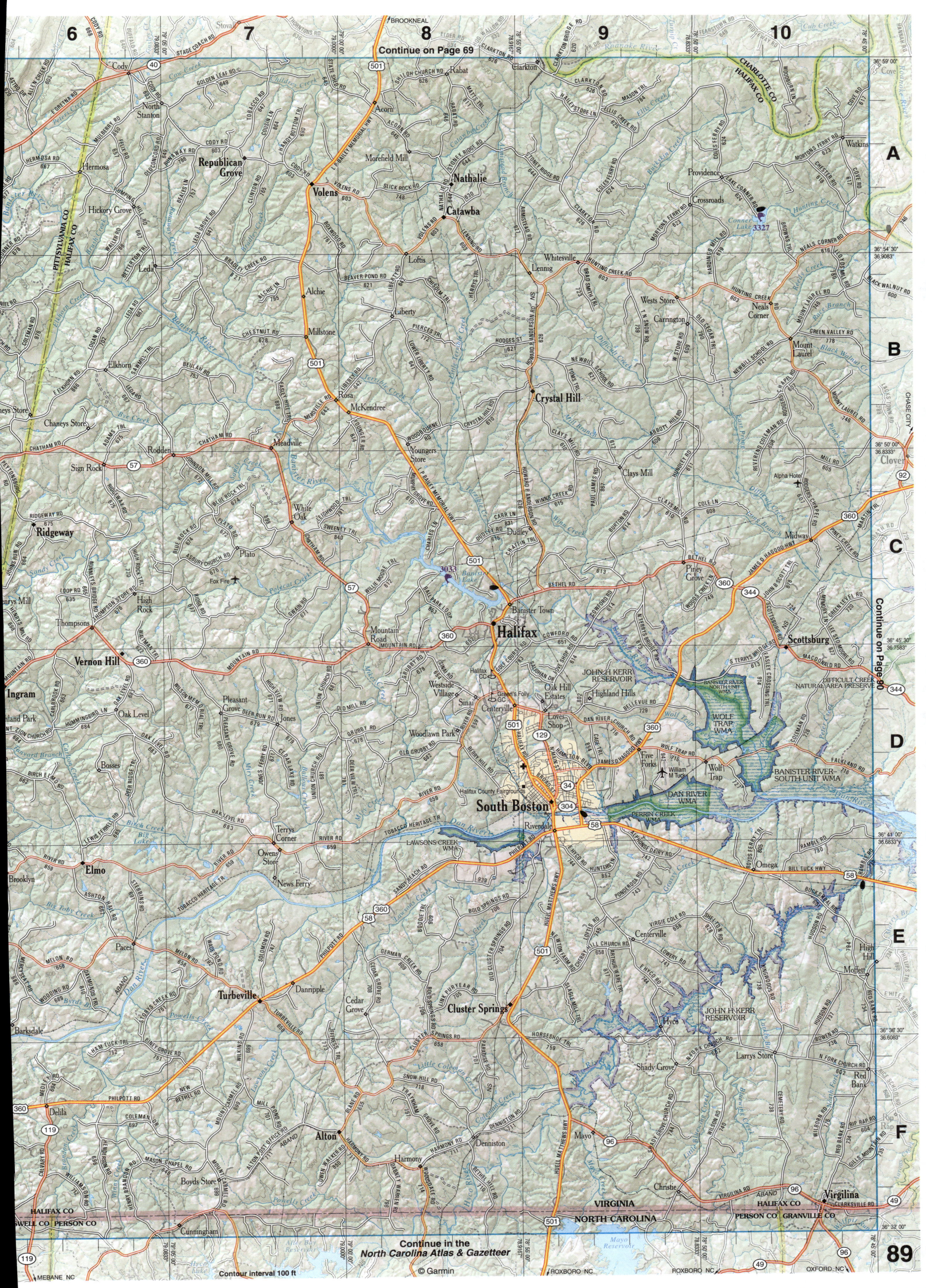

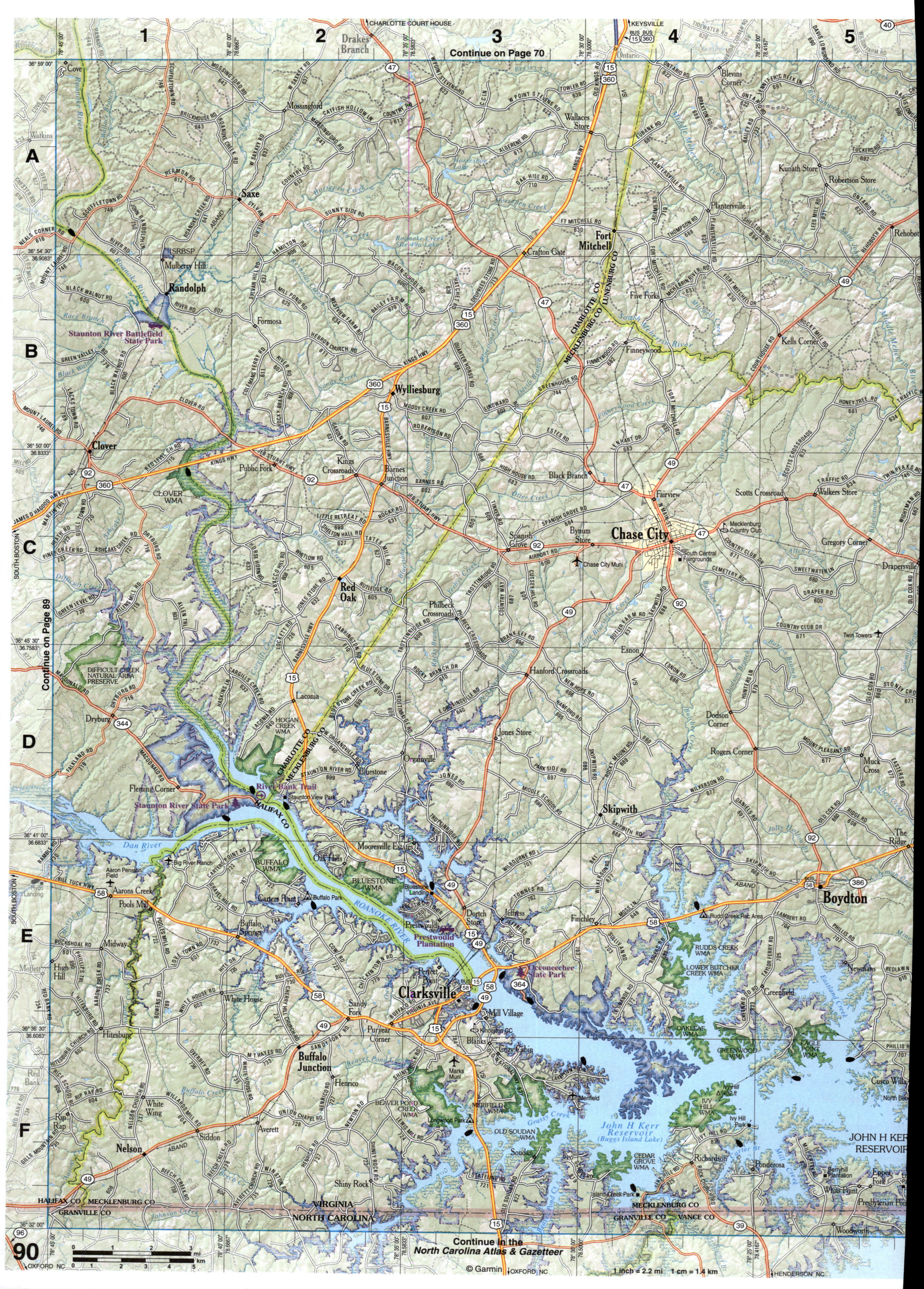

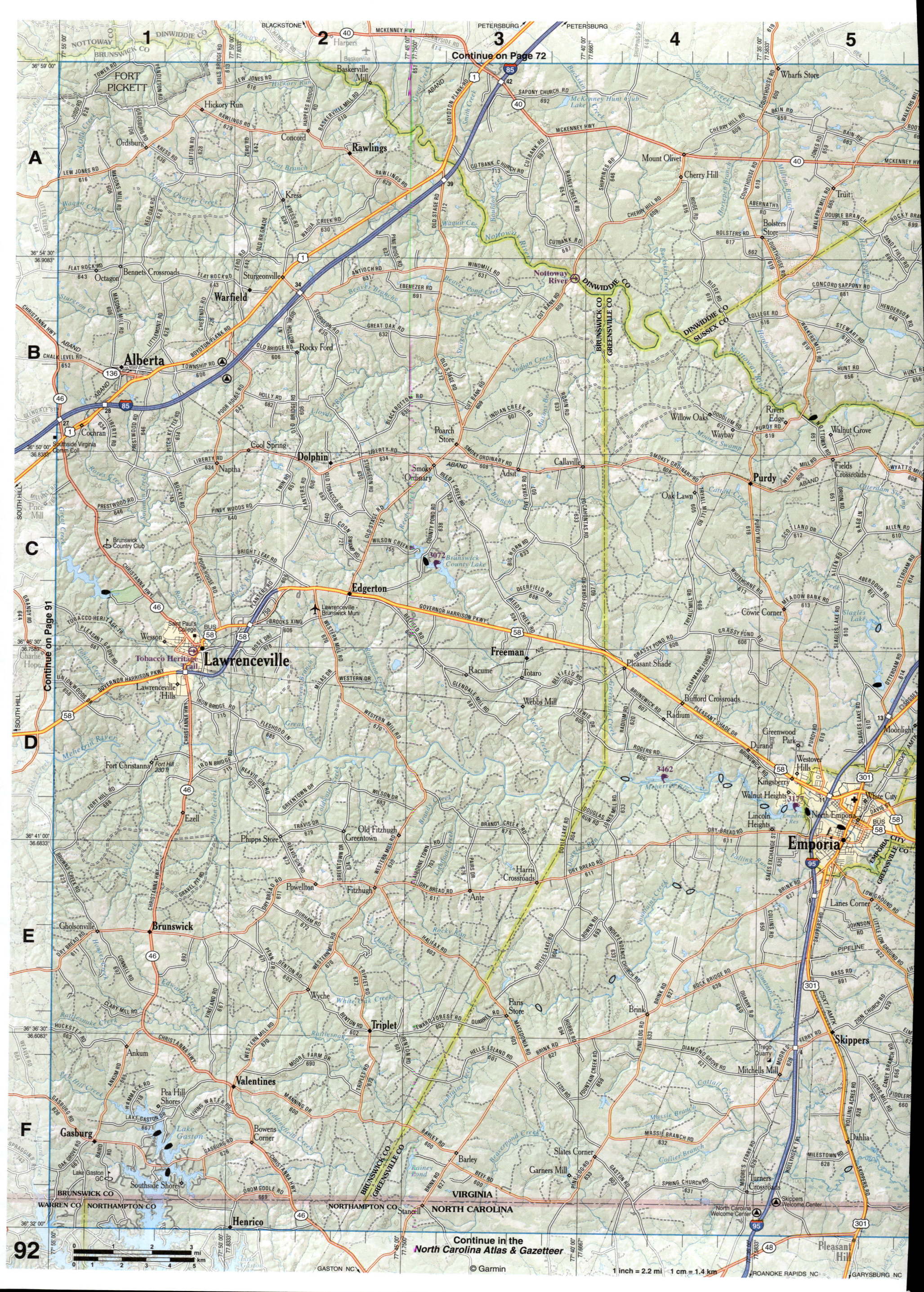

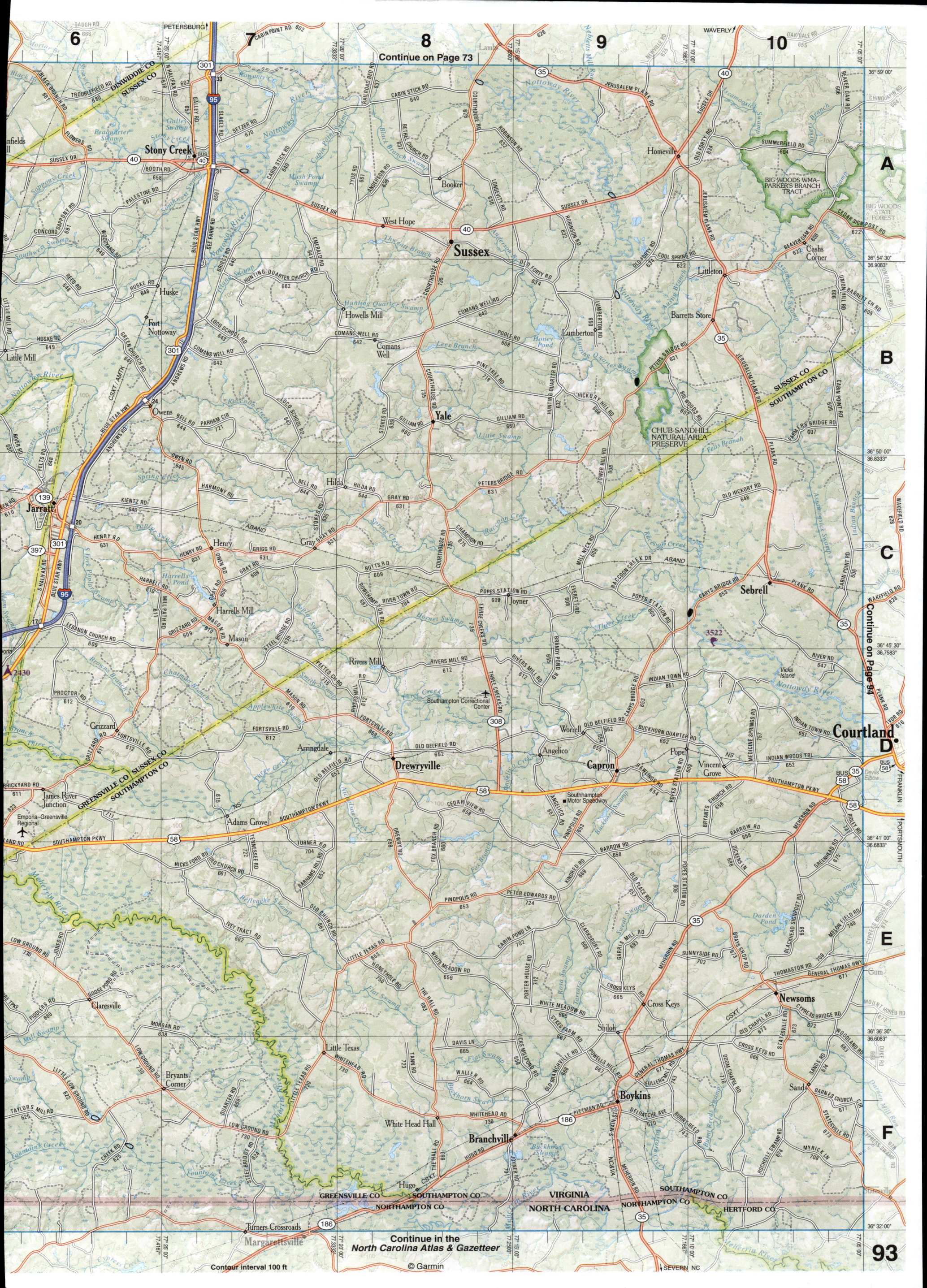

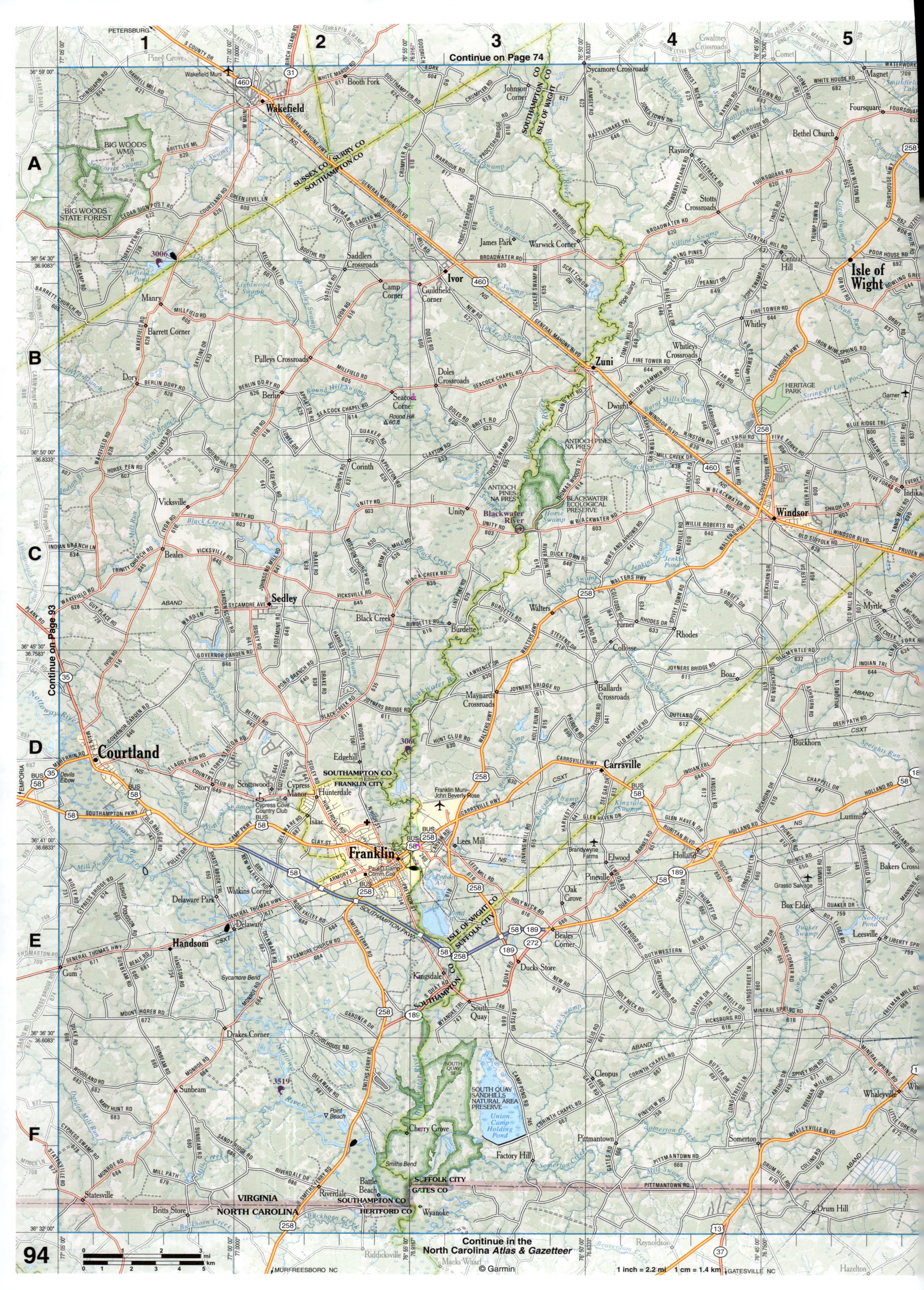

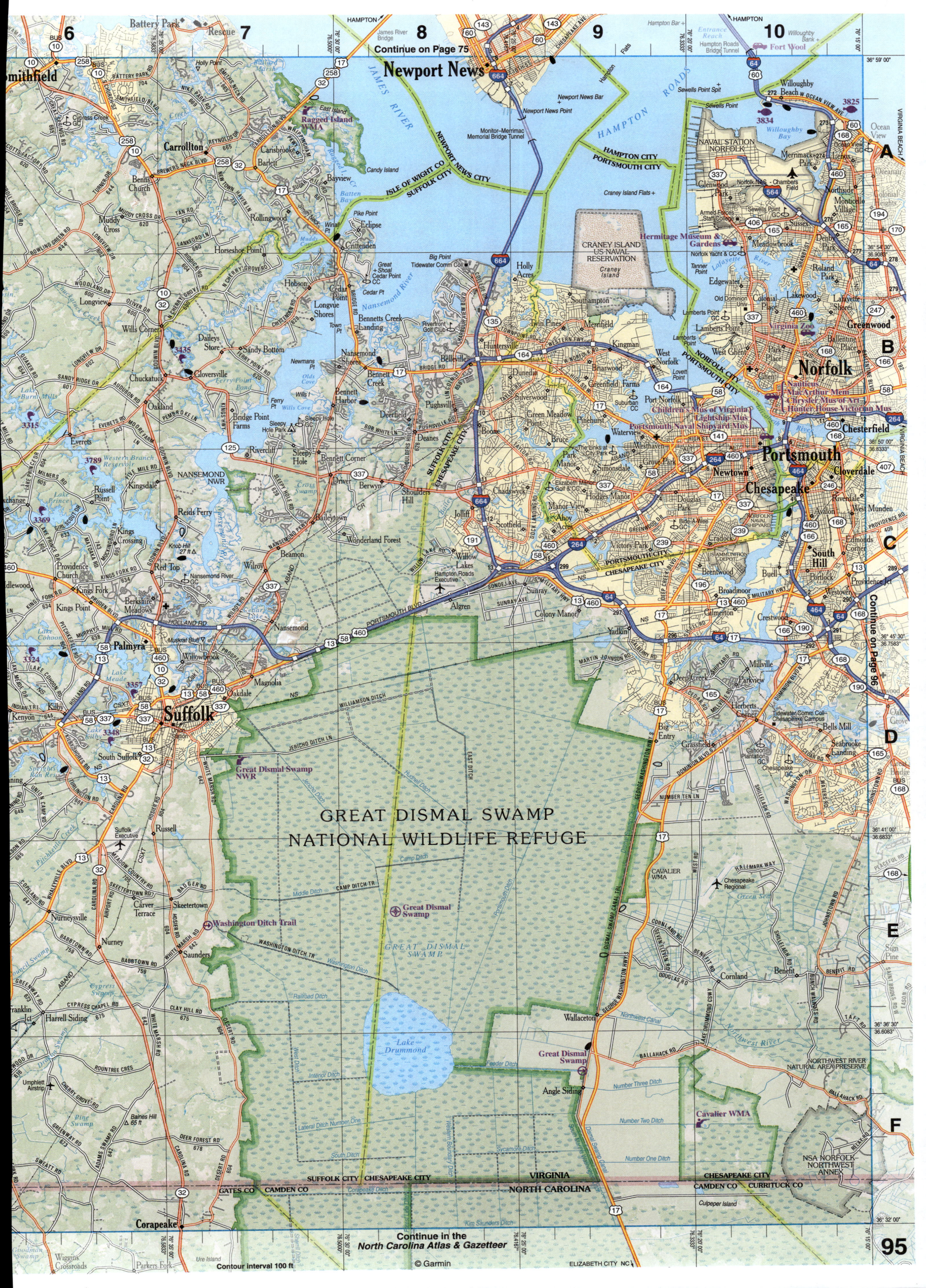